Among the proliferation of books on biblical prophecy and the crisis in the Middle East, *The Gathering Storm* alone is written from the perspective of a Western Christian living among the Arab people on the West Bank. A unique blend of history, prophecy and his family's own eyewitness experiences, Dr. Dailey's refreshing new approach challenges certain widely held beliefs about the end times.

As he points to the stormclouds portending the approach of Armageddon, Dailey offers provocative, surprising answers to the following:

- Why will Russia and China *not* invade the Middle East?
- What is the role of the United Nations in biblical prophecy, especially in the wake of the Gulf War?
- Who is the *real* enemy confronting Israel?
- What can we surmise at this point about the mysterious figure known as the Antichrist?

Concluding with a fictional scenario that blends his observations into a gripping portrayal of the last days, Dailey charges you with the hope of Christ's return.

THE GATHERING STORM

Timothy J. Dailey

Chosen Books
A Division of Baker Book House
Grand Rapids, Michigan 49506

Unless noted otherwise, Scripture texts are from the Holy Bible, New International Version, copyright © 1973, 1978, 1984 by International Bible Society. Used by permission of Zondervan Bible Publishers.

Scripture quotations identified NASB are from the New American Standard Bible, copyright © 1960, 1962, 1963, 1968, 1971, 1972, 1973, 1975, 1977 by the Lockman Foundation.

Library of Congress Cataloging-in-Publication Data

Dailey, Timothy J., 1953–
　　The gathering storm : startling new evidence we may be approaching earth's final chapter / Timothy J. Dailey.
　　　　p.　　cm.
　　ISBN 0-8007-9199-1 (pbk.)
　　1. Bible—Prophecies—Middle East.　I. Title.
BS649.N45D35　　1992
236'.9—dc20　　　　　　　　　　　　　　　　　　　　　92-189

A Chosen book
Copyright © 1992 by Timothy J. Dailey
Chosen books are published by Fleming H. Revell
a division of Baker Book House Company
P.O. Box 6287, Grand Rapids, Michigan 49516-6287
All Rights Reserved

ISBN: 0-8007-9199-1

Second printing, September 1992

Printed in the United States of America

To
Rebekka

Acknowledgments

Y OU, THE READER, HAVE WON MY RESPECT FOR DIL-igently reading a part of the introductory matter that I myself have skipped over all too often. In return, I will try to avoid the usual flattering tribute to all kinds of people you probably never heard of and are reading about only to be sure of getting your money's worth.

Let's cut it down to rock bottom, then: To whom am I really thankful?

At the risk of sounding too "spiritual," as a Christian I would like first to thank the Lord Jesus for making this book possible. Quite simply, I could not have written it in my own strength, and I could certainly not have opened the door of opportunity to have it published. My hope is to be a faithful servant of Him who guides us faithfully step by step through all of life's wonders, challenges and pain.

Next I salute my wife, Rebekka, who puts up with me—not only in regard to writing this book, but in general. I have often wondered why wives seem to embody the qualities of goodness and selflessness while their husbands strut about like self-important cocks, never completely rising above the emotional development of an adolescent. I am blessed with a wife who consistently exhibits the Christlike life to which I so inconsistently aspire. I am the theologian, but she is the one who knows how to live the Christian life. I am the teacher, but she has taught me more than many books.

Finally I would like to thank Jane Campbell, editor of Chosen Books, and Ann McMath, associate editor, who have made this project lots of fun and are really nice to work with (and I'm *not* just writing this knowing that they will read it!). I hope I have learned from their positive, encouraging way of working with others.

Contents

Contents

Foreword

TIMOTHY DAILEY IS A BRIGHT YOUNG AMERICAN MAR-
ried to a sweet young Swiss woman named Rebekka. They and their
small family have lived for some time in the historic city of Bethlehem. If this sounds romantic, it is. It is also traumatic. It was while
the Gulf War raged and Saddam Hussein was lobbing Scud missiles
at Israel that Timothy started writing this book "in a sealed room
wearing a gas mask." Now that's on-the-spot reporting!

But the trauma didn't start there. The whole story of the relations between modern Israel and her neighbors is one long, sad
story of trauma—bloodshed, hatred, distrust and deceit.

Living in the midst of the turmoil, Timothy and Rebekka have
made friends with Israelis and Arabs; they have listened to their
stories, empathized with their fears, shared their sorrows. At the
same time they have researched their history eagerly, searching out
how the present situation came to be.

Timothy's interests do not stop there. True, he looks back into
history and deeply into the present, but with the trained eye of a
Bible student he looks forward to the future, seeking to unravel the
mysteries of prophecy.

He is not always dogmatic, which is admirable in this field; he is sometimes controversial, which is not surprising in this field; but he is always concerned and compassionate, as befits one whose life in recent years has been devoted to reaching people of whatever ethnic group or religious grouping with a practical, biblical message of hope.

I commend Timothy and Rebekka for their faithful and thoughtful service and I recommend *The Gathering Storm,* a book that tells the story of one young couple's attempts to live in a demanding and sometimes dangerous environment in order to understand the people who live there—to love them and to present to them the message of life in Christ.

Stuart Briscoe
Waukesha, Wisconsin

Preface

The Lord, who stretches out the heavens, who lays the foundation of the earth, and who forms the spirit of man within him, declares: "I am going to make Jerusalem a cup that sends all the surrounding peoples reeling. Judah will be besieged as well as Jerusalem. On that day, when all the nations of the earth are gathered against her, I will make Jerusalem an immovable rock for all the nations."

Zechariah 12:1–3

THE ABOVE PASSAGE JABS MY MEMORY EVERY TIME there is a crisis in the Middle East. It surfaced in the middle of a January night in 1991 when we were awakened by a knock on our front door. Half-asleep, my wife, Rebekka, and I struggled out of bed apprehensively, aware that midnight tidings are rarely good.

We heard the voice of our neighbor Abu Butros with the news that the long period of anticipation was over. "The war has begun" was all that he said, disappearing into the darkness.

Instantly awake, I went into the cold living room of our stone Arab house and switched on the radio. A flurry of reports from the Gulf was already flooding the airwaves. Correspondents in Baghdad were describing intense bombing of the city. Rebekka wisely returned to bed but I sat glued to the radio late into the night, listening to reports of the massive Allied assault unfolding only a few hundred miles away, wondering what the impact would be on Jerusalem.

It was the war we had all been expecting, one that brought a question of the end times easily to mind. As Christians living and working in Israel, we knew well the prophecies of the Bible regarding the battle of Armageddon at the close of human history. During those turbulent days, friends wondered aloud if we had reached the beginning of the end.

The war was over quickly, but developments in the aftermath have altered irrevocably the geopolitics of the Middle East and the world. This book is the story of those remarkable changes and what they mean in relation to biblical prophecy.

It is my hope that the reader will be encouraged to learn that his or her perplexity about the prophetic timetable is shared by a great many people. Contemporary writers and teachers all too often confuse their audiences with bewildering charts and diagrams that they themselves probably do not fully understand.

In this book I attempt to cut through some of the unwarranted speculations and distortions that have found their way into virtually every book on this subject.

This is a book about biblical prophecy—but not the usual treatment of the subject that the reader may already be well acquainted with. It challenges some cherished assumptions about future events on the prophetic timetable. Who *really* are Gog, Magog and company? Will Russia still lead an invasion of Israel? Will two hundred million Chinese march to the Middle East? What is the deadliest threat facing Israel today? Finally, and most intriguing, what can we know about the mysterious figure known as the Antichrist?

No one can say for certain how far along we are on the road to Armageddon. It may be nearer than we think or yet over the horizon. But as we observe together the signposts in the world around us, perhaps we will hear more clearly the rumbling thunder of the storm gathering over Israel.

Timothy J. Dailey
Beit Jala, West Bank

Part 1
Shifting Sands:
The Turbulent
Middle East

1
The Palestinian Question

One JANUARY EVENING IN 1991 DURING THE height of the Iraqi Scud missile bombardments against Israel, I stepped outside after hearing the wailing siren that warned of an impending attack. Standing quietly in the shadows of our olive trees, I searched the star-filled sky. Only a minute or two remained until the missile would hit.

Suddenly there it was. In the distance over Jerusalem a telltale plume of fire streaked across the sky. It seemed so close, so unreal. Was this a messenger of destruction sent from a distant, cruel land? From where I stood it appeared to make its way silently, almost peacefully.

It was, in fact, screaming toward a designated city at more than two miles per second. Its target: Tel Aviv and the coastal plain with its sprawling 1.5 million population. On the ground, U.S. soldiers manning Patriot antimissile batteries were sweating over their computerized control panels. Split-second decisions could mean life or death to Israelis huddled in safe rooms throughout the area. Usually, valiantly, the Patriot missiles would shoot up with a flash to intercept the incoming Scud.

But not this time. There were simply not enough Patriots to defend the entire country. Many Scuds would fall to earth unopposed.

I watched as the missile dropped slowly to earth in the distance. Just after it disappeared from view a flash lit up the horizon. It was likely that helpless civilians had experienced the devastation of a high-explosive warhead. I waited and listened. Judging from the time it took the low rumble of the explosion to reach me, the Scud had landed somewhere between Jerusalem and the Tel Aviv area.

My attention was brought back to our West Bank Arab village of Beit Jala by another sound: the sounds of whistling and shouting. All around in the valleys and mountainsides young Arab Palestinians were celebrating another Scud missile attack against Israel.

My heart sank as I stood silently in the dark. What hope was there for these people among whom we were living? I felt rage at the mentality that exults whenever Jews are attacked. How could anyone rejoice when innocent people are injured and killed?

At once I felt alienated and alone. Why were my wife, Rebekka, little Mahalia and Matthias and I here? Why did we choose to stay and identify with people who were cheering for Saddam Hussein? Beyond that, I wondered what lay ahead for the troubled Middle East, and what part this war played in the future of our world. Yet even as I pondered all this, some answers began to come—at least to the first question of our residence here.

The Other Side of the Fence

Before coming to Israel, I considered myself knowledgeable on the subject of the Palestinian conflict. In truth, I knew little about these people and their situation. Worse, I wasn't interested in knowing more. My love for the land of Israel did not extend to her Arab inhabitants. For me the Palestinians were basically a troublesome presence in the midst of the awe-inspiring state of Israel.

Not that I wished them any harm, but who were they to cause so many problems for God's chosen people?

Never did I imagine that one day God would put me down squarely in their midst. I would have been horrified at the thought. But God in His infinite wisdom leads us gradually, step by step, so that we do not realize what we are getting into.

Initially I came to live and work in Jerusalem. Through a series of unexpected developments, however, I somehow found myself teaching in Bethlehem—and living in a neighboring village among the Arabs! Blessings would follow: The next year would bring me my newfound Swiss wife, and still later our flat would resound with the pitter-patter of tiny feet.

Still, I remember the trepidation I felt boarding the rickety old Bethlehem bus for the first time. My destination was only a few miles south of Jerusalem, but already it seemed like a different world. I felt awkward and uncomfortable as I looked for a seat among the dark, staring faces. How different these people were from the modern, Western-oriented Israelis! I feared for my safety. Would I be attacked? How did I get myself into this, anyway?

Yet almost at once they began to win my heart. A young man jumped up graciously to offer me his seat, refusing to take no for an answer. That had never happened to me on an Israeli bus.

As I began teaching in Bethlehem, it didn't take long to discover that all Arabs did not look and act like Yasser Arafat. They became our neighbors, and the statistics took upon themselves real faces and personal histories. Settling down in Beit Jala, we grew to love these dispossessed people who welcomed us into their homes and lives. And we began to see firsthand that there were many sides to the complex issue known as "the Palestinian question."

Having grown up in a neighborhood with many Jewish families, and having long had an interest in the rebirth of the state of Israel, I could never view Israelis simply as "evil oppressors" of the Palestinians. Certainly there are oppressors among them; we see a few such individuals among the Israeli troops in what are called the Occupied Territories of the West Bank and Gaza. Our hearts ache when we see Jewish soldiers mistreating Arabs. We found it hard to believe such accounts initially, but the longer we live among the Arab people the more inescapable the evidence becomes.

At the same time, it is clear to us that the Israeli Army is much like any other army. We are treated respectfully by the soldiers with whom we come into contact (although, of course, we are not Arab) and have come to believe that the general population will not be mistreated as long as they remain peaceful.

Many of our Arab friends would disagree strongly with that assessment. For them, the very fact of living under occupation means the suppression of human rights.

To a certain extent this is true. In the Bethlehem area, for example, "cottage industries" are common, whereby local Arab people sew in their homes for Israeli clothing factories. The work involves long, hard hours for minimal pay. After the war began some of our neighbors found that the factories refused to pay them for work completed. Sitting and drinking the ubiquitous Arabic tea with them, we would also absorb their despair and anger. After working long hours and feeling rightfully proud of their workmanship, they were chagrined to find that their salary checks "bounced" at the local bank.

The explanation? Their Israeli supplier would shrug his shoulders, claiming he didn't have any money at the moment. More probably, business was slow and he did not want to pay out the money just then. The frustration of our Arab friends deepened when these same employers badgered them about completing more work with still no pay in hand.

This is not likely to happen to Israeli workers who are protected by law as in any modern industrial society. Not being citizens, however, Arab workers from the West Bank have no recourse in the Israeli legal system. In cases like this they can only hope that their employer will see fit to pay them.

Our neighbors put up with this kind of treatment simply because they have no other choice. The economy of the West Bank, never developed to any significant degree, has been in shambles since the beginning of the Palestinian uprising, known in Arabic as the *intifada*. It is difficult to find any kind of employment. Delayed, erratic payment is better than no paycheck at all.

Our neighbors do admit that their Israeli employers come up with the money eventually. But the hardship of trying to survive while waiting on the whims of their employers heats a simmering resentment. I had to ask myself how I would react if my boss delayed paying me until it was convenient for him. How much bitterness would I harbor if there were no way to correct the injustice?

The Arabs I am describing here are not unshaven terrorists with long knives hidden under soiled garments. On the whole, as Arab Christians they have a higher moral standard and sense of integrity than many in the "Christian" West. The majority of the Arab people work hard and expect nothing more than to be paid for their labor. Examples of this kind of mistreatment abound, and in these situations Rebekka and I sympathize wholeheartedly with our Arab friends. How can we do any differently?

Also in these situations we wish that our fervently pro-Israeli friends would admit that real problems exist and need to be addressed. No group of people should be kept indefinitely in a state of limbo without the civil rights that we in the West take for granted.

The West Bank of the Jordan

The name *West Bank* comes from the period between 1948 and 1967 when the country of Jordan occupied much of the central, mountainous part of the ancient land of Israel. The main part of the Hashemite Kingdom of Jordan is east of the Jordan River. The newly acquired territory was on the west bank of that dividing river.

Our main sources of information about life in those years are our landlords, Silwa and Nadia, two elderly sisters from established Jerusalemite Arab families.[1] Silwa held a high administrative post during the Jordanian occupation of the West Bank. They both speak impeccable English and are a wealth of information about former times. An invitation to tea upstairs is to step back into an earlier, more civil time.

They have often described how the people suffered poverty during those years as King Hussein used most of his meager resources to develop his "East Bank." The Jordanian military presence was oppressive: Those arrested for wrongdoing were sometimes carried off into brutal prisons in the Jordanian desert. The sisters had to endure an uncouth Jordanian officer who occupied the lower flat without paying. The Palestinians remember well how they were treated during the Jordanian occupation and are not eager for any future peace settlement that would once again give Jordan control over the West Bank.

In spite of the difficulties, Silwa and Nadia were well enough off financially to motor across the Jordan valley occasionally to attend receptions with young King Hussein in Amman, the then-fledgling capital of Jordan. It was only a couple of hours by car to Jordan's chief city through Jericho and across the Jordan valley depression, a thousand feet below sea level. At that time Amman had few paved streets and even fewer attractions.

Once, deciding to spend the night, Silwa and Nadia booked into what was then the only hotel in town. They refused to crawl between the filthy sheets, however, and spent the night sitting up together sipping tea.

They reminisced how on occasion they would journey by car on to Damascus, and from there to Beirut. Ah!—Beirut, the Paris of the Middle East. Words fail them as they try to describe the abundance to be had in the shops of that cultured city. The beauty of Lebanon was breathtaking. Borders, if they existed then, were insignificant. Truly it was another world.

---

[1] Because of the sensitive political situation, the names of all personal acquaintances have been changed.

Amman, increased today in size if not in beauty, still lies a mere fifty miles away, but it might as well be a thousand. Now it is separated by a heavily guarded frontier. Rebekka and I have often driven along that border in the Jordan valley. It consists of a minefield separated by two fences with electronic sensors to alert the I.D.F. (Israeli Defense Forces) to any terrorist incursions.

The West Bank was captured by Israel in the lightning "Six Day War" of June 1967. Israel also took control of a narrow strip of territory along the Mediterranean coast bordering Egypt known as the Gaza Strip. In addition, the Golan Heights overlooking the Sea of Galilee were also occupied by the I.D.F. These three territories are the focal point of the Arab world's denunciations against Israel—highlighted during the Middle East peace talks that began in the autumn of 1991—regardless of the fact that the Arabs lost them in a war of aggression against the Jewish state.

Besides Jerusalem, the Golan is the only territory that has been annexed outright, primarily for reasons of security: The Syrians had used the Heights to lob artillery shells down on Israeli communities below. We will see later why the rest of the land has not been annexed.

A Visit to Azza Camp

Another source of insight into the lives of the Palestinians has come from the poorer element of their society. Pulling my VW bug off the main Hebron road near the entrance to Azza camp, just a few blocks from our home, I can enter the constricted world of the Palestinian refugees. Azza is the smallest of three refugee camps in the Bethlehem area. Many who pass by, especially tourists riding past in air-conditioned buses on their way to the Church of the Nativity, are unaware that a squalid refugee camp lies beyond the streetfront buildings. A thousand Palestinians have made this triangle of land at the entrance to Bethlehem their cramped home since the 1948 war. Just a few years earlier, I was one of those who passed by oblivious to the presence of this camp.

I have often made my way carefully through the narrow alleys in the darkness, taking care to avoid the drainage gutter in the middle of the makeshift passageways, venturing toward the ill-fitting door that marks the entrance to Issa's home. As I call out his name he appears, welcoming me warmly. After I exchange customary greetings with his family, we retire to his room to talk.

In the first years after 1948, the residents of Azza camp lived in tents, through the stifling heat of summer and driving rain of winter. They had little interest in building permanent dwellings. This was not their home: They were merely temporary residents here until they were once again in rightful possession of their homes and properties inside what had become the state of Israel. The refugees had no intention of residing permanently in this new territory called the West Bank.

The residents of Azza could not understand why the Arab Legion was unable to defend their lands during Israel's war of independence, but they were sure that they would return to their homes; the Arab armies would soon accomplish that. By the mid-1960s they were talking excitedly about Egyptian President Gamal Abdul Nasser, who was already preparing his armies to "liberate" Palestine. His thunderous radio messages beamed from Egypt proclaimed boastfully that Israel would soon be cast into the sea. It was unthinkable that tiny Israel would be able to defend herself against the vast armies of Egypt supported by Syria, Jordan and other Arab countries. No, it was just a matter of time now. . . .

Then, as Israel launched a preemptive strike to blunt the impending offensive, the combined Arab armies attacked Israel on three fronts. The news coming across the airwaves was encouraging: Egyptian and Jordanian radio were proclaiming a triumphant victory. The Arab armies were striking at the heartland of Israel, whose forces were being defeated on every side. Tel Aviv was being pounded by the Arab air forces while the Egyptians pushed up from the South and the Syrians advanced across the Golan toward Galilee.

But something was wrong. The tanks rolling down the streets of

Bethlehem bore unreadable markings; the soldiers spoke a strange language. Almost overnight the Jordanian Army had fled. Our neighbors told of soldiers throwing away their uniforms and fleeing barefoot across the desert back to Jordan. Soon the unbelievable reality could no longer be denied. The boastful propaganda they had been following excitedly on their radios had been no more than wishful thinking. Instead of the Arabs destroying the State of Israel and regaining Palestine, the Jews had now conquered the West Bank!

The Six Day War was a stunning blow to the refugees living on the West Bank. For almost twenty years they had waited to return to their villages. Rather than acknowledge defeat at the hands of the Israelis, most chose to believe that a covert conspiracy was responsible for the debacle. They accused King Hussein of Jordan of making a secret pact with the Israelis to allow the Jews to take Arab land. No one was able to explain how King Hussein could possibly benefit from selling out the West Bank, or what solid evidence there was to support this contention. But *Mah leesh* (Never mind) it must have happened this way.

A popular story—and Arab humor can be delightfully wry— tells of one unfortunate man from Hebron who fled the West Bank during the war with as many of his possessions as he could stuff into his aged truck. He made his way down to the Jordan River valley and lumbered up to the Jordanian border post. Upon examining his vehicle, the guards told him he could pass but that his possessions had to be left behind—to which the flustered man blurted out, "Did you sell the country *furnished*, too?"

Sitting in Issa's room, we would soon be brought steaming cups of dark, sweet tea. Looking around the room as I sipped, I would marvel at the austere life of these people. Issa's few possessions were gathered in this room: a shelf of tattered books, a half-broken radio, a bottle of aftershave displayed proudly. The room was furnished with worn furniture that had been wired and nailed together repeatedly. On the cracked walls were cut-out pictures and an old scenic calendar showing a European landscape. How often I stared at that sedate, well-ordered vista and marveled at how out of place Europe looked in this crumbling room.

Decades ago the U.N.R.W.A. (United Nations Relief and Works Agency) built these simple buildings as temporary housing for the residents of the camp. In winter the cold winds penetrate the thin walls and in summer there is little relief from tormenting mosquitos.

How ashamed I would be to invite my own guests into such a room! Having grown up in a large family with never quite enough money to go around, I have never thought of myself as wealthy. Yet sitting in that humble room, I cannot hide the fact that I am indeed the child of a rich country with abundant resources.

But these people don't seem to mind. Observing them, I know that material possessions are not the key to happiness. In fact, they laugh more easily and—despite their difficulties—appear to enjoy life more than those whose lives are filled with every kind of material comfort.

Issa is a graduate of the Health Science course at Bethlehem University. Along with many of his classmates, he was unable to find employment in his field. Due to the depressed economic conditions on the West Bank, the unemployment rate among university graduates exceeded fifty percent. More fortunate than some of his friends, Issa found a job in a chemical factory paying about $300 a month. With this he could help support his aged parents and family.

I have discovered that Arab families are much more supportive financially than their Western counterparts. Those who are employed share their incomes freely with their parents and other family members. This illustrates one important difference between Middle Eastern and Western culture: While European and American culture is more likely to stress the *independence*, Arab society may be characterized by mutual *interdependence*.

Israeli society is also much more interdependent than what one might expect to find in the West. I heard the story of one Israeli man who, while visiting friends in New York City, decided to check this out for himself. He stuck his head out into the hallway of the apartment where he was staying and shouted "Help!" at the top of his voice. Then he waited to see what would happen.

In Israel such a cry would bring an immediate response: Doors would fling open as people wondered what was going on and offered assistance. Living in a continual state of siege has taught Israelis to bind together and to render immediate help when needed.

But in New York the situation is different. The visiting Israeli waited as he looked down the long hallway. Not a single door opened. No one inquired what the problem was. Apparently nobody wanted to "get involved."

When I was told that story, I could not help but think that there is an element of selfishness to the Western style of life. We live separate existences behind closed and locked doors so that no one can interfere with our private lives. On the other hand, we might also find ourselves alone just when we need help the most.

Sometimes Issa and I sat and talked with his father, a kindly man who still dressed in traditional Arab clothing. He was weak and infirm but still had a clear memory of his former estate. Bet Gubrin, the village where he and his family came from, was located in the Shephelah region between the Judean highlands and the coast. With gently rolling hills and a rich history, it is one of my favorite areas of Israel. It is there, on the border of Philistine territory, that David fought Goliath and where the Ark of the Covenant was returned by the plagued Philistines.

Issa's father, reclining on his mat, would describe his property. Years ago he owned two hundred *dunams* (about 25 acres). But after the 1948 war the villagers were thrown out of their homes and Bet Gubrin, along with dozens of other Arab villages, was demolished.

Arabs and Israelis strongly disagree as to the reasons for the upheaval of people from their homes. The Israelis claim that the villages were destroyed for reasons of security. That is, from them came roving bands of marauding Arabs who threatened nearby

Jewish towns. Arabs insist that their villages were razed to make room for Jewish settlements.

The magnitude of this tragedy for the Arab villagers cannot be understated. Land is the lifeblood of the Arab. In those days, most were farmers earning their livelihood much the same way their forefathers had done. The Arab borrowed little from the modern methods his Israeli counterpart adapted. They were too complicated and cost too much money to implement. What need was there to change? Given enough rain, the land produced enough olives, fruit and vegetables for the family to eat and sell for the coming year. Their flocks of sheep and goats would provide milk and meat products.

The Shephelah region is Israeli territory now. No Arab villages remain. But still, Issa's parents could not help wondering what had happened to their beloved lands. Was someone trimming the apricot trees? What about the vineyards that needed so much care— and could it really be true that their family home was no more? Closing their eyes, they could imagine everything as it once was— and *enshallah* (God willing) would once again be.

After many years the family dared to return to the area for a visit. The hills were the same but everything else had been transformed. A new road had been cut through the broad valley leading to Bet Gubrin. Finally they arrived. Issa's mother wept as she walked over the terraces and orchards they had once cultivated. She had known every square inch, every fruit tree. Now everything was overgrown, abandoned. Nearby an Israeli kibbutz employed modern agricultural methods.

Issa's father located the spot where the family home had once stood. The walls he had laid with his own hands were now only piles of rubble overgrown with weeds. Nothing remained of Bet Gubrin: The Israelis had planted a forest of pine trees over the area. But in the midst of the new trees, as if in memory, fruit trees, wild grapes and cactus plants marked the border of the Arab village. Issa's father gazed at the untended fruit trees, they told me, as if recognizing old friends.

Issa was resigned to the fact that they would never return to Bet Gubrin, but his aged father still talked about the old days. "I own two hundred dunams in Bet Gubrin!" he would remind himself, as if to compensate for his present humble state. Issa, out of sadness for his father's hopeless dreams of yesteryear, would reply in frustration, "It's finished! It's all over!"

In time Issa finally escaped the camp and went abroad. Later he received word that his father had quietly passed away, still dreaming he owned two hundred dunams in Bet Gubrin with every variety of fruit tree.

Annexing the West Bank

Many pro-Zionist Christians visiting Israel support enthusiastically Israel's right to "the whole land, including Judea and Samaria"—meaning the West Bank and Gaza. They seem not to have considered the fact that the Jewish state has purposely never annexed these territories. If Judea and Samaria are irrevocably part of Eretz Israel (the land of Israel), why has the West Bank never been formally incorporated into the State of Israel? The motives for this are political as well as practical.

The main reason is population demographics. If the West Bank were formally part of the Israeli state, then its Arab inhabitants would have to be granted citizenship. But that would mean an additional 1.6 million Arabs from the West Bank and Gaza voting in Israeli elections.[2] Combined with another 800,000 Arabs living within Israel proper—who have voting rights—this would create a sizable voting bloc to compete with the nearly four million Jews of the country. Given the higher birth rate of the Arab population, the Israelis fear they would one day be voted out of their country.

Another reason is economic. Annexing the West Bank and Gaza would mean pouring billions of *shekels* (the Israeli unit of currency) into the territories in order to bring the economic infra-

---

[2] The more than 100,000 Jews living in the 160-odd settlements on the West Bank and Gaza have full voting rights.

structure up to par with Israel. This is money that hard-pressed Israel simply does not have, especially as it struggles to absorb hundreds of thousands of new Russian immigrants.

The West Bank and Gaza are light-years behind Israel in terms of industrial development. In our area only a handful of factories can even be considered light industries. Our Arab neighbors, if they are able to work at all, are usually employed in manual labor or other low-paying jobs. A surprising amount of employment on the West Bank depends directly on either Israel or foreign religious and charitable organizations.

In short, the Palestinian economy, far from self-sufficient, would go into a tailspin if total independence from Israel were achieved or if foreign aid dried up.

If these territories were annexed as part of Israel, on the other hand, the cost of absorbing an additional 1.6 million persons, many of whom are without steady employment, would put an unbearable strain on the Israeli social welfare system.

Finally, Israel realizes that to annex the West Bank and Gaza would bring about severe censure by the community of nations, including the United States. The Jewish state cannot risk the ostracism and punitive measures that would almost certainly follow. This very issue may well be a catalyst for the final battle at the end of time that the Bible calls Armageddon. We shall try to imagine this future scenario later.

This is not to say that the Arab inhabitants of the West Bank and Gaza would accept Israeli citizenship if it were granted. The vast majority would undoubtedly reject it.[3] A similar situation occurred after 1967 when Israeli citizenship was offered to the Arab residents of East Jerusalem. Very few accepted the offer. Indeed, if the territories were annexed, the Israeli government would likely have great difficulty gaining any degree of coopera-

---

[3] This can be seen in the post-1967 situation in East Jerusalem, when Arab businesses refused to be registered as Israeli companies, Arab lawyers refused to appear in Israeli courts, and Arabs refused to sit on the unified city council. Gradual progress has been made in economic—but not political—integration.

tion from the Arab population. Even today Arab municipalities refuse to coordinate with the Israelis in such mundane matters as garbage collection.

Thus, the West Bank remains under perpetual "administrative control" by the I.D.F. Its Arab inhabitants do not have Israeli passports; they cannot vote in Israeli elections; and if arrested for security offenses they do not have the right to a trial by jury. The understandable misgivings of the Israelis toward the Arab people have led to the denial of basic civil rights, a situation that has continued for four decades.

My friend Ahmed came to see me one day, humiliated and angered. Ahmed was a quiet, strong fellow whose family owned a small farm near Hebron. He dressed and acted in the plain, straightforward manner of people who live simply and know the value of hard work. Ahmed was honest and kept to his own business. While he shopped in the Old City of Jerusalem, some Israeli police had first stopped him and then harassed him. They forced him to stand on one foot until he could bear it no longer, then taunted and beat him.

Most Israeli police would not stoop to this kind of behavior, but the fact that the Palestinians on the West Bank and Gaza do not have the rights of citizenship increases the potential for such abuses.

As we shall see, there appears to be no human solution to the problems of the West Bank and its Palestinian inhabitants. It is inconceivable that Israel, for the above reasons, would annex the West Bank. Yet it is equally inconceivable that she would yield sovereignty over it. The situation will likely continue to deteriorate until, according to the Bible, an evil world leader will arise and intervene militarily in the Holy Land.

We will discuss later the rise of this nefarious man and his solution to the Middle East problem. For now, let's look more closely at this volatile part of the world through the eyes of the Palestinians, and see the historical and internal conflicts that have caused them to vent their anger in violence.

2
Throwing Off the Yoke

To RIDE THE RICKETY ARAB BUSES TO AND FROM JER-
usalem is to ride between two worlds. To the left, upon entering
the city limits, sprawls the modern Jerusalem suburb of Gilo. With
its high-rise apartments and a population exceeding twenty thousand, one would scarcely believe that twenty years ago it was a
barren mountain ridge considered part of the village of Beit Jala.

At the Gilo junction Arab men line up along the wall, waiting
for the bus or a ride. These are the laborers who commute between
two worlds. During the day they provide the manual labor and
skilled stonecutting without which the construction industry of
Israel would come to a halt. Other Arabs come to work as gar-
deners and maintenance workers, waiters and cooks, janitors and
street sweepers.

Many of them clearly feel out of place in the Westernized cities.
Sometimes these proud Arab men have to take orders from a
woman. Such a thing is unheard of in conservative Arab society. In
their restrictive world women rarely rise above secretarial positions.

Even worse to them are the shameful ways of acting and dressing in Israel, which confirm their opinion about the decadent West. In traditional Arab society a woman would not be seen in public with any man other than her husband, father or brother. With their faces often hidden behind veils, it would be inconceivable for them to dress immodestly or show open affection to a boyfriend. Stealing glances as they pass the cinemas, these men are shocked at the enticements openly available; such films would never be shown on the Arab side. Passing newsstands, they gape at the publications sold on the streets. They have little need for further proof: The Jews are steeped in the immoral ways of the West.

In the evening these Arab men line up along the road, awaiting rides back to their villages. A simple meal awaits them, after which they will sit into the night drinking strong, sweet tea with their friends in homes built with their own hands. Here life is more civilized, more ordered. They do not crave the material comforts and luxuries of the Jewish side.

In fact, if accepting the Western lifestyle is the price to be paid for material prosperity, they don't want it. There is a sense of continuity in Arab society lacking in Western countries. Many of us wonder about—and fear—the direction in which our society is heading. Not so the traditional Arab—so long as he can keep corrupting Western influences as far away as possible.

The Muslim Brotherhood

Their absolute rejection of the culture and religion of the Western world is the key to understanding one of the most secretive yet powerful movements sweeping the Middle East: the Muslim Brotherhood. The religious ideology of the Brotherhood is a major factor in the violent Palestinian uprising that has engulfed the West Bank and Gaza in recent years.

Westerners are often perplexed as to why Arabs are attracted to extremist groups and movements. The answer lies in the predominant religion of the region, Islam. The religion of Muhammad holds a latent explosive potential that has been aptly described as "incandescent fury," refering to the smoldering hand-held flash devices that early photographers used with bulky box cameras. We shall see later how Islam will play a critical role in the fulfillment of biblical prophecy.

People sometimes confuse the terms *Arab* and *Muslim. Arab* refers to the race of people who have inhabited the Mideast for millennia. *Muslim* refers to a follower of the religion of Islam.

Not all Muslims are Arabs. In fact, the largest Muslim nation, Indonesia, is not Arab. And not all Arabs are Muslims. Most of the people on our street are Christians. There is a minority of Christian Arabs from various denominations living throughout the Arab world. Thus the terms *Arab* and *Muslim* are not synonymous. Since the vast majority of Arabs accept the religion of Islam, however, the terms are often used almost interchangeably.

Most in the West tend to think of religion as but one of many parts of our lives. We usually separate economic and political matters from our faith. Islam, by contrast, does not limit its control over the believer to purely spiritual matters:

> In fact, Islam is a religious faith that permeates every nook and cranny of a believer's life, entering into virtually all of the experiences from which he derives a sense of meaning. The central figure of this religion, the Prophet Muhammad, was a cultural leader, a religious prophet, a military man, a father and a husband, a person who at one time at least had considerable commercial interests.[1]

The religion of Islam addresses the above areas and more. The holy book of Islam, the *Koran,* reads like a textbook of specific commands for every aspect of life. The Koran alone, moreover, gives direction; all foreign influences must be resisted.

The Muslim Brotherhood was founded in Ismalia, Egypt, in 1928 by Hassan al-Banna, who coined a simple yet compelling slogan:

---

[1] C. George Fry and James R. King, *Islam: A Survey of the Muslim Faith* (Grand Rapids, Mich.: Baker Book House, 1982), p. 1.

Allah is our goal
The Prophet is our leader
The Koran is our constitution
Holy War is our way
Death for Allah's sake is our supreme desire.[2]

The Muslim Brotherhood considers Western civilization to be the primary source of evil in the world. Zionism is viewed as the West's agent and, therefore, the enemy of Islam's divinely inspired moral and political order. The challenge of the decadent West can be countered only by the revival of Islam among the masses. The Muslim Brotherhood seeks to establish the ideal Muslim state, called the *caliphate*, based on Muslim law, called the *shari'a*.

The movement spread throughout Egypt attracting mostly peasants and manual laborers. Following their militant slogan, they did not shrink from violent means to achieve "death for Allah's sake." They pursued relentlessly their goal to overthrow the Arab governments that were considered corrupted by Western values.

Despite attempts to contain its influence, the movement could not be suppressed. It continued to grow in Egypt where today it represents a constant and deadly threat. The late Egyptian President Anwar Sadat is said to have sympathized with the Brotherhood and to have tolerated the growing movement. He may have paid for such appeasement with his life.

His successor, Hosni Mubarak, finds himself in a difficult position *vis-a-vis* the Brotherhood. Recognizing the danger the movement poses to his regime and to the democratic tradition in Egypt, he has tried to prevent legalization of the Brotherhood as a political party. Ironically, while the Brotherhood is demanding inclusion in the political process, its final goal is to dismantle democracy not only in Egypt but throughout the Arab world.

The Muslim Brotherhood with its implacable hatred of non-

---

[2] Nissim Rejwan, "Moslem Brotherhood: Jordan's Juggernaut," *Jerusalem Post* (January 4, 1991), p. 6.

Muslim values has been making phenomenal advances in other Muslim countries as well. In 1981 the movement won 51 out of 264 seats in the Sudanese Parliament. In Jordan the Brotherhood finally won its long battle for legal recognition. In 1990, on the ballot for the first time, the movement won the largest bloc of seats of any political party. King Hussein was then forced to surrender five Cabinet posts to the Muslim Brotherhood and its affiliates, whose first demand was to be given control of the country's educational system.

The fate of the Muslim Brotherhood in Syria has been quite the opposite. It made the mistake of resorting to violent means to overthrow Hafez al-Assad's regime. The conflict came to a bloody end in February 1982 when the Syrian president launched a full-scale military operation against the city of Hama, the stronghold of the movement. According to a 1983 report of Amnesty International, more than ten thousand perished in the onslaught.

Hamas, Israel's Implacable Enemy

Since its inception, the Muslim Brotherhood has been obsessed with the Palestinian cause. Iftah Zilberman, research fellow at the Truman Institute, Jerusalem, writes:

> It is not surprising that as early as 1935 the Egyptian Moslem Brotherhood leadership backed the Palestinian cause and, for example, supported Haj Amin al-Husseini, the well-known Palestinian leader. In 1945 the Moslem Brotherhood started to operate directly in Mandatory Palestine, recruiting thousands of members, some of whom fought against Israel on the battlefield.[3]

The organization *Hamas* is the military arm of the Muslim Brotherhood in the Occupied Territories. This Gaza-based fundamentalist Islamic group sees every non-Muslim on Arab soil as the

---

[3] Iftah Zilberman, "Hamas: Apocalypse Now," *Jerusalem Post* (December 28, 1990), p. 5.

enemy. Even U.N.R.W.A. personnel stationed in the Territories to provide aid fear the group. Hamas has been responsible for numerous terrorist acts including the murder of Israelis.

The Hamas activists I have met proved to be rigidly idealistic and anti-Western. Years ago, when the Brotherhood began expanding its influence outside of Gaza, it met with resistance on the West Bank, which was under the "control" of various mainstream P.L.O (Palestine Liberation Organization) factions. Their extreme Islamic ideas soon found fertile ground, however, especially in the refugee camps and among the students at nearby Bethlehem University.

I remember talking with some of them after the U.S. space shuttle Challenger disaster. We sat together in front of a television set watching the horrifying news films of the shuttle exploding. They evinced no sympathy. Instead, their attitude was one of self-righteous vindication. Here at last was Allah's judgment upon the cursed United States, the bastion of evil in the world.

Their hero was Ayatollah Khomeini, who had brought Islamic fundamentalism to Iran. No matter that his regime was oppressive. An Islamic theocracy has no need for democracy. What was needed instead, they insisted, were true Islamic values. Only that would bring order and peace to the world. Individual freedom was incomprehensible to them: Why should people be given the right to deviate from Allah's will? The only fault they found with the Ayatollah was that he had purchased arms secretly from Israel. Flagrant human rights abuses did not move these radical students, but to engage in dealings with the hated Zionists was unforgivable.

As this kind of fanaticism began to spread through the Occupied Territories, the voice of moderation was seldom heard. Demonstrations at the Vatican-run Bethlehem University occurred more frequently. The protesters, members of Hamas as well as the various P.L.O factions at the university, would barricade themselves inside the campus buildings and hurl rocks down upon the military.

Many students wanted nothing to do with these demonstrations. They wished only to continue their studies, which the radicals were denying them. No one dared, however, to speak a word against the disruptions.

In early December 1987, a friend of mine named Yusef was caught inside the university compound when the demonstrators took over the buildings. Yusef was as kind a fellow as one would ever hope to meet. He lived in nearby Aida refugee camp with his family and studied mathematics at the university. I still remember his warm smile and gentle manner.

Undoubtedly thinking that the skirmish with the military was over, he stuck his head out of the University gate. An I.D.F. sharpshooter ended Yusef's life with a single shot. He was 21.

The Rise of the Intifada

It was about this time that the intifada erupted in the West Bank and Gaza. Rebekka and I, newly married, had just moved into our flat, the lower half of an old stone Arab house. We had met while I was teaching at a training school for Arab Christians. Rebekka came from Switzerland to volunteer at the college and we happened to be in the same Arabic class. I suddenly took a great interest in studying Arabic and asked Rebekka if she would be willing to study with me after class.

She was, and after a while I asked her to teach me German, which was an added burden on her busy schedule. She consented graciously, and after I plied her with candy bars she began to enjoy my company as much as I enjoyed hers. Several months later we decided to marry and had a lovely wedding in a quaint village church in Rebekka's Swiss hometown. Since we were both interested in working among Arabic people, we returned the following autumn to continue our ministry.

Then everything changed. *Intifada* is an Arabic word meaning to "throw off" something undesirable—in this case, Israeli rule. No longer could we enjoy exploring the countryside in our little VW bug, visiting the Arab villages nestled in the hills and valleys of the West Bank. Our car was registered in Jerusalem and had yellow license plates, in contrast to cars from the West Bank that had blue plates. This enabled the police and military to identify the vehicles of West Bank Arabs. Palestinians viewed it as one more form of harassment.

The color-coded policy backfired when Arabs targeted yellow-plate cars for attack with rocks and Molotov cocktails.[4] For the Jews living in some 160 settlements on the West Bank, traveling by car became a dangerous venture. Many put plexiglas or metal screens on their car windows in order to deflect flying rocks. Several of our friends had harrowing tales to tell of their vehicles being attacked, and we found ourselves increasingly limited as to where we could drive safely.

Our days of exploring the narrow streets of Bethlehem gradually became a thing of the past as well. It was not that ordinary Arabs would attack us. We had no fear of the inhabitants of our area, who continued to be friendly and helpful—even protective when trouble was near. The danger came from another sector: the *shabiba,* the youths actively involved in the "resistance." Their newfound power and authority was one of the most frightening aspects of the uprising.

The intifada brought a fundamental change to Arab society on the West Bank. Historically in an Arab town or village the sheik was the final authority, one who was paid great deference by all. He was the one who mediated disputes and negotiated with warring individuals or families. When problems arose there was a hierarchy of authority to appeal to for a solution.

No longer. The sheiks were pushed aside and could only watch helplessly as the shabiba, who supposedly took orders from the P.L.O. hierarchy, dominated every town in the Occupied Territories. The elders of the village could only remain mute lest they come under suspicion for challenging the new authority. Parents

---

[4] A Molotov cocktail is a simple but effective weapon consisting of a bottle filled with gasoline and lit with a cloth wick stuffed in the neck. When thrown it shatters, spraying the burning liquid.

lost control over their children, not daring to try to prevent them from participating in violent demonstrations against the I.D.F.

I will never forget the seething rage that possessed a young shabiba one day when my family and I managed to get caught in the middle of a violent confrontation. We were visiting some Arab friends nearby who lived next door to a refugee camp. They told us about a Jewish doctor who had lost his way in his car and strayed into the camp. His yellow Israeli license plates were spotted and he soon found himself under attack. He was chased down the driveway of our friends' house by an angry crowd.

The Arab father and sons went outside and placed themselves literally as a human shield between the terrified doctor and the enraged crowd. After intense negotiations they convinced the crowd to relent, but not before they smashed his car and, for good measure, quite a few windows in our friends' house.

This is not, by the way, the only instance I know of in which Arabs courageously defended Jews from violent attack. The vast majority of Arab people want only to live their lives in peace, as do most Israelis. It is an extremist minority on both sides that keeps stoking the fires of hatred.

As my friend told me the story of the doctor, I felt relief that no one had been hurt and that my family had not been there at the time. At that very moment we heard the crash of garbage bins being overturned on the street outside. To our chagrin we saw that a demonstration was about to begin. Masked youths were barricading the street—and our way out.

They set tires on fire and began smashing bottles on the street hoping to puncture the tires of the Army vehicles when they arrived. Our hosts hurried to close the windows. The Army would soon be shooting noxious tear gas to disperse the demonstrators.

We might have been able to sit this one out except for a fateful twist of events. An Arab-American relative who happened to be visiting just then decided that the demonstration was a chance to take some great photos to show back home. Despite our host's cautions, he pulled out his camera and began snapping pictures through the porch glass.

Suddenly everything erupted. The youths on the street spotted the picture-taker and assumed he was a spy. Before we realized what was happening they charged the house, hurling rocks and bottles as they ran.

A bottle crashed through the parlor window, splattering where we had just been sitting. We were herded to the back of the house. If the shabiba discovered that foreigners were inside the house—and especially Americans—our safety would be endangered.

We knelt to pray together as the men went outside to try to explain the situation. They finally convinced the shabiba that the man was not an Israeli spy, and the youths left to continue their demonstration on the street.

Shortly afterward the Army arrived and broke it up. The family gave the all-clear for us to leave, apologizing profusely for the trouble we had experienced. At the entrance to the driveway I was spotted by one of the young shabiba. Thinking I was Jewish, the boy was so visibly filled with hatred that his body trembled, distorting his speech. Our Arab friends managed to calm him down enough for us to pass.

What alarmed me most was the deference that my friend had to pay to the youth, who could not have been more than half his own age. The reason was obvious: If he did not show respect toward the shabiba, he and his family would soon become targets for attack.

This breakdown of respect for authority is one feature of the intifada that defies Arab culture. My friend Mahmud told me of another incident that illustrates this. Mahmud lived in a refugee camp bordering the Hebron road, a main thoroughfare for the Jewish settlers in the Territories who commute to and from Jerusalem. Stonings of their yellow-plate cars occurred on a daily basis, and the military began taking increasingly harsh measures to prevent the rock-throwing.

One man in the camp, whose home bordered the road, saw the

youths throwing rocks at cars from his property. Since that could bring him problems from the I.D.F., he confronted the youths, some of whom were barely in their teens. If they wanted to throw rocks at cars, he told them, it was none of his business, but he did not want them to do it from his property.

In traditional Arab society the youths would be expected to comply with his wishes. In a densely populated, close-knit community like their refugee camp, great care is taken not to offend one's neighbors.

Not so in the intifada. Mahmud told me that one of the shabiba, who could not have been older than ten or twelve, pointed to the telephone pole and informed the man where he could expect to find himself hanging unless he shut up. He complied, and so ended his complaints.

This level of intimidation is hard to fathom, but for individuals on the West Bank and Gaza to question the legitimacy of any action by the intifada is a dangerous venture indeed. Not once have I heard the idea expressed publicly that peaceful coexistence is preferable to a fruitless violent resistance.

Sometimes our Arab friends will disclose privately to us their reservations about the intifada. To a certain degree they feel safe opening up to us. As foreigners, we are outside the fraternal strangle of Arab society. Because we oppose the ways of violence, they know there is little chance we will betray them. But they do not speak freely even with their closest Arab friends. One never knows whether or not those friends will one day disclose feelings and opinions shared in confidence.

Given the volatile nature of Arab friendship, especially among young people, this is a real possibility. Rebekka and I are sometimes surprised to learn that a close friendship between two Arabs has suddenly been shattered by some seemingly minor conflict. Instead of resolving the problem, each party prefers to "save face" by refusing to have anything more to do with the other.

Most Palestinians live in fear of being labeled a collaborator —someone having some alleged connection with or sympathy toward Israel. This could include anything from holding a job inside Israel to failing to show enthusiasm about the intifada. And since the Arab community is susceptible to ill-founded rumors and fraught with suspicion, doubtless many are labeled collaborators to satisfy personal grudges. In fact, as fewer and fewer Palestinians die in violent demonstrations, the number of Arabs killed by fellow Arabs is escalating at an alarming rate.[5]

We have learned of terrible incidents of people being killed for almost no reason. A man who worked as a laborer inside Israel was murdered a few blocks from our home for allegedly collaborating. This may have been his unforgivable crime. Or perhaps he spoke his mind too freely. He was lured out of his home one night by the false news that his brother had been in an automobile accident and lay injured, and was thereby led into an ambush.

One pregnant mother of seven children who worked as a nurse in a hospital was knifed to death. She was accused of providing the names of her patients, some of whom were injured in demonstrations, to the Israeli military.

Another Arab worker found a Molotov cocktail on his doorstep one morning with the attached note: "You have a nice family—keep it that way."

When the result of these threats is a late-night knock on the door, a group of men will be waiting outside, their hoods concealing the identities of neighbors and "friends" who join in on the punishment of the collaborator.

They ask to speak with the suspect, who in most instances opens the door despite the obvious danger. Why? There is little point in resisting; those who do usually have their doors broken down. And in an Arab community there is no place to flee. No one will

---

[5] According to I.D.F. figures, Palestinian militants killed 176 people considered to be informers in 1990, as compared to 139 in 1989 and 16 in 1988. In January 1991, in a vain attempt to stem the killing of Palestinians suspected of aiding the authorities, the P.L.O.-backed Unified Leadership went so far as to issue a leaflet warning against such attacks, but to no avail. "Intifada Marks 3rd Birthday with Grim, Hostile Silence," *Jerusalem Post* (December 15, 1990), p. 5.

dare hide those marked by the intifada, even their own relatives. Their only hope is to comply and try to persuade the group that they are innocent of the charges against them.

All too often, however, there is no trial: The offender is led to an olive grove or some other secluded area and put to death.

In death the shame continues. There is no funeral; no *imam* (religious leader of a local mosque) will preside over the ceremony of a collaborator. The family will not dare to grieve publicly for their lost loved one; and instead of offering the customary condolences to the family, friends shun them. Few want to cast suspicion on themselves by expressing sympathy for the death of a collaborator. The ostracized family, its wounds deepened by the communal rejection, bury their loved one in solitude.

The increased violence in the intifada is particularly blatant because there is no police force operating in the Occupied Territories.

When the uprising began, the "Unified National Leadership"—which represented the P.L.O. in the Territories—decreed that all Arab policemen in the West Bank and Gaza either resign or face recrimination. This was because all local police stations were part of the Israeli Civil Administration, which governed the Territories.

So profound was the rejection of anything Israeli that the P.L.O. preferred to leave their own people without protection rather than have a police force that cooperated with the hated Jews. Almost all Arab policemen immediately resigned for fear of their lives. One policeman in Beit Jala who hesitated was murdered.

The I.D.F. is always in the area, but their job is not to take the place of the local police, and they have neither the resources nor the desire to investigate civil crimes.

Without any police on patrol, of course, crime increased radically. One family near us had the terrifying experience of watching their home be broken into in broad daylight while they cowered inside. Arab homes are strongly built, with iron bars and doors, but when criminals know there are no police to come and rescue their victims, they can proceed at leisure.

This family could do nothing as the thieves cut through the

window bars with electric saws. They called the local police department and reportedly heard a Hebrew-accented voice say, "You want help? Call the P.L.O.!" There was an unfortunate logic to that mockery.

Things that Go Bump in the Night

After dark became the most frightening time for us. We gradually stopped going out at night unless necessary. It is then that groups of masked Arab youths prowl. Coming during the wee hours of the night, they are rarely seen, but the morning brings evidence of their presence: slogans and threats painted on walls, streets blocked with stones, or the latest "intifada leaflet" with various instructions.

Once, while I was on a teaching trip to Galilee, Rebekka was alone in the house with Mahalia, our first child. In the middle of the night she was awakened suddenly by a violent pounding on the outside door near where she was sleeping. She grabbed Mahalia and went into the living room. The intruder then moved to the front of the house and began striking the iron door there with a metal instrument.

It sounded as though the door would be broken through at any moment. Our flat does not have a telephone—not that there would be anyone to call. Praying frantically, the only thing Rebekka could think to do was run into the kitchen and start screaming out the window. For some "unknown" reason it worked. After a while the banging stopped and the intruder or intruders left.

During that period our tension built. Sleep fled from us as our ears strained to hear the sounds in the night. The more I listened the more I heard. Quietly getting out of bed, I would move from room to room, peering out into the darkness. What was that sound? Was it a masked gang prowling silently around our house intending to break in—or just a patrolling cat?

It came to the point where something had to be done. Either we would really begin to trust God or we would leave. We found ourselves praying often for the Lord's protection and peace. Finally our prayers were answered. During a brief time of furlough in the States for refreshment with family and friends, the spirit of fear was lifted. Upon returning, we were no longer fearful in the night, and since that time we have continued to sleep peacefully.

The key for us was learning to rest *fully* in the Lord. Why should we be continually eaten up inside with fear about things that we have little or no control over, and which may never happen anyway? Come to think of it, this is a basic lesson to learn no matter where one lives.

3
Center Stage of History

THE JUDEAN HILLS ARE ESPECIALLY PICTURESQUE just after daybreak, when the morning sun brings out warm shades in the olive trees and vineyards flourishing in the terra rosa soil of the terraced hillsides. It is a special feeling to be out and about before the oppressive midday heat beats down.

I enjoy walking through Bethlehem in search of some fresh-baked *ka'ek*, sesame-sprinkled Arab bread, and *falafel*, spiced, ground chick peas deep-fried into crunchy balls. The clanging of the iron shop doors along the crooked streets signals the beginning of another day of business. Vendors in the old *suk*, or marketplace, advertise their produce loudly to the swelling crowds of shoppers, mostly Arab villagers and Bedouin, the Arab nomadic people living in rural areas.

Finding a spot to sit in and enjoy my breakfast, I feel the cares of life melting away against this timeless Mideast backdrop.

To the uninitiated tourist, the streets of Bethlehem seem quiet enough. The intifada has awakened a sixth sense of danger, however, in people on the street. Suddenly there will be tension in the air. Like a change in the wind, it will sweep down the street, causing shopper and shop owner to pause and look around.

Then one will hear the banging of metal doors as merchants up and down the street hurriedly shutter their shops. No one wants his merchandise damaged in the impending clash. In a minute the streets will be all but deserted. In the distance is the reason for the alarm: plumes of black smoke from tires set alight. The signal has been given that a demonstration is beginning.

The street is transformed quickly into a scene of confrontation with masked shabiba hurling rocks, bottles and iron bars at the approaching Israeli military patrol. Following strict procedures, the military responds by firing tear gas at the protesters, followed by rubber bullets. These are rubber slugs with metal cores considered more humane than live ammunition. Usually by this time the youths have retreated into nooks and alleys, thus ending the demonstration.

But if they persist or an inexperienced soldier panics, live ammunition will be used. In a matter of minutes it is over, at least for the day.

The demonstrations have become a regular morning feature, with each side acting out its well-rehearsed part. Makeshift memorials occasionally mark the bloodstained spot where a "martyr" has fallen. The number of casualties has dropped off as the skirmishes become increasingly routine.

Focusing Our Attention

Sometimes a third player takes part in these demonstrations. Arriving in expensive rented cars with large "press" signs pasted in the windows, or perhaps in a TV minivan, they are really the most important people of all, for they turn the fight into a media event for the world to see on the evening news. There is no use starting until the cameras are rolling; it is not unusual for the shabiba to wait patiently until the camera crew is set up. Then, as if on cue, a signal is given to begin. After a few minutes the cameras have filmed enough footage and the reporters pack up and leave.

Living in Israel, we are amazed continually at how the world's attention, as if spellbound, remains transfixed on this tiny island in the midst of the vast Mideast sea. Other major events around the world seem to be but temporary distractions. Sure enough, after a few days the Holy Land and its problems are once again the focus of attention.

The Palestinian uprising has brought the reality of this obsession with Israel home with clarity. This is not to belittle the very real violence and suffering that have become the tragedy of the Occupied Territories. It is true, however, that while attention remains riveted on Jerusalem, thousands are dying in senseless violence around the world. In the Indian state of Punjab alone, for example, the death toll from political violence in 1990 averaged more than 600 people per month.[1]

This statistic indicates that more people have been killed every two months in Punjab than have been killed in three years of the reign of the Palestinian intifada. News coverage of these events, however, is almost nonexistent so that the public will receive its daily portion of unrest from Israel. It seems as though whenever masked young men in the Occupied Territories pick up rocks to hurl, the television cameras are there faithfully to record it.

Part of this may be due to the fact that Israel, the only true democracy in the Middle East, is more accessible to the news media. As a rule, repressive regimes do not permit foreign television crews to film scenes of bloodshed of their own making.

In 1988, for instance, when the foreign press howled about the closure of West Bank universities, little was said about the student riots across the Jordan valley. Reports reached us on the West Bank of King Hussein's handling of the demonstrations at Yarmuk University at Umm Quis in northern Jordan. Dozens of students were killed and wounded, mowed down by the Jordanian security

---

[1] Guy D. Garcia, "The Awesome Wrath of Rama," *Time* (November 12, 1990), p. 32. This total does not include many hundreds of deaths from fighting in other Indian states such as Kashmir and Assam.

forces. During that same time, the relatively tame demonstrations in the Territories continued to be front-page news.

Thus, the Arab-Israeli conflict—or, more notably, the plight of the Palestinian refugees—has stayed in the spotlight of attention, causing most viewers to take hold òf one side or the other. Many viewers distrust the Palestinians, identifying them as a whole with Arab terrorists. Others sympathize so fervently with the Palestinian cause that they excuse its arm of terrorism.

Not all interest in one side or the other is compassionate in motivation. There are, after all, wars and conflicts on almost every continent. No, the world has its eye on the desert sands of the Middle East not totally because of humanitarian concerns, but rather for Israel's strategic location amid world powers and for what lies underneath the desert sands.

Navel of the World

Prophecies in the Bible, spoken thousands of years ago, declare that the Middle East will one day capture the world's attention. The prophet Ezekiel foretells an invasion of the land of Israel by the forces of Gog and his allies. We will discuss this battle later, but for now notice the description of the land in the machinations of Gog:

> "I will go against those who are at rest, that live securely, all of them living without walls, and having no bars or gates, to capture spoil and to seize plunder, to turn your hand against the waste places which are now inhabited, and against the people who are gathered from the nations, who have acquired cattle and goods, *who live at the center of the world*."
>
> Ezekiel 38:11–12, NASB, italics mine

The Hebrew word for *center* here actually means "navel" and appears in some translations as such. The ancients would have understood these words, though perhaps their meaning escapes those of us in the modern world.

The land of Israel is the land bridge between the three continents of Africa, Asia and Europe. The great civilizations of antiquity were connected by trade routes that passed through the Holy Land: Egypt to the south, Mesopotamia to the east, and, later, Greece and Rome to the west.

The armies of those empires also marched along those communication routes in search of conquest, taking them directly through what is now called Israel. Strategically speaking, Israel is indeed the center of the world and no stranger to military invasion.

Those great kingdoms were eventually buried in the desert sand as the Middle East sank into obscurity. After the decline of the powerful Islamic dynasties in the tenth century, Mesopotamia lay in neglect for centuries as Europe and the New World marched into the industrial age.

When the twentieth century began, the Arabian sands were coveted only by the solitary Bedouin, who migrated from place to place in search of grazing lands. Little did those desert nomads realize, as their flocks scratched the barren ground, what fabulous wealth lay underneath—the very lifeblood of modern civilization:

> They were backwaters—poor, simple places with nothing to offer the industrialized countries, and little influenced by the modern West. Their way of life had scarcely changed over a millennium. Then oil riches abruptly thrust them into the center of the world economy, tying them totally to it, deluging them with Western culture, and giving them startling economic and political power.[2]

Black Gold

The first oil derrick was erected not in Middle Eastern sands, but in Titusville, Pennsylvania, where Edwin L. Drake extracted min-

---

[2] Daniel Pipes, *The Long Shadow: Culture and Politics in the Middle East* (New Brunswick: Transaction Publishers, 1989), p. 91.

eral oil for the first time in 1859. A few years later a 26-year-old entrepreneur by the name of John D. Rockefeller bought into the new oil business for $72,000 in Cleveland, Ohio. In 1870 he founded Standard Oil Company, thus becoming the world's first oil mogul. America's craving for "black gold" grew as the country swiftly entered the industrial age.

"Oil guru" Dan Yergin in his book *The Prize: The Epic Quest for Oil, Money and Power* states that the quest for secure sources of oil has been a major factor in many of the wars of the past century. "Oil has profoundly shaped our lives," he says, "whether it be Hitler's strategy in the Second World War or Saddam Hussein's decision to invade Kuwait this summer."[3] The oil wealth of the Middle East has been—and will remain—at the center of world attention.

The strategic importance of the region for America dates back to the end of World War I. Henry Ford was producing automobiles by the millions, creating a huge market for petroleum products. Domestic oil production was insufficient to meet the growing demand and the U.S. began to look abroad for additional sources. At this time Britain and France were deciding how to divide up the newfound oil riches of the Middle East, formerly under the control of the defeated Ottoman Empire.

President Woodrow Wilson, fearing the U.S. would be cut out of the fantastic petroleum reserves in the Middle East, muscled his way into the negotiations, demanding that U.S. oil companies get their share of the wealth. The American petroleum companies eventually won their first concession—in Iraq. Since that time the U.S. has consistently demonstrated her willingness to use military force in defense of her supply of Middle East oil.

A Costly Addiction

Viewed from the air, the huge and absolutely empty Arabian desert extends as far as the eye can see. This bright moonscape is

---

[3] Kenneth R. Sheets, "Thoughts from an Oil Guru," *U.S. News & World Report* (September 10, 1990), p. 70.

utterly inhospitable to all but the hardy Bedouin. On the ground in the eastern Saudi desert, the undulating sand dunes are broken only by vehicle tracks and pipelines leading to the oil derricks dotting the horizon.

Unseen from the surface, about a mile underneath the sand dunes lies a hundred-foot-thick zone of porous limestone, 150 miles long and 25 miles wide. The underground rocks hold tremendous amounts of thick, dark liquid under high pressure. Once penetrated by drilling bits, the oil gushes forth without pumping at a pressure of 500 pounds of pressure per square inch. From the wellhead it travels by pipeline to gas-separator plants, the first step of a long journey to petrol stations around the world.

This immense reservoir in Saudi Arabia, known as the Ghawar Field, is the largest known deposit of oil anywhere in the world. Here under the sand lies more than three times the oil reserves of the U.S.—more than eighty billion barrels of petroleum.

But Ghawar is just one part of the vast sea of underground oil deposits underneath the Saudi desert. With proven reserves of 257 billion barrels—fully one-fourth of the world's petroleum supply— the oil sheikdom needs to operate only seven of its 58 fields to meet its export demands. By comparison, the U.S. pumps from more than 700 times as many wells to provide the same amount of oil.[4] Thus, the industrial world depends for its survival upon oil, and nowhere is it found in such abundance as in the Middle East.

The international community was not primarily concerned about the plight of billionaire oil sheiks when it responded so forcefully to Iraq's invasion of Kuwait in 1990. The massive military intervention of the West had one overarching purpose: to protect its threatened oil supply.

Once Iraq's armored columns captured Kuwait, the oilfields of Saudi Arabia and the United Arab Emirates were within easy

---

[4] U.S. proven reserves are 25.8 billion barrels, with 612,448 producing wells vs. 858 for Saudi Arabia. William J. Cook, "Hostage to Oil," *U.S. News & World Report* (October 8, 1990), p. 70.

reach. In one fell swoop more than half of the world's petroleum supply could then have been under Iraq's control. Saddam Hussein would then have been in a position to exert unprecedented economic blackmail over the West. As it was, the Iraqi invasion of Kuwait caused a temporary shortfall of one million barrels a day. This modest reduction in world oil supply sent oil prices rocketing to their highest levels ever and jarred the U.S. economy when it was already sliding into a recession.

Nor was this the first time. The past two decades have shown how vulnerable the West is to instability in the Middle East. In 1973 the Arab oil producers, enraged by American support for Israel in its victorious Yom Kippur War, initiated an oil embargo that brought about a sixfold increase in oil prices overnight. The economies of the world, unable to absorb the shock, plunged into recession.

The next convulsion occurred in 1979 when Iran, a major producer, was rocked by the Islamic revolution. The disruption of Iran's production capacity once again caused prices to soar. The following year Iraq invaded Iran, jeopardizing the production capacity of two major Gulf producers. During the war O.P.E.C. (the Organization of Petroleum-Exporting Countries) increased production as high as 31 million barrels a day, but failed to keep up with the West's growing thirst for petroleum. Recognizing the danger of a cutoff of Gulf oil, Washington was forced, at great expense, to dispatch the U.S. Navy to the Persian Gulf to protect the sea lanes.

Despite these oil shocks, the United States was actually twice as dependent upon Middle Eastern oil in 1990 than it was in 1973. America was importing 77 percent more foreign oil than just seventeen years earlier—and at a time when domestic production was steadily declining. As the world's largest petroleum addict, the U.S. imports more oil than Britain, France and Germany combined.[5]

The U.S. seems blissfully complacent about its energy future. While we continue to import 8 of the 17 million barrels consumed

---

[5] Cook, p. 57.

each day, we have taken few steps to protect against a catastrophic loss. The much-vaunted Strategic Petroleum Reserve has some 600 million barrels; this reserve on its own would last only two and a half months.

The situation around the world is not much better. The storage tanks of industrial countries worldwide have an excess storage capacity of 3.5 billion barrels of crude. This may sound impressive, but by itself represents only a three-month supply at current world consumption levels. If a major war in the Middle East were to shut off the oil spigot, it would be only a matter of months before the lights would go out around the world.

The war also showed how the mere *fear* of war in the Middle East convulses world stock markets. U.S., Japanese and European stocks lost considerable value in the crash of October 1990 without a single shot having been fired. If this could happen at a time when oil stocks stood at record highs, what will happen when the oil supply is really in danger of being cut off? In the face of a worldwide financial crisis, the Western powers would be inexorably drawn once again to military intervention in the Middle East.

Consider one such future scenario in which the immense oil reserves of the Middle East are again threatened. Crippled production would push oil prices through the ceiling. The effect on the world economy would be disastrous, leading to a worldwide economic collapse that would dwarf the Great Depression of the 1930s.

And it would prepare the way for a powerful world leader to arise claiming the solution to the problems of planet Earth. When that happens, the drama of the book of Revelation will begin to unfold.

Sound unreal? Let us see just how unstable the shifting sands of the Middle East really are.

4
Dreams of a Lost Empire

"I love any Arab leader who will unite the Arabs, even by force. We want to see one empire restoring our culture to its former glory."[1]

—Yusef Kawash
Veteran Jordanian army officer

THE STREET IS THE HUB OF SOCIAL ACTIVITY IN OUR little neighborhood. The reassuring sounds of talking and laughing, mixed with the excited chatter of children scampering around, waft inside as I work at my desk. If such sounds are still to be heard, I tell myself, things cannot be all bad in the world.

In the evening one of our neighbors sells freshly deep-fried falafel under the street lamp. Friends and passersby stop by to chat with her and buy a small bag of the treat.

One night, during the time when the air war against Iraq was well underway, I decided to wander outside to see what was happening on the street. My friend Ibrahim was leaning against a wall, taking a break from his sewing work. He and his brother have a workshop in the back of their home, as do many others in the area. Now was my chance, I thought, to ask a question that had been bothering me since Iraq's invasion of Kuwait.

At that time the Western world was bewildered at the fanatical

---

[1] Otto Friedrich, "He Gives Us a Ray of Hope," *Time* (August 27, 1990), p. 18.

support that Saddam Hussein enjoyed throughout the Arab world. It was common knowledge even among the Arabs that he had used poison gas against his own people. And there was no denying that the country he had heedlessly invaded was an Arab neighbor.

Surely reasonable Ibrahim, a Christian Arab who had traveled in the United States and spoke excellent English, would shed some light on this question. And enlighten me he did. Much of what he said made sense. It did not seem right to me, either, that one clan, the al-Sabah ruling family of Kuwait, should own and control the unlimited oil wealth of that country.

And then Ibrahim mentioned what was really the central point, one I have mentioned earlier: that in spite of his undeniable faults, Saddam Hussein was, like themselves, an Arab. And in the face of outside "imperialist" aggression, all Arabs had no choice but to stand together. For the Arab mind, questions of right and wrong mattered little compared to this basic axiom.

Gradually I began to understand what fostered this mentality and why it has endured for so many centuries.

Wounded Spirits

Living in a Palestinian community, we learned that even our moderate Arab friends would sometimes disappoint us with attitudes and opinions that seemed worlds apart from Western ways of thinking. We kept hoping they would be "reasonable" and "objective," as we imagined ourselves to be. Gradually we realized that factors deep within their psyche caused Arabs to think and reason differently from Westerners.

Among an Arab's basic motivations, two stood out for us: a sense of national humiliation and, therefore, an impelling sense of fierce pride.

This is not to say that the Arab has more pride than other people. Westerners are infused with as much hubris as anyone. The difference is that most Western countries have not experienced a long history of national humiliation. Our societies are basically strong and prosperous. We do not as a rule dwell on past failures. The Western mind is forward-looking: Given a problem to solve, we typically analyze factors in the present that could lead to a future solution.

Arabs tend to analyze a problem by reflecting on the past. They are deeply conscious of and identify strongly with all of Arab history. The brilliant successes as well as the shameful defeats become part of one's personal history. Unfortunately, the Arab nation has been in general decline for centuries and there is not a lot to be proud about. To compound matters, the West has exerted an overpowering influence, and often outright control, over Arab lands for the past two hundred years.

All this adds up to a sense of indignation at the collective humiliation suffered by the Arab people at the hands of Western "imperialists." Indeed, it has been argued that Islam, revulsed by anything outside the realm of its own teaching, is inherently xenophobic.

How does the Arab compensate for this humiliation? Through the concepts of honor and dignity. Visitors from the West are often amused at the Arab's preoccupation with maintaining his honor, even in matters considered trivial. Rebekka and I learned—often the hard way—that the Arab people are extremely sensitive. On occasion I would be puzzled when someone exhibited a sudden coolness. Nothing would be said directly, but later it would emerge that I had caused offense. Once an entire family charged out of our home because I accidentally showed the sole of my shoe. I was oblivious to what had happened until Rebekka explained what a great insult this is to traditional Arabs.

When they are offered something to eat or drink, Arabs will go through an elaborate, mutually understood ritual, the purpose of which is to make absolutely clear that they are not destitute and have no need of anyone's food. Once this matter of pride is established, and only after several pleadings, will they consent to partake. After that point they are obliged to eat heartily lest the host, in turn, be offended.

A lot of Arabs have gone hungry while visiting in the West. Accustomed to being asked several times if they would like something to eat or drink, they are dismayed to have the offer cease after the very first rejection! Their hosts quite naturally assume that if someone says he doesn't want anything to eat or drink, he means it.

During one holiday season I was having great difficulty convincing my students to eat the homemade cookies Rebekka had baked for them. After politely accepting just one each, they refused graciously to eat more. Was it an inappropriate treat? Perhaps they didn't like sweets. Yet I knew that these fellows were perpetually hungry. Finally one of them advised with a twinkle in his eye, "Close your eyes, *yaa ustaaz* [honored teacher], and they will disappear!"

This politeness often involves saying or doing the opposite of what you mean. When we walk down our street, for instance, our neighbors invite us into their homes automatically, even though they are busy at the time. This is a formality on their part and we refuse politely—as we are expected to do. In fact, they would be surprised and perhaps a bit offended if we were to accept their offer.

The rich Arabic language is full of double meanings for such occasions, and we answer *Shukran!*, which generally means "Thank you," but in this situation means the opposite, "No, thank you."

We might smile at such overly polite behavior, but it is important to the Arab people, enabling them to maintain a sense of dignity in daily life. They will go to great lengths to avoid confronting someone directly about a wrong committed. If a problem must be discussed, it is done indirectly in order to avoid humiliating the person. Even minor embarrassments can be dangerous because they expose the nerve of the deep underlying sense of humiliation.

Thus, this politeness has at its core the very fires that erupt in the intifada. The response is different but the desire to overcome shame is the same.

Few Westerners understand the longing Arabs have for the revival of the mighty Arab nation, which they believe will extinguish the collective humiliation they have endured for centuries. In the eighth century the Islamic empire reached great heights of cultural achievement, seemingly on the verge of dominating the known world. One historic figure for pan-Arab nationalists is the great Saladin, whose military brilliance restored Muslim rule over Palestine by crushing the Crusader armies in the twelfth century. Since Saladin's time, the fragmented Arab world has been looking for a leader with the ability to unite them.

His Hand Will Be Against Everyone

Gamal Abdel Nasser is a name that still evokes powerful emotion among Arabs despite the military debacle of the Six Day War. This Egyptian president came the closest in modern times to recapturing Arab honor[2] when his "free officers' revolt" in 1952 led to the overthrow of King Farouk's regime. This was the first true Arab revolt against colonialism, replacing a regime propped up by Western imperialism with what promised to be a genuinely popular government. Euphoria again swept the Arab world when Nasser seized control of the Suez Canal in 1956, despite a combined British, French and Israeli attempt to intervene militarily.

In those first heady years after the Egyptian revolution, the young Saddam Hussein, then living in Cairo, witnessed the public esteem that Nasser enjoyed. Doubtless he dreamed that one day the Baath party would bring a similar revolution to Iraq. After all, the Baath party stood for "Arab renaissance." And was not the greatest Arab empire of all—the Abbasid Dynasty that ruled for five hundred years—centered in Baghdad itself? Years later, after

[2] Libya's Muammar Gaddafi also gained a measure of respect in 1973 when he organized the quadrupling of the price of oil through O.P.E.C.

coming to power, Saddam Hussein would seek to emulate the Egyptian president. He would work to accomplish Nasser's unfulfilled goal of a unified Arab nation.

While Europe marches steadily toward unification, however, the cause of Arab unity remains an elusive dream. For decades various Arab states have attempted to realize the great pan-Arab union that they all aspire to. An attempt at an Egypt-Syria merger in 1961 floundered, for instance, followed by an aborted Libya-Egypt-Syria union.

A biblical prophecy speaks to their seeming inability to come together for a common purpose. The book of Genesis gives a perceptive description of Ishmael, who is considered the forerunner of the Arab people. Here is a description of Ishmael's character: "He will be a wild donkey of a man; his hand will be against everyone and everyone's hand against him, and he will live in hostility toward all his brothers" (Genesis 16:12).

The history of the Arab people has certainly borne out this prediction. Despite all the rhetoric about a unified Arab Middle East, and despite their desire to stand together against the world, the truth is that there is hardly an Arab nation that has not been in conflict with one or several of its "brothers."[3]

The Iraqi invasion of Kuwait provided a glaring example of the fractured Arab world. While many of the people cheered Saddam's stand against the evil West, 21 Arab governments stood by, paralyzed with indecision, as one from their midst committed blatant aggression against another. Soon after the invasion the Arab League convened an emergency meeting in Cairo. After prolonged

---

[3] A few recent examples of Arabs fighting Arabs are the Yemen civil war in the mid-1960s, known as "Egypt's Vietnam" because of her occupation of the country; the bloody "Black September" clashes in Jordan in 1970 between Palestinians and the Jordanian security forces; the tragic civil war in Lebanon beginning in 1975 and involving both Syria and Iraq; the mid-1980s war between Morocco and Mauritania over the western desert; and now the 1990–1991 war against Iraq involving several Arab nations. This list does not include the numerous near-conflicts between Middle Eastern countries.

debate, they mustered a majority behind a feeble censure of Iraq. Unable themselves to intervene, it was left to the Western powers to free Kuwait.

Still, though his support was not universal in the Arab world, Saddam Hussein showed a remarkable ability to rally forces around him. His populist message, a defiant assertion of dignity, unity and honor, was irrestible for the Arab masses. Degenerate regimes kept in power by American and Zionist powers must be overthrown. Above all, the head of the evil serpent, Israel itself, will not escape its fate.

Such rhetoric stirs the deepest yearnings of the Arab people. So potent are these emotions that millions of Arabs were willing to excuse Saddam's evil side to have their dreams fulfilled. They hoped against hope that it was Saddam who could revive the long-lost Arab/Islamic glory and empire.

The Iraqi president also struck a popular chord by verbally assailing the oil sheiks. There is a widespread feeling in the Arab world that the fabulous oil wealth, viewed as a gift from Allah to Muslims, has been squandered by the "oil emirs." While most of their Arab brothers continue to languish in poverty, these sheiks flaunt their extravagant lifestyles. There is little sympathy for the royal families of the Gulf—rather, the conviction that the Arab world would only benefit from their demise.

The vast desert kingdom of the royal family of Saudi Arabia includes the two most holy places of the Islamic religion—the *Kaaba* in Mecca and the tomb of Muhammad in Medina. Since the establishment of the dynasty, Saudi monarchs have proudly carried the title *Khadim al-Haramain ash Sharifaim*—Servant of the Two Exalted Sanctuaries. Such pretenses are laughable to many Arabs, who see the royal family as the antithesis of true Islamic values. And they are incensed by lurid tales of the excessive lifestyle of the Saudi monarchy. A case in point is King Fahd himself.

Today the 275-pound king has difficulty walking and suffers from diabetes, but in his younger years the billionaire had a well-deserved reputation as a playboy. Nothing money can buy was denied him. The youthful monarch frequented the exclusive night-clubs of London and Paris. Reportedly, he knew the leading belly dancers in the nightclubs of Beirut by name, and is said to have paid the wife of a Lebanese businessman $100,000 a year for her companionship when he was in town. One old story relates how, during a weekend binge in Monte Carlo, he gambled away one million dollars.

Until 1980 King Fahd received personally a fee levied on every barrel of oil that was pumped from Saudi soil. Worth an estimated $18 billion, his fortune is second only to the Sultan of Brunei's $25 billion. His $2.5 billion palace complex is only one of at least twelve royal palaces around the world, including a "cottage" in Marbella, Spain, that is four times the size of the White House. His main $60 million yacht is escorted by a vessel carrying Stinger anti-aircraft missiles. A fleet of jets awaits his private use, as well as a sizable collection of the world's most expensive automobiles.

It is these tales of self-indulgent lifestyles that circulate in the Arab world, stirring resentment and bitterness among the common people. In 1961 Egyptian President Nasser expressed his disgust with the corrupt Arab leaders of his day: "Of course, the Sheikh does not think of anything except his turkey and the food with which he fills his belly. He is no more than a stooge of reaction, feudalism, and capitalism."[4]

The Festering Sore

The overthrow of foreign-backed imperialist regimes and the redistribution of oil wealth were not the only wrongs needing redress by a united Arab world. Their single-most-humiliating event occurred in 1948 when the Jewish state of Israel was established on what was considered Arab territory.

The following decades brought the Arabs seven major wars and several minor ones. Several of them involved Israel, which—to the

---

[4] Nissim Rejwan, "Islam Can Justify Anything," *Jerusalem Post* (November 2, 1990), p. 4.

disgrace of the Arab world—managed in every case to emerge victorious from the battlefield. To the Muslim this is an intolerable situation, and he awaits the excising of this "festering sore" from the midst of the Arab world. Israel, which also stakes her territorial claims on ancient history, exists in the Arab mind as a denial of their past, present and future.

Saddam, realizing shrewdly that enmity toward Israel is the glue that holds the Arab world together, sensed that his time had come. At every opportunity during the Gulf crisis, he sought to drag Israel into the war. He insisted repeatedly that his withdrawal from Kuwait be linked to the Palestinian question. Later, when diplomacy failed, he used his Scud missiles in an attempt to force the Israelis to join the battle.

On the West Bank and Gaza, one might have expected to find at least some opposition to Saddam. After all, hundreds of thousands of Palestinians were earning good money in Kuwait and sending it back to their families—that is, until Iraq's invasion.

The exact opposite has occurred. Even though many Palestinians fled, leaving their jobs and life's savings behind, not a single anti-Saddam demonstration took place in the Occupied Territories. The reason was summed up by Samiha Khalil, director of a rehabilitation center in al-Birah: "I am against America, against America, against America!"[5]

After the invasion of Kuwait, only one Arab East Jerusalem daily, *An-Nahar,* blamed Iraq for harming the Palestinian cause. The error of their ways was soon pointed out, and by the following morning the paper had unabashedly reversed itself. Falling back into lock step, *An-Nahar* embraced the pan-Arab anti-American position adopted by the rest of the East Jerusalem press.

---

[5] Jon Immanuel, "Powerless Palestinians Find a Strongman," *Jerusalem Post* (August 10, 1990), p. 5.

The Big Lie

The book of Revelation speaks about a future world ruler who will lead many astray with arrogant speech:

> The beast was given a mouth to utter proud words and blasphemies and to exercise his authority for forty-two months. He opened his mouth to blaspheme God, and to slander his name and his dwelling place and those who live in heaven.
>
> Revelation 13:5–6

The boastful oratory of this future world leader known by Christians as the Antichrist will eclipse what we have seen in Adolf Hitler, Joseph Stalin, Saddam Hussein or any human ruler to date. He will doubtless employ an all-pervasive propaganda machine to spread his fabrications.

The Gulf War served as an illustration of how the "Big Lie" could be used to sway the masses. Saddam's propaganda found an astounding degree of ready acceptance throughout the Muslim world. His incredible claims were spread through Arabic news services to incite a fever pitch among the masses.

At the beginning of the Allied Operation Desert Shield, for instance, our Palestinian friends were convinced that the warplanes arriving in Saudi Arabia were not American but actually disguised Israeli jet fighters. The Iraqi ambassador to France asserted on various television programs that Israeli warplanes based in Saudi Arabia and Turkey were taking part in bombing raids on Iraqi cities. Not to be outdone, P.L.O. chief Yasser Arafat declared in televised interviews that Israeli cruise missiles were being fired against Iraq regularly from the Negev in southern Israel. Despite this, relying on the Arabic papers and Jordanian news, one would have thought that the Iraqi army was on the verge of certain victory.

How did we react to these kinds of claims? Frankly, we learned not to say much. Many Palestinians believed what they read and heard, so long as the source was not Israel. If we tried to rebut a particularly outrageous claim, then *we* were the ones deceived by the Israelis and their Western lackeys.

The Arab mind often seems to work according to wish fulfillment: If something is presented forcefully enough, long enough, it is considered a *fait accompli,* regardless of the truth. Muslims sometimes think we are insincere about our Christian faith, for instance, because we do not raise our voices and become visibly agitated. Our refusal to do so indicates to them that we are not firmly convinced of our beliefs.

Thus, the Occupied Territories accepted the news of unconditional ceasefire with typical vigor: Iraq had won—if only because Saddam had managed to "stand up to the Americans."

The Gulf War brought to the world's attention a Mideast dictator afflicted with megalomania who may himself prefigure the "Beast" of Revelation yet to come. It certainly reveals the depth of support for a leader who threatens to destroy the archenemy of the Arab world: Israel. It is this common goal that may one day finally unite the nations of the Middle East under the Antichrist. I believe this is exactly what the Bible predicts will occur in the last battle of human history.

In Part 2 we will take a closer look at the mysteries of ancient Mesopotamia. We will see how this birthplace of the occult provided fertile ground for Saddam Hussein, the self-proclaimed "Sword of the Arabs" and modern prototype of the Antichrist.

Part 2
The Sword of the Arabs:
A Case History

5
The Lure of Mystery Babylon

"Since its birth, Babylon has stretched out its arms to the future, to be the seat of eternal wisdom, to represent the first civilization, and to remain the glittering lighthouse in the dark night of history."[1]

—Saddam Hussein
at the dedication
of the rebuilding of Babylon

THE CLATTERING HOOFBEATS ECHOED AGAINST THE distant hillsides as the horses raced across the gravel plains of what is now Syria and northern Iraq. It was a curious-looking entourage by today's standards that hurried south toward the magnificent capital city of Babylon. One man—Nebuchadnezzar—stood out among the riders, a look of steadfast determination spurring him onward to his destiny.

The ancient world had just been rocked by a violent, decisive confrontation between the superpowers of the day. The once-powerful kingdom of Assyria, already in irreversible decline, now lay mortally wounded. A civilization called Babylon, which had its origins in hoary antiquity, was about to be reborn.

In the south the Egyptian empire, fearful of the emerging new order, had sent military help to its old adversary, Assyria. Moving

---

[1] George Grant, *The Blood of the Moon* (Brentwood, Tenn.: Wolgemuth & Hyatt Publishers, Inc., 1991), p. 30.

north through the kingdom of Judah, the forces of Pharaoh Necho II were challenged by King Josiah, who was attempting to stop the Egyptian advance. Despite assurances from Pharaoh regarding his intentions, King Josiah and his greatly inferior army chose to fight. That fatal decision led to the death of Josiah and the defeat of his Judean army.

This confrontation took place at the junction of a key pass through the Carmel range as it empties into the broad Jezreel Valley. A city, already ancient by the time of Josiah, stood overlooking that vital intersection. It would lend its name to numerous battles, past and future, as invading conquerors sought to control the Holy Land.

In Hebrew its name is Megiddo, but in the Greek language of the Apocalpyse the site is called "the mountain of Megiddo"—or Armageddon.

The defeat of Josiah is little more than a footnote in the annals of history compared to the battle soon to take place far to the north at Carchemish. Located on what is now the border between Syria and Turkey, at that time Carchemish on the Euphrates marked the northern boundary of the Assryian empire. It was there that the young vice-regent Nebuchadnezzar defeated the combined Egyptian and Assyrian forces in one of the pivotal battles of Syrio-Palestinian history.

At that moment Nebuchadnezzar received word that, back in Babylon, his infirm father had died. At once another crisis was in the wind. Unless the young prince could return quickly to Babylon, another would take his rightful place. Nebuchadnezzar was destined to claim his throne and rule long and vigorously. The date was 605 B.C. An enigmatic civilization had arisen again from the sleep of a thousand years, known by historians as the neo-Babylonian empire.

The Land Between the Rivers

Modern Iraq covers the former lands of Babylonia and Assyria, a region known by the ancient Greek name of Mesopotamia, meaning "between the rivers." The two rivers, the Tigris and the Euphrates, flow through a region of astonishing fertility. It is here in the land of Eden where the earliest civilizations known to man were nourished.

Mesopotamia has been a battleground since the dawn of recorded civilization as one empire replaced another in a seemingly endless cycle of conquests. It was here that many innovations of ancient warfare were developed. Then as today, battles were won with the most advanced weapons available; the chariot, bronze ax, bow and arrow and iron-bladed spear were each, in turn, radical inventions that proved decisive on the ancient battlefield.

Thousands of years later, the same cauldron of war would play host to weaponry undreamed of by the ancients. A besieging army from the United States of America would use computerized weapons to defeat the modern heir of ancient Mesopotamia, Iraq.

The civilization of Babylon ranks among the world's greatest, with a history spanning two millennia. It dominated the region in the eighteenth century B.C., when King Hammurabi and his army of 50,000 men—a huge force at that time—conquered most of Mesopotamia.

In those days most armies were made up of conscripts, but like Saddam's elite Republican Guard, his predecessor Hammurabi also relied upon a crack force of 1,000 Royal Guards. His army was famous for its mounted archers, who along with chariots and infantry posed a formidable threat to any foe.

Hammurabi's reign, marked by material prosperity and a sophisticated code of law, is considered a high point in the history of ancient civilization. Although this first dynasty was to fall, the mystique of Babylon would continue to linger in the land of Mesopotamia until the kingdom was revived in the late seventh century B.C.

It is this neo-Babylonian empire and its greatest king, Nebuchadnezzar, that we read about in the Old Testament. During Nebuchadnezzar's long reign, Babylon experienced the pinnacle of her power and prosperity. From the beginning of his rule, Nebuchadnezzar sought to control the whole of Syria-Palestine, including the kingdom of Judea. After eighteen years of piecemeal advance, Jerusalem was conquered and destroyed in 586 B.C. as foretold by the Hebrew prophets.[2]

It is because of this single event that we find Babylon haunting the pages of Scripture, until it reappears in the Apocalypse of St. John. As the first city mentioned in the Bible, and with more than 275 references from Genesis to Revelation, Babylon dwarfs attention given to other great cities such as Rome (fourteen references). In the Bible only one city receives more attention than the capital city of Nebuchadnezzar. It is Jerusalem.

Before we delve further into the mysteries of Babylon, let's take a capsulized look at the history of Jerusalem, the most famous of all cities.

Jerusalem, City of Promise

A millennium and a half before Nebuchadnezzar rose to claim his crown, in the days of antiquity before Hammurabi carved out the old Babylonian kingdom, the footsteps of a band of nomads could be heard making its uncertain way in the opposite direction along the same ageless route.

Led by a 75-year-old patriarch, they were trekking northward from one of the great cities of the day: Ur on the banks of the Euphrates in southern Mesopotamia. Their destination was unknown, save for a divine command. The Lord had said to Abram, "Leave your country, your people and your father's household and go to the land I will show you" (Genesis 12:1).

Herding flocks of sheep and goats along with them, they pitched their handwoven tents along the way. Stoking their evening fires under the Mesopotamian stars, how often they must have pondered the marvelous promise given to the patriarch:

---

[2] A classic source for the early rule of Nebuchadnezzar II is D. J. Wiseman, *Chronicles of Chaldaean Kings* (London: British Museum, 1956).

"I will make you into a great nation
   and I will bless you;
I will make your name great,
   and you will be a blessing.
I will bless those who bless you,
   and whoever curses you I will curse;
and all peoples on earth
   will be blessed through you."

Genesis 12:2–3

Abram and his clan made their way along the major international highway of the day through what is now Iraq, Syria and Lebanon on their way to the Promised Land. Once in the land of Canaan, they left the "main road" to travel along the spine of the central mountains of Canaan, passing through Shechem and Bethel.

Not far south of Bethel, the road passed near the ancient mountain fortress of Jebus. I have often stood at the fork in the road outside the Old City of Jerusalem where the trail led down around a bend in the Hinnom Valley to where the Jebusite city once stood.

Abram would not have turned aside to enter the pagan city. Instead he set his face southward where, sojourning in tents, he and his sons would have many adventures in the Negev Desert and in Egypt. It was left to one of his descendants a millennium later to gaze upon Jebus as the new capital for the children of Israel who now filled the land.

But it would not be easy to capture the Jebusite city, so well fortified that its inhabitants taunted young King David and his men as they approached the city: "You will not get in here; even the blind and the lame can ward you off" (2 Samuel 5:6).

The intrepid warrior-king was not to be deterred. Learning of a hidden water tunnel that led into the city, which has in our day been excavated for all to see, David's men crept stealthily through the water shaft under the city by night. Jebus was taken by surprise and so became the chief city of the Israelites.

It is ironic that many visitors to Jerusalem are scarcely aware of the original City of David, which remains largely covered by an Arabic neighborhood on a small ridge south of the Old City. Indeed, the site was too small for David's son and successor, Solomon, who expanded the city northward to include his Temple and palace complex. That site has been immortalized throughout the ages by the Jewish people and is known today as the Temple Mount—still the focal point of the Old City.

After Solomon's time the golden age of the united Israelite monarchy came to an end, torn apart into the Northern Kingdom of Israel and the Southern Kingdom of Judah. Then began the long decline, as the children of Israel sank ever deeper into idolatry. This was no idle pastime: Canaanite religion involved hideous abominations, which were also practiced in time by morally degraded Israelites.

In the same valley Abraham transversed as he passed by Jebus, and which skirted the fortress city David conquered, fearsome rites were performed by apostate kings of Judah:

> [Ahaz] walked in the ways of the kings of Israel and also made cast idols for worshiping the Baals. He burned sacrifices in the Valley of Ben Hinnom and sacrificed his sons in the fire, following the detestable ways of the nations the Lord had driven out before the Israelites.
>
> 2 Chronicles 28:2–3

It was because of such practices that the previous inhabitants of the land had been driven out. The very people God had called to be a light unto the nations would not escape the same judgment: "And if you defile the land, it will vomit you out as it vomited out the nations that were before you" (Leviticus 18:28).

The repeated admonitions of the prophets fell on deaf ears. In due time such was the moral degeneration of the Israelites that the very land that had been given to them also vomited them out. And

Jerusalem, intended to be "the joy of the whole earth," lay in ruin, her inhabitants herded into captivity in a strange land:

> How deserted lies the city, once so full of people! How like a widow is she, who once was great among the nations! She who was queen among the provinces has now become a slave.
>
> Lamentations 1:1

After seventy years of captivity in Babylon, returning exiles in 537 B.C. rebuilt the city and its Temple on a modest scale. But hopes for an independent Jewish kingdom proved elusive as the tiny land of Israel was passed along from one superpower to the next. By the time of Jesus, Rome controlled the Middle East and the Jews were proving, as always, to be most unwilling subjects.

They persisted in their struggle for independence, but were ground under the ironclad boot of Roman legions sent to pacify the land. In A.D. 70 rebellious Jerusalem was set to the torch and the Temple destroyed, as prophesied by Jesus while speaking to His disciples in the shadow of its massive walls.

" 'Do you see all these things?' he asked. 'I tell you the truth, not one stone here will be left on another; every one will be thrown down' " (Matthew 24:2).

The fervently nationalistic Jews were not finished yet, however, and in A.D. 135 the emperor Hadrian sent more legions to suppress another revolt. But it would not be without cost. When the Roman general returned to report to the Senate, instead of the usual salutation, "The emperor and the legions are well," the general offered only the ill-boding greeting, "The emperor is well."

Historians note that an entire Roman field army, the 25th Legion from Egypt, disappeared from history around this time.

In ferocious retribution, Hadrian ordered Jerusalem to be razed, plowed and sown. A new city was laid out along Roman lines and named Aelia Capitolina, to which Jews were forbidden entrance upon pain of death. Hadrian did not fail to discriminate against the growing Christian sect, whose places of worship were also destroyed.

Determined to impose the worship of the Roman imperial gods, the emperor encased the probable site of the crucifixion and resurrection of Christ beneath a huge concrete platform, which served as the base for his Capitolina Temple, flanked by a shrine honoring Aphrodite.

Ironically, in his efforts to stamp out the holy places of Christianity (he did the same to the revered site of Jesus' birth in Bethlehem), Hadrian unwittingly preserved them for future generations. In the fourth century A.D. the newly converted Emperor Constantine commissioned the excavation and restoration of the most important historical site in Christendom. Today that edifice, much altered but still standing, is known as the Church of the Holy Sepulchre.

Jerusalem, an Immovable Rock

The remains of many other churches and monasteries from the Byzantine period can still be seen throughout the Holy Land. Christian rule came to a grinding halt, however, when the armies of Muhammad swept into the land in A.D. 636. For the next fourteen centuries, excepting the Crusader interlude, the religion of Islam ruled the land of Israel. Still, as the centuries came and went, a tiny, humble remnant of Jews was always present in Palestine, doggedly preserving their religious traditions.

In the late nineteenth century a new impetus moved among the Jews scattered throughout the Diaspora: the drive once again to reclaim the land of Israel as a homeland for the Jewish people. Inspired by Theodore Herzl and others, idealistic Jews from around the world settled once again in Palestine. Tolerant at first, the Arabs of the region became increasingly nervous about the Jewish population as their numbers grew.

After World War I Britain was granted the mandate to govern Palestine and found itself caught between the warring sides. After three decades of trying to maintain order and mediate between

Arabs and Jews, the British unilaterally abandoned their mandate and withdrew abruptly from Palestine.

The year was 1948. No sooner had the last British ship sailed from Jaffa when the newly proclaimed State of Israel was attacked by the combined forces of the Arab Legion. The ill-equipped Israeli forces managed to hold onto Galilee and the coastal plain, but lost control over most of the mountainous central region, which came under Jordan's control.

The Israelis appeared willing to live with this division of territory, even though their enemies controlled the historic Old City of Jerusalem. The Arabs were not willing, however, finding the existence of the Jewish state intolerable.

Two decades later the region once again erupted into war when, after an Israeli preemptive strike, the Arabs launched a combined attack spearheaded by the armies of Syria and Egypt's President Nasser. They were joined by the somewhat hesitant Jordanians who had the most to lose. And lose they did: As we have seen, the lightning-quick Six Day War of June 1967 ended with complete Israeli control over the West Bank. Syria lost the Golan, and Egypt, the vast Sinai desert.

Yet no piece of territory lost was more significant than the Old City of Jerusalem, over which now flew the Star of David.

A final military effort, exceeding all previous attempts to wrest control of the Holy Land from the Jews, took place in October 1973. Under the leadership of President Anwar Sadat of Egypt and Hafez al-Assad of Syria, the Arabs attacked on two fronts simultaneously.

The surprise offensive came on the most holy day of the Jewish year, Yom Kippur, when the country was virtually shut down. The unprepared I.D.F. suffered heavy losses initially as the Egyptians punched deep into the Sinai and the Syrians swept across the Golan Heights. In some of the most intense tank battles in the history of modern warfare, the Israelis finally turned the tide, driving the invaders back deep into their own territory.

This last military setback convinced President Sadat that the

Arabs would not be able to defeat Israel so long as the United States continued to back Israel financially and militarily. Having recently ejected the Soviets from his country, he was looking to the West for economic asssistance to rebuild his war-torn economy. But there was a pricetag for the billions of American dollars that would soon flow into his country: Egypt's willingness to turn her swords into plowshares.

President Sadat made the courageous but hazardous decision to break ranks with his fellow Arabs and make a bold attempt at peace. Thus an astonished world and a rapturous Israeli public witnessed the sudden arrival of Sadat at Ben Gurion Airport in November 1977. The ensuing negotiations, brokered by President Jimmy Carter at his Camp David retreat in Maryland, led to the signing of the Camp David peace accord in September of the following year.

While general agreement was reached on a plan to give autonomy to the Occupied Territories, the question of the status of Jerusalem threatened to torpedo the talks. President Carter, realizing the explosive nature of the issue, left it unsettled.

But it would not go away. When peace talks were convened, beginning in 1991, the question of Jerusalem was at the forefront of the discussions as both Israel and the Palestinians claimed the city as their capital. Despite the prodigious efforts of the United States to resolve the issue, the City of David continued to be the focal point of the conflict in the Middle East.

There seems to be no human solution to the problem of Jerusalem, and one day the words of the prophet of old will ring true:

> "I am going to make Jerusalem a cup that sends all the surrounding peoples reeling. Judah will be besieged as well as Jerusalem. On that day, when all the nations of the earth are gathered against her, I will make Jerusalem an immovable rock for all the nations. All who try to move it will injure themselves."
>
> Zechariah 12:2–3

Second City of the Bible

The two cities of Jerusalem and Babylon present a fundamental contrast in Scripture. Jerusalem was intended to be the heart of true worship where the God of Israel dwelled in His holy Temple. Jerusalem is light and truth and all things good; the Psalms are full of her praise: "Great is the Lord, and most worthy of praise, in the city of our God, his holy mountain. It is beautiful in its loftiness, the joy of the whole earth" (Psalm 48:1–2).

With Babylon we move from light to murky shadow. That city is the antithesis of true religion. Throughout Scripture Babylon denotes temporal power in active rebellion against God. In the book of Revelation Babylon represents the spiritual apostasy of the last days, symbolized by a woman sitting on a fearsome beast:

This title was written on her forehead:

MYSTERY
BABYLON THE GREAT
THE MOTHER OF PROSTITUTES
AND OF THE ABOMINATIONS OF THE EARTH.
Revelation 17:5

Mystery Babylon symbolizes the natural alternative to the true worship of God. Because of this, rebellious mankind will be unable to resist her seductive charm: "With her the kings of the earth committed adultery and the inhabitants of the earth were intoxicated with the wine of her adulteries" (Revelation 17:2). This passage indicates that one day an iniquitous force will exercise its power of enchantment over the whole earth.

The ancient city that parallels this future Mystery Babylon has also enchanted many throughout her long history. Some of the greatest rulers in history have been drawn to Babylon, which symbolizes like no other the pinnacle of earthly power.

City of Conquerors

In 539 B.C. the city of Babylon, considered impregnable, fell without a struggle to the Persian army. The army was able to circumvent the immense fortifications by an ingenious plan. By diverting the course of the Euphrates River upstream, it dried up the moat defenses and infiltrated the city through the riverbed. That very night, as recorded in the book of Daniel, Belshazzar lost both his kingdom and his life.

At the same moment that the handwriting was appearing on the walls of Belshazzar's palace, the Persian army was marching into the city. Sixteen days later the Persian monarch Cyrus the Great himself entered Babylon amid much public acclaim, thus ending the Chaldean dynasty as predicted by the Hebrew prophets (Isaiah 13:21). Cyrus, enchanted with the city, chose to rule his vast Persian empire from Babylon rather than from his own capital, Susa.

Long after him came that enigmatic Macedonian, Alexander, who marched to Babylon in 331 B.C. There he was triumphantly acclaimed without a struggle by the Persian garrison. Like Cyrus before him, Alexander chose to make Babylon the center of his empire. He offered sacrifices to the Babylonian god Marduk and set into motion elaborate plans to rebuild the city.

He envisioned construction of a new port as well as restoration of the ancient monuments. He ordered the rebuilding of the temple of Bel, which had been destroyed by the Persian ruler Xerxes. Interestingly, Jewish historian Flavius Josephus reports that the Jews who fought in Alexander's army refused to participate in the restoration of the pagan temples.[3]

Alexander then continued on to India, forging a great empire stretching from Libya to the Punjab. Finally, after conquering the known world, he returned in triumph to Babylon. Alexander seemed captivated by this city with its crumbling ziggurats, or

---

[3] Flavius Josephus, *Contra Apion,* i. 192.

pyramidal structures, imbued as it was with the spirit of occultism. We will look more closely at this spirit in the next chapter.

In the ancient world Babylon was unparalleled as a center of Oriental religion. According to extant Babylonian texts, it held at least fifty monumental temples. Nebuchadnezzar built at least fifteen within the city. Some of those pagan temples remained in continual use for nearly two millennia. In addition, cuneiform texts mention hundreds of shrines and daises, upon which idols stood, in the city.

The Tower of Babel

The most famous of the religious monuments of ancient Babylon was the Tower of Babel. The story of this mysterious structure is told in the book of Genesis:

> Now the whole world had one language and a common speech. As men moved eastward, they found a plain in Shinar and settled there.
>
> They said to each other, "Come, let's make bricks and bake them thoroughly."
>
> They used brick instead of stone, and tar instead of mortar. Then they said, "Come, let us build ourselves a city, with a tower that reaches to the heavens, so that we may make a name for ourselves and not be scattered over the face of the whole earth."
>
> But the Lord came down to see the city and the tower that the men were building. The Lord said, "If as one people speaking the same language they have begun to do this, then nothing they plan to do will be impossible for them. Come, let us go down and confuse their language so they will not understand each other."
>
> So the Lord scattered them from there over all the earth, and they stopped building the city.
>
> Genesis 11:1–8

The foundations of this impressive tower may still be seen in Babylon today. Known as the Temple Tower, or the Ziggurat of Babylon, it was a stepped tower whose heights reached to the heavens. Although all that remains of the tower are the lower stairs, archaeologists estimate that the tower originally rose some 280 feet into the air. There is little reason to doubt the identification of this site with the biblical Tower of Babel.

Babel was one of the monuments that captured Alexander's interest. Perhaps he envisioned it as a magnificent symbol of his unified world empire. He began to clear the rubble from the base of the great ziggurat, intending to restore mankind's first boastful attempt to reach into the heavens. That dream, as well as his other elaborate plans for the sacred city, were suddenly cut short.

On June 13, 322 B.C., the greatest master of the ancient world, who wept bitterly when there was nothing left to conquer, died in Babylon at age 33 of malarial fever.

While Alexander's empire was being torn apart by feuding generals, Babylon grew as a center of Hellenistic culture. The city also hosted a large number of Jews who chose to remain after many of their fellow countrymen returned from the exile to Judea. Indeed, by the first century the Jews of Babylon enjoyed self-government, and it is there that some of the greatest works of Judaism, including the *Talmud,* the authoritative body of Jewish traditions, were composed.

The fascination of Babylon continued to draw those with a thirst for temporal power. The Roman emperor Trajan fought his way east, entering the city in A.D. 115. His most significant act in the then-decaying city was to perform a sacrifice to Alexander's manes, or "divine spirit." Doubtless he aspired to the same measure of greatness as his predecessor.

Trajan was the last of the great leaders drawn to the city, which became a casualty of the gradual shifting of the Euphrates River. But even though Roman historian Septimius Severus would report in A.D. 200 that the site was deserted, Babylon would not remain buried in desert sands forever.

A Nation Reborn

The tel or archaeological mound of Babylon lay undisturbed as centuries came and went. The Romans and Byzantines failed to gain a lasting foothold in Mesopotamia, held at bay by the fierce Sassanids. In A.D. 637 the new religion of Islam triumphed, carried to Eastern lands by Arabs with brandished swords. They were followed by Tamerlane and his Mongols and later by the Ottoman Turks, who ruled for four hundred years.

By the early twentieth century, the Ottoman empire, dubbed "the sick old man of Europe," was in its last dying stages. Its fatal mistake was to side with the Axis powers during the first World War. When Germany lost the war the Ottomans lost their empire. The British and French divided up the Middle East into spheres of influence, with the British assuming control over Iraq, Transjordan and Palestine, and the French, Lebanon and Syria.

In 1918 the British Army occupied the territory of Iraq, and after a costly attempt to rule Iraq as a province, organized a national government. Amir Faisal was installed as king in 1921, but the British continued to cast a long shadow over Iraq for the next forty years.

In 1958 the Iraqi monarchy was overthrown in a popular revolt against its pro-British policies. Nuri Said, the venerable politician who had served as prime minister many times since independence, became a focal point of popular rage. Attempting to flee dressed in women's clothing, he was discovered and literally torn to pieces on a Baghdad street by a mob. Such was the heritage of savagery that was to characterize post-revolution Iraq.

The revolution was the springboard for the career of Saddam Hussein, who until then had been a bit player in the violent underworld of Iraqi resistance movements. Upon his ascendancy to the Iraqi presidency in 1979, he began to take an interest in the ancient history of his country. That interest turned into an obsession. As if possessed by the very specter of Nebuchadnezzar, Saddam sought to bring about nothing short of the revival of ancient Babylon.

Babylon Rises from the Sands of Time

For the first time since he ruled his mighty empire 2,600 years ago, Nebuchadnezzar's Babylon began literally to rise again. And just as Nebuchadnezzar was a "world ruler" over the neo-Babylonian empire at the peak of its greatness, so also Saddam Hussein aspired to become a latter-day Nebuchadnezzar to restore lost Arab glory. In 1988, in honor of Iraq's "victory" over Iran, Saddam issued a medallion with his likeness on one side and Nebuchadnezzar's on the other.

Saddam went to great lengths to cultivate parallels between himself and the rulers of ancient Babylon. Everywhere in Iraq huge monuments and murals showed him in the company of such notables as Hammurabi and Nebuchadnezzar. The population was reminded continually of the key role the land of Babylon played in ancient history.

As if to cement his own continuity with Nebuchadnezzar of old, the Iraqi president went so far as to actually order the Iraqi Department of Antiquities to restore the ruins of ancient Babylon. In 1987 a drama was performed at the site with the title "From Nebuchadnezzar to Saddam Hussein: Babylon invokes its former glories."

In 1990 he offered a generous prize for a plan to reconstruct the intricate irrigation systems of Babylon's Hanging Gardens, built originally by Nebuchadnezzar and hailed as one of the seven wonders of the world. Part of the city wall and a major gate are already standing. Every fourth tile used in the reconstruction was incised with the inscription *Built in the time of Saddam.*

Shortly before the outbreak of the Gulf crisis, this self-exalting ruler had a gigantic image of himself, standing nearly ten stories high, erected over the restored gate of the city of Babylon. That massive picture of Saddam Hussein looking down over the city reminds us of the fate of Nebuchadnezzar as described in the book of Daniel:

> Twelve months later, as the king was walking on the roof of the royal palace of Babylon, he said, "Is not this the great

Babylon I have built as the royal residence, by my mighty power and for the glory of my majesty?" The words were still on his lips when a voice came from heaven, "This is what is decreed for you, King Nebuchadnezzar: Your royal authority has been taken from you."

Daniel 4:29–31

It was arrogant pride that caused the downfall of Nebuchadnezzar. Following the divine decree he was struck with a bout of insanity until he finally acknowledged the most high God.

The career of Saddam Hussein, Nebuchadnezzar's would-be successor, has also been marked by unbridled ambition. As it did with Nebuchadnezzar of old, did a life of self-exaltation push the "Sword of the Arabs" to the edge of reason? Or were there other "forces" at work?

The Middle East is where Yahweh of the Old Testament chose to reveal Himself to mankind as the one living and true God. The region is also considered the birthplace of the occult. The Bible predicts that one day a world leader in possession of awesome paranormal powers will turn his attention to this part of the world that has nurtured dark forces throughout the ages.

How close are we to the final confrontation between God and the powers of evil in the Middle East? Let's take a look at some of the spiritual powers already at play there and how they seek to influence events.

6
Wizards, Seers and Astrologers in Bible Lands

Daniel replied, "No wise man, enchanter, magician or diviner can explain to the king the mystery he has asked about, but there is a God in heaven who reveals mysteries."

Daniel 2:27–28

THE DARKENED ROOM, DEEP WITHIN THE INSULAR Mea Shearim quarter of Jerusalem, was illuminated only by the required black candles. A group of ten "righteous men" from an obscure ultra-Orthodox Jewish sect had been summoned for a rare and deadly ritual. The ceremony, called the *pulsa de nura* ("lash of fire" in Aramaic), was known to have been held at least once before in recent history.

In 1959 then Jerusalem mayor Gershon Agron had aroused the ire of the secretive group, known as the *Eda Haredit*, for permitting the first public swimming pool to be built in the capital. The Eda felt that this move would allow mixed bathing, which to them violated Jerusalem's sanctity. The delegates of this shadowy organization met and the kabbalistic incantations were uttered. Soon afterward Gershon Agron died unexpectedly—the result, Eda members claim, of the death curse placed upon him at the ceremony.

In 1973 Jerusalem mayor Teddy Kollek was the intended target. He was guilty of advocating the building of a football stadium in what the Eda considered Orthodox territory. Eda members were in the process of investigating the name of Kollek's mother—one peculiar requirement of the curse is that the correct name of the victim's mother be obtained, to avoid any mistaken identity at the address to which the curse is delivered—when the stadium plan fell through. The curse was not pronounced, and the mayor was spared the possible fate of his predecessor.

The next target of the Eda Haredit was none other than Saddam Hussein. Haifa University professor Amatzia Baram, world expert on the Iraqi president, was contacted by the Eda to learn the name of Saddam's mother. Baram reportedly told the Eda official that Saddam's mother had two names, Subha and Khadiya. His caller pressed him on the authenticity of the names, and asked that authenticating documents be forwarded to the organization. Baram assured him that the names were accurate. It is not known when, or if, the ceremony was ever held.

According to Professor Menahem Friedman of Bar-Ilan University in Tel Aviv, the kabbalistic ritual comes from a Talmudic legend regarding Reb Yihiya and his son, who allegedly possessed supernatural powers. In a test of his abilities Reb Yihiya was asked to speak the prayer during the synagogue service. When he pronounced the blessing for wind, the wind blew. When he prayed for rain, the rain fell.

The Reb was stopped short of pronouncing the phrase regarding "the resurrection of the dead." According to the tale there was considerable alarm in the heavens, and a divine investigation was ordered to find out who had taught the Reb how to force heaven to do his will. The culprit turned out to be the prophet Elijah, who was given sixty "lashes of fire" for his trouble.[1]

The Land of Prophets

Those who come to live in the Holy Land soon learn that Israel is the land of would-be prophets, both ancient and modern. Some say that Elijah has already returned in our day.

---

[1] "Kabbalists Prepare Ritual Curse for Saddam," *Jerusalem Post* (January 29, 1991), p. 4.

Once, while walking the streets of Jerusalem, I came face to face with none other than the self-proclaimed prophet himself. He certainly looked the role, dressed in a flowing white robe matched by his long silver hair and beard. As additional confirmation he also sported a tall knurled staff. The only item that looked out of place was his Samsonite briefcase. He apparently spent his days walking the streets of the Old City, raising his staff in righteous exhortation to whoever would listen. Most of his time was spent in places frequented by tourists, the native inhabitants (as it were) not fully appreciating the man or his message.

During the late 1980s at least two claimants to the mantle of the prophet Elijah walking the streets of the holy city. One day they chanced across one another and a spirited argument ensued as to who was the real latter-day prophet. Revelation 11 describes how two prophets, one of whom is thought to be Elijah, will be translated to heaven from the streets of Jerusalem. These two squabbling would-be prophets also ascended into the heavens—but on an Israeli El Al Airline flight, at the firm request of the local authorities, never to be heard from again.

Israel also has its modern-day prophets. A book written in the 1930s and recently rediscovered created a stir with its startling twentieth-century predictions. The book, entitled *Heshbonot Hageula* (Reckonings of Redemption), was written by the late Rabbi Haim Shvili. In it he forecast a great war that would include the use of chemical and germ warfare. He predicted it would be waged among Arabs during the Jewish feast of Succot in the year 5751 (1990), followed by the messianic era.

Needless to say, in 1990 when Saddam Hussein was trying to hold fast in Kuwait and threatening Israel with the "mother of all battles," speculation was rife that the final apocalyptic battle was indeed imminent. Prominent rabbis lent credence to the speculation. Former Ashkenazi Chief Rabbi Shlomo Goren said that he, too, had reason to see the past year as the "threshold of redemption." For him, "the greatest sign of redemption" was what he termed the "miraculous" immigration of Russian and Ethiopian Jews.[2]

According to Shvili's book, there will be a great earthquake during the feast of Succot in Jerusalem. Muslim and Christian homes will be destroyed and a great spring will gush forth. The city will then be bombed from the air and shelled by land, and the residents taken briefly as prisoners. God will protect Jerusalem, while the warring sides destroy each other in a fit of madness.

After the war, the book continues, Jerusalem will reign supreme. The city will be a center of tourism and pilgrimage boasting the finest in food, clothing and merchandise. Her residents will live a life of leisure, required only to study the Torah according to the new interpretation of the Messiah.

Birthplace of the Occult

Upon examination, Shvili's prophecy appears to be a creative restatement of some Old Testament prophetic passages. But the prophets of the Bible were not the only ancient sources of information in the Middle East concerning the future. It was in Mesopotamia that the occult practices of divination and astrology originated. The Tower of Babel itself was an astrological observatory. In arcane chambers on its summit the priests of Bel pored over astrological charts, comparing them with the constellations above.

This was no idle pastime: The judgments of these stargazers determined the course of Babylon, the greatest empire of the day. The king was advised by the priests concerning the propitious moment for virtually every activity.

In the seventh century B.C., the Babylonian king Nebuchadnezzar was, like his forerunners, controlled by his court astrologers. He attributed his phenomenal success in building his empire to their

---

[2] Haim Shapiro, "Seer Predicted Gas War in 1990," *Jerusalem Post* (September 28, 1990), p. 3.

auspicious consultations. But the king began to have strange experiences:

> In the second year of his reign, Nebuchadnezzar had dreams; his mind was troubled and he could not sleep. So the king summoned the magicians, enchanters, sorcerers and astrologers to tell him what he had dreamed.
>
> Daniel 2:1–2

This list includes almost every occult specialty known to the ancient Middle East. Diviners would hover around the king, interpreting his omens and checking their charts for the precise timing of his every undertaking. But this time the "wise men" of Babylon failed in their task. They were unable to describe Nebuchadnezzar's mysterious dream.

In a miraculous demonstration of the power of the true God, Daniel was summoned and was able to give an accurate description of the king's dream and its interpretation. Proud Nebuchadnezzar could not deny that the occultic forces he allowed to govern his kingdom were impotent in the face of the living God:

> The king said to Daniel, "Surely your God is the God of gods and the Lord of kings and a revealer of mysteries, for you were able to reveal this mystery."
>
> Daniel 2:47

Times have changed—or have they? Occultism is alive and well in the Middle East, even though the religion of Islam frowns upon such practices. William R. Polk mentions that astrology played a major role in the founding of one of the capital cities of Islam:

> Laying out their capital under the guidance of the astrologers when Mars (al-Qahirah) was in the ascendant, they named it Cairo (al-Qahirah), and proclaimed a new era of Egyptian power and prestige.[3]

---

[3] William R. Polk, *The Arab World* (Cambridge, Mass.: Harvard University Press, 1980), p. 58.

The practice of divination still holds sway in the ancient land of its birth, and it may help to explain abnormal behavior in high places. Consider the erratic lifestyle of King Fahd of Saudi Arabia. The king is known to disappear for weeks at a time, only to emerge again with little explanation. He then resumes his habit of sleeping during the day and beginning work at 11 P.M., receiving his top officials and foreign envoys throughout the night. It is not unusual for him to keep them waiting for hours while he watches TV or videos. Numerous TV sets throughout his palace are tuned continually to CNN.

Is this mere eccentricity, or a sign of some deeper obsession? That it may be the latter is indicated by the fact that the king is known to be superstitious and to consult regularly with astrologers. But if a remarkable story that surfaced in the Arab press is indeed accurate, the example of King Fahd is mild compared to that of his opponent in the Gulf War.

Saddam's Occult Connection

Just before the outbreak of the war, an unconfirmed report circulated in the Middle East press that may help to explain Saddam Hussein's unexpected behavior during the Gulf crisis. According to the story, Saddam had fallen under the powerful spell of a group of sorcerers, who came to dominate virtually his every decision. The source for the story, originating from Amman, Jordan, was an unnamed eyewitness who spent the night as a guest of a prominent Baghdad family. His host, who held an important government position, revealed the shocking story to him.

The Washington and Amman correspondents of the prestigious Kuwaiti daily *As-Siyasa*, then being printed in Saudi Arabia, filed the story which appeared in the December 17, 1990, issue. The headline read: "The African Magicians Are Behind Saddam's Tenacity." The report stated that at least fifty African magicians, soothsayers and fortune-tellers were brought from Mali, Niger,

Mauritania, Sudan and Chad immediately after the invasion of Kuwait. They resided in the Republican Palace in Baghdad in close proximity to Saddam, advising him daily about the future and the plots of his enemies and rivals. They also counseled him on the conduct of the business of state, including the newly proclaimed "nineteenth province of Kuwait."

These occult practitioners assured Saddam that the U.S. would never go to war against him. The reason, they confided, was that the anti-Iraq alliance would be weakened in January 1991 by "the murder of a great leader." The resulting upheaval would "turn all the alliances and the equations upside down."[4] The sorcerers were so trusted by Saddam that they functioned as an alternate council of ministers whose voices were respected at the highest levels of decision-making.

The magicians also persuaded Saddam not to agree to the dates suggested by Washington for high-level talks in December 1990. They assured him that as a result of this refusal, President Bush would relent and agree to the dates Saddam himself fixed. This would prove to be the first of many concessions as America gradually lost her resolve.

Incredibly, at the same time, a popular legend was being revived in Jordan that lent support to Saddam's delusions. According to the story, the Bedouin of Arabia together with the Franks (Westerners) and Egypt would gather in the desert against a man called "Sadam" (sic). The result of the war would be the destruction of all of Saddam's opponents. This battle, according to the story, would take place between the first half of December and the second half of February 1991. The legend was quoted by Jordanian politicians as proof that Saddam would destroy his enemies.[5]

All this may help to explain the obstinacy that Saddam Hussein displayed during the Gulf crisis. He confounded Western observers

---

[4] Nissim Rijwan, "Saddam and the African Magicians," *Jerusalem Post* (January 11, 1991), p. 3.

[5] Lance Morrow, "The Devil in the Hero," *Time* (January 28, 1991), p. 35.

by refusing to budge when, as they say, the handwriting was on the wall. Was Saddam convinced by his occult magicians and folk tales that, despite all outward appearances, he would in the end emerge the glorious victor?

An Evil Namesake

An even more bizarre footnote to the occult side of Saddam Hussein was revealed in an interview with Amatzia Baram, noted expert on Saddam Hussein. It seems that Saddam Hussein was originally given another name. While still in the womb, Saddam's mother—for unknown reasons—named him after the Prince of Darkness. Saddam's original name was Satan.[6]

It is all too possible that this heartless act on the part of Saddam's mother, known for her ruthlessness, indelibly marked the young boy's emotional and psychological development. Children depend upon their parents to mirror a healthy, positive reflection of themselves. Evidently Saddam's childhood was devoid of any such influence. The name the boy finally ended up with, Saddam, itself means "one who confronts." He has certainly lived up to that name over the years. *Time* magazine comments:

> In his blood-drenched career, Saddam has acted truly, not metaphorically, Satanic. It is reported, credibly, that in the evening, before bed, he has been in the habit of watching a video of an execution that he ordered, preferably one carried out that day. He is apparently conscienceless.[7]

Perhaps Saddam's occult connection—and the cruel name conferred upon him—help us to understand more than anything else the behavior of a man who would lead his country into a disastrous war.

---

[6] This was reported in a *Jerusalem Post* (January 15, 1991) interview with Amatzia Baram, Haifa University professor and world-renowned authority on Iraq and Saddam Hussein.

[7] Morrow, p. 34.

Biblical Prophecy Fulfilled?

Instead of listening to his sorcerers, Saddam would have been wiser to read the Hebrew prophets. A close reading of the book of Jeremiah indicates two destructions of the kingdom of Babylon. The first is described at the beginning of chapter 50:

> "Babylon will be captured; Bel will be put to shame, Marduk filled with terror. Her images will be put to shame and her idols filled with terror. A nation from the north will attack her and lay waste her land. No one will live in it; both men and animals will flee away."
>
> Jeremiah 50:2–3

This prophecy states that *one* nation from the north will conquer Babylon. It describes the overthrow of Babylon by Cyrus, who had unified the empires of Persia and Media and who entered the city on October 29, 539 B.C.

Later in the same chapter of Jeremiah a second devastation of Babylon is described:

> For I will stir up and bring against Babylon an alliance of great nations from the land of the north. They will take up their positions against her, and from the north she will be captured. Their arrows will be like skilled warriors who do not return empty-handed.
>
> Jeremiah 50:9

Here we have not one nation but an alliance of many nations that will come against Babylon. Regarding the destructive nature of that second war, John Bright comments:

> Moreover, it is to be noted that the actual fate of Babylon at the hands of Cyrus could scarcely have been more unlike the awful picture of slaughter and destruction that we see in these poems. Cyrus actually entered Babylon without a fight, refrained from harming it in any way, and treated its citizens with the utmost consideration.[8]

---

[8] John Bright, *Jeremiah* (Garden City, New York: Doubleday, 1965), p. 360.

Thus it appears that the second destruction of Babylon was not fulfilled in the time of Cyrus. When will this second war take place? The context gives us a clue. Sandwiched between the two above-mentioned invasions is another prophecy—regarding the return of the Jewish people to the land of Israel:

> "In those days, at that time," declares the Lord, "the people of Israel and the people of Judah together will go in tears to seek the Lord their God. They will ask the way to Zion and turn their faces toward it."
>
> Jeremiah 50:4

This is clarified further in verse 19: "I will bring Israel back to his own pasture and he will graze on Carmel and Bashan; his appetite will be satisfied on the hills of Ephraim and Gilead."

According to the chronology of the chapter, the second destruction of the kingdom of Babylon will take place after the regathering of the people of Israel in the land of Israel. If we can assume that this refers to the restoration of the nation of Israel in 1948, we should then look for a war subsequent to this time.

In our day a war was fought in the land of Babylon that drew armed forces from thirty different lands—from as far away as South America and Australia. We cannot conclude, however, that the Gulf War of 1990–1991 was a direct fulfillment of biblical prophecy. This is because Jeremiah 50 seems to be describing a devastation that far exceeds the damage wrought against Iraq by the Allied war machine.

Not that the Allies did not have the capability to do the damage described in this passage. For reasons that have been and will continue to be debated among military and political analysts, the Western forces withdrew at their moment of greatest advantage, leaving the regime of Saddam Hussein and a good part of his army intact. Had Saddam Hussein been able to involve Israel in the war, it might then have erupted into a conflagration of truly apocalyptic proportions.

Aftermath The 100-Hour War

The Gulf War serves as an illustration of how the armies of the world will one day converge on the Middle East with their awesome destructive power.

This was illustrated for the world to see by the systematic decimation of Iraq's military capability by the multinational forces. In fact, U.S. General Norman Schwarzkopf, overall commander of the multinational forces, waited until Iraq's fighting capability was reduced by approximately fifty percent before even initiating the ground offensive.

Thus, when the end came it was almost anticlimactic. Five weeks of bombing had reduced much of the Iraqi army in Kuwait to half-starved, shell-shocked soldiers huddled in filthy bunkers. It turned out to be a war of superlatives for the Allies, and one of mediocrity for Iraq.

The Allied blitzkrieg blasted through the Iraqi defenses almost unopposed. About the only thing that slowed their advance were tens of thousands of Iraqi soldiers desperate to surrender to just about anyone. One group of soldiers was observed trying to surrender to a reconnaissance drone, turning around and around waving white rags as the pilotless craft circled overhead. Most were sent unguarded in long, ragged lines to the rear, where at last they received food and medical attention. The Iraqi soldiers were dumbfounded. They assumed that the multinational soldiers would be even more brutal than their own superiors, and here even their clothes were being washed for them.

To call it a rout would be an understatement. The ground battle turned out to be one of the great mismatches of military history. Iraqi casualties were estimated in the tens of thousands versus some 350 for the Allies; an estimated 4,000 Iraqi tanks were damaged or destroyed, against 4 for the Allies; more than 2,100 artillery pieces versus a lone one for the Allies.

The various Allied armed forces operated with a level of efficiency and precision that earned the admiration of the watching world. The armchair pundits who predicted everything that could and would go awry were silenced in the face of an astounding victory. The weapons systems, some never before battle-tested, performed with deadly effectiveness, while the soldiers operating them proved to be dedicated and hard-working.

Patriotism was no longer a laughable concept from a bygone era. America exorcised the ghost of Vietnam, shaking off the war in which everything went wrong, basking in the glory of a war in which, finally, everything went *right*. No longer the powerless giant pushed around by assorted midget despots around the world, America had at last flexed its impressive military might.

Almost before the Gulf War euphoria wore off the problems began. Like wandering into quicksand, getting into was easier than getting out of the quagmire of the Middle East. To begin with, Saddam was still in control—once again wreaking havoc on his own people. He moved on to a ruthless suppression of uprisings in the north and south of Iraq. The Kurdish refugees in northern Iraq, who were fleeing from Saddam, engaged the U.S. military in another operation: protecting them against Saddam and providing them with humanitarian assistance. As Saddam became increasingly defiant regarding the U. N. Security Council cease-fire resolutions, the West was forced to contemplate further military action against the tenacious land of Babylon.

At the same time, Secretary of State James Baker, attempting to capitalize on new U.S. influence in the region, immediately began intensive "shuttle diplomacy" *à la* Kissinger to bring Israel and her Arab neighbors to the negotiating table. Convening the Middle East peace conference was no small accomplishment, but as talks progressed it became increasingly clear that neither the Israelis nor the Arabs were prepared to move from their fundamental positions. The morning after, it was the same old world. The war, it turned out, had really not changed much.

The End of Superpower America?

Despite the brilliant success of the U.S. armed forces in the war against Iraq, it is not at all certain that in a few years America could mount overseas military ventures such as envisioned by the Defense Planning Guidance. The bottom line is money to pay for it, and even before the war was concluded, President Bush was forced to ask Congress for significant reductions in the defense budget. Despite aspirations for global projection of U.S. military power, Pentagon planners were gradually becoming resigned to the severe budget cutting that would be necessary in the light of new economic realities.

In March 1992 details from a classified Pentagon document created a stir when they were leaked to *The New York Times*. The document, called the "Defense Planning Guidance for the Fiscal Years 1994–1999," stated that "America's political and military mission in the post-cold-war era will be to insure that no rival superpower is allowed to emerge in Western Europe, Asia, or the territories of the former Soviet Union."[9] The 46-page policy statement made the case for the benevolent domination of the world by one superpower—the United States. The document outlined U.S. military contingencies for dealing with crises around the world. While preferring "collective action," such as occurred during the Gulf War, the U.S. military is prepared to act independently if the vital interests of the United States are threatened. With regard to the Middle East, the objective of the U.S. is "to remain the predominant outside power in the region and preserve U.S. and Western access to the region's oil."[10]

The gradual erosion of America's military might will leave a power vacuum that will be hard to fill. With the collapse of the U.S.S.R., the long-feared "Soviet threat" has dissipated. The resultant convulsive political changes make it clear that whatever political entity emerges from the ashes of the former Communist regime will not be in a position to project military power worldwide.

---

[9] Patrick E. Tyler, "U.S. Strategy Plan Calls for Insuring No Rivals Develop," *The New York Times* (March 8, 1992), p. 1.

[10] "Excerpts from Pentagon's Plan: 'Prevent the Re-Emergence of a New Rival,' " *The New York Times* (March 8, 1992), p. 3.

But history teaches us that another "superpower" is always waiting in the wings to fill the gap left by declining powers. As the U.S. military is weakened by budgetary constraints, a disturbing question remains: Who or what will replace a faltering America and the now-defunct Soviet Union as the superpowers of the world? And what will be the character of the next dominant political force? Will it lead to democracy and progress—or to a dark age of ironhanded tyranny?

The indications are that the world may be at the brink of a new—perhaps the last—phase of human history. Let us now turn our attention to Part 3, in which we will examine some of the signposts in today's world that point to the end of the age.

Part 3
Signposts on the Road to Armageddon

7
The Ticking Time Bomb

"In Jerusalem violence courts violence in a perpetual magic circle, and at its heart a time bomb with a destructive force of apocalyptic dimensions is ticking, in the form of the Temple Mount."[1]

Meron Benvenisti
former deputy mayor of Jerusalem

THE TEMPLE MOUNT IS INDEED THE EMOTIONAL FOcal point of Jewish-Muslim-Christian interaction in Jerusalem.

I am especially aware of this "ticking time bomb" as I teach the historical geography and archaeology of the Holy Land to visiting student groups. It gives me pleasure to talk about the beauty of Israel, the wide variety of landscapes and climate that we who live here love so much.

It is always Jerusalem, though, the hub of the "center of the world," that dominates student interest. It is here that King David established his capital, and the compelling drama of the kingdom of Judea was played out on the pages of the Old Testament. Jerusalem is also the backdrop for the culmination of Jesus' earthly ministry.

Our groups always look forward to visiting the Old City of Jerusalem, whose stately walls enclose a labyrinth of narrow, ancient streets divided into Jewish, Christian, Armenian and Muslim

---

[1] Charles Lane, "A Time Bomb at the City's Heart," *Newsweek* (October 22, 1990), p. 38.

quarters. Almost one-fourth of the area of the Old City is occupied by the massive Temple Mount, the center of Jewish and Muslim aspirations. It was a thousand years before the time of Jesus Christ when, as I mentioned earlier, King Solomon extended the original City of David northward to enclose Mount Moriah, thus making room for the Temple and his palace complex.

That Temple stood until 586 B.C., as you will recall, when the armies of Nebuchadnezzar conquered Jerusalem and destroyed it. In 20 B.C. Herod the Great decided to rebuild the Temple on an even more grandiose scale. This second Temple of Jesus' day was destroyed only a few years after its dedication, by the Roman legions in A.D. 70.

Even the Roman armies, however, could not demolish the massive rectangular platform Herod had constructed as the base for the Temple. That platform, almost 1,600 feet long and 1,050 feet wide, continues to dominate the topography of the Old City. Standing next to the gigantic limestone blocks of the retaining wall, one is overwhelmed by the genius of Roman engineering. Some of the ashlars weigh hundreds of tons and were laid so skillfully—without benefit of cement or mortar—that after 2,000 years it is still impossible to slide a piece of paper into many of the joints between the immense blocks. It remains a mystery to this day as to how the Roman engineers, under Herod's direction, managed to build the platform.

Centuries came and went. Nearly 600 years later Muslim armies marched into Palestine and the Caliph Omar claimed the ruined Temple Mount for Islam. The Muslims named it the *Haram esh-Sharif*, or noble sanctuary. Two of the most important shrines of the Muslim religion were built on the site: the al-Aksa Mosque and the Dome of the Rock. For the past 1,300 years these Muslim structures have stood on what is sacred ground for the Jewish people.

After regaining control over the Old City in 1967, the Israeli government decided to preserve the status quo over the holy sites in order to respect the various religious traditions. This meant that the Muslim *Wakf* (religious administration) would retain control over the Temple Mount. But pious Jews continued their prayers and hopes for its restoration once again into Jewish hands.

The Third Temple

Today the Muslim Wakf guards the Temple Mount fanatically. Every supposed breach of their authority is met with vigorous protest. Brazenly asserting their Israeli-granted authority, the Wakf has severely restricted any access by non-Muslims to the Haram esh-Sharif. Zealous guards prowl the grounds watching for any "improper" behavior. I was once accosted by an Arab watchman for chewing a piece of gum at the site.

Some of the most interesting historical attractions on the site are closed to non-Muslim visitors. Archaeologists are forbidden to disturb a single stone on the Haram esh-Sharif. Such an act would be proclaimed around the Arab world as a "Zionist conspiracy" to destroy a Muslim holy site. More importantly, Jews have been forbidden to pray publicly on the Temple Mount, which once was the center of Jewish worship.

This state of affairs will change one day. As unbelievable as it may seem, the Bible indicates that the Muslim edifices will somehow be removed, making way for the Temple to be rebuilt. Without a doubt, the destruction of the third-most-important holy place in the Muslim world would immediately galvanize the Arabs against Israel.

The last eight chapters of Ezekiel describe in great detail the measurements of a Temple that is without historic parallel. When will this future third Temple make its appearance? A clue is provided in a cryptic passage in the book of Daniel, where a future "prince" is described—the Antichrist. This satanically inspired charismatic leader will be a master of deception. He will lead the armies of the world against the land of Israel and will initiate a Middle East peace treaty that he will himself later discard:

> "He will confirm a covenant with many for one 'seven,' but in the middle of that 'seven' he will *put an end to sacrifice and offering*. And one who causes desolation will place abominations on a wing of the temple until the end that is decreed is poured out on him."
>
> Daniel 9:27, italics mine

The context indicates that *seven* refers to *seven years*. This is called the Tribulation in the New Testament, a seven-year period when the earth will undergo unheard-of upheaval culminating in the battle of Armageddon.

Note that the coming ruler will "put an end to sacrifice and offering" and desecrate the "Temple." It is evident, then, that some kind of Jewish Temple will be standing when the Antichrist is fulfilling his evil designs. When discussing the Tribulation, Jesus warns His followers about the same ill omen:

> "So when you see standing in the holy place 'the abomination that causes desolation,' spoken of through the prophet Daniel—let the reader understand—then let those who are in Judea flee to the mountains."
>
> Matthew 24:15–16

These events from Matthew 24 and Daniel 9 have not occurred at any time in history. The first revolt against Rome, ending with the destruction of the second (or Herod's) Temple, devastated the Jewish people. The Jewish historian Josephus describes in ghastly detail this Roman siege of Jerusalem, which he reports as costing the lives of more than one million Jews.[2]

Yet even the horrific destruction of A.D. 70 did not fulfill Jesus' prophecy in Matthew 24, in which He spoke of a time immediately preceding His return, as we read in verse 30:

---

[2] Flavius Josephus, *The Jewish War*, 6:439. His estimate of casualties is thought by some historians to be inflated.

"At that time the sign of the Son of Man will appear in the sky, and all the nations of the earth will mourn. They will see the Son of Man coming on the clouds of the sky, with power and great glory."

The apostle Paul, writing to the Thessalonians, addresses apparent confusion in that church regarding the return of Christ:

> Don't let anyone deceive you in any way, for that day will not come until the rebellion occurs and the man of lawlessness is revealed, the man doomed to destruction. He opposes and exalts himself over everything that is called God or is worshiped, and even sets himself up in *God's temple*, proclaiming himself to be God.
>
> 2 Thessalonians 2:3–4, italics mine

Notice again the reference to "God's temple," which will be standing once more. The world still awaits this startling event, which will occur in the final dark phase of human history before Jesus' return.

Bible scholars differ as to the exact nature and description of that future Temple, but there is little doubt that current interest is centered on the Temple Mount in Jerusalem as its site. That interest has sometimes taken a misguided and violent turn as individuals and extremist groups have attempted to take matters into their own hands.

In 1969 a mentally disturbed Christian tourist set fire to the al-Aksa Mosque, believing that the Messiah would not come until all "abominations" had been cleared from the Temple Mount. That arson attempt, which damaged the interior of the mosque, caused an international incident. Years later, in the early 1980s, a Jewish extremist group threatened to remove the Muslim shrines from the sacred mount by force. They led a group of armed men to the Dome of the Rock in an attempt to blow it up, but were stopped short of carrying out their plans.

The most serious effort to reverse the status quo was yet to come. In the midst of the buildup to the Gulf War, a tragic event in the Holy Land was to have far-reaching consequences. The events of October 1990 marked a turning point for attitudes toward the nation of Israel, and may point to the beginning of the gathering storm over Israel.

In Harm's Way

On that day, a hitherto little-known organization called the Temple Mount Faithful planned to reverse symbolically the centuries-old Muslim domination of the Temple Mount. Their leader, Gershon Saloman, describes himself as a strictly observant Jew with a divine mandate.

Saloman sees himself as a key leader in the struggle for the spiritual renewal upon which the future of the Jewish people depends. He is scorned by government officials and the Orthodox community, which maintains that it is forbidden for Jews to set foot on the Haram esh-Sharif. (This is to prevent Jews from inadvertently treading on the spot where the Holy of Holies once stood.) Saloman, undeterred by opposition within Israel itself, is supremely confident about his mission in life. He believes that divine providence has destined him for a historic mission—to bring Israel's salvation to fulfillment.

With great fanfare, the Temple Mount Faithful announced that on October 12, 1990, during the Succot holidays, the group would lay the "cornerstone" of the third Temple. Realizing that this would send tremors throughout the Muslim world, Israeli police refused to give Saloman permission to carry out his ceremony. Upon appeal, the Israeli High Court of Justice upheld the police decision. Nonetheless, Saloman and his Temple Mount Faithful were determined to carry through with their plans.

For Bill, a teacher and colleague of mine, this particular Friday began like any other day as he led a tourist group through the Old City. Yet Friday is always touchy in the Old City. It is the day of prayer for Muslims, and thousands flock to the al-Aksa for midday prayers. There was an unusual tenseness in the air as the *imam*, or Muslim spiritual leader, preached to those kneeling in straight rows inside the ornately decorated mosque.

The word *preach* might imply too close a parallel to sermons in Christian churches. The messages by imams in mosques around the country consist primarily of vehement diatribes against the enemies of Islam and exhortations to the faithful to fight and defeat them.

In Arab East Jerusalem rumors had been rife that a radical Jewish sect would on this day attempt to tear down the Dome of the Rock and begin building the Jewish Temple. Arabs were tense even though they knew that Israeli police had forbidden the Temple Mount Faithful to enter the Arab site; notices had been sponsored in the local Arab papers giving assurances to that effect.

Saloman and his group were turned away by the police before they could approach the Temple Mount, but the Arab leaders of the uprising used the occasion as a pretext for inflaming the Muslim crowds to riot. Preparations had been made for the expected confrontation. Police later discovered rocks stockpiled where they could be hurled down at Jews praying at the Western ("Wailing") Wall below.

As Bill was leading his tourist group through the Old City toward the Temple Mount, they heard the sound of gunfire—not all that unusual after the noonday prayers. The police often fired tear gas canisters to disperse spontaneous demonstrations.

This time, though, the gunfire increased in intensity, along with shouting and screaming in the distance. Bill knew they had to get out of the area immediately, so he marched his anxious group down the street to the nearest exit of the walled city—St. Stephen's Gate.

Unfortunately, St. Stephen's Gate is also a main exit for people coming from the Temple Mount. And it was precisely at the Haram esh-Sharif that the shooting was taking place. Bill's students soon found themselves caught in the middle of agitated crowds fleeing the Temple Mount. As the horrified group watched, injured and lifeless bodies were rushed out to local hospitals in a scene of blood and mayhem. Bill and his students huddled in a corner for protection as young, frightened Israeli soldiers fired their automatic rifles in all directions.

The story of what happened would soon be flashed around the world. The imam's message had been an unbridled exhortation to protect the holy places of Islam against the infidels. Throngs of excited Muslims had surged out of the mosque in search of infidels. The first target at hand: a small police station on the other side of the Temple Mount. The anxious policemen watched as the inflamed crowd, several thousand strong, moved toward them and set the station on fire. Other Muslims began raining rocks down upon the Jewish worshipers sixty feet below at the Western Wall plaza. Miraculously, there was not a single serious injury among the thousands of Israelis and tourists gathered at the Western Wall in the shadow of the Temple Mount.

The police above soon found themselves in a precarious position. Backed up against the burning police station and facing enraged crowds, they quickly switched to live ammunition. As reinforcements were rushed to the scene, pandemonium broke out. On that day, which would mark a downward trend in Western attitudes toward Israel, twenty Arabs died and an estimated 200 were injured. The bloodshed was called the worst single episode of violence in East Jerusalem since Israel captured the Old City in 1967.

Prime Minister Yitzhak Shamir called the disturbance "a satanic scheme" to "distract world attention from events in the gulf to our area."[3] The Arab members of President Bush's coalition saw it differently. Butros Ghali, Egypt's Minister of State for Foreign Affairs and soon-to-be-elected Secretary-General of the U.N., referred cynically to the Temple Mount shootings as "Israel's great gift to Saddam Hussein."[4]

Back in the Gulf, the Temple Mount incident emboldened Saddam to seize the moment. He warned Israel to "leave the lands of

---

[3] Tom Masland, "A Bill Comes Due Early," *Newsweek* (October 22, 1990), p. 36.

[4] Lisa Beyer, "Saddam's Lucky Break," *Time* (October 22, 1990), p. 38.

Palestine," bragging that he had a new missile capable of reaching "the targets of evil" in Israel "on the day of reckoning."[5]

A Turning Point

Thus ended Israel's brief respite from center stage of the world's attention. The tragedy brought bitter condemnation, even from America's Gulf allies. Support for Israel among the U.S. public took a nosedive: A *Newsweek* poll showed that sixty percent of the American public thought it was time for Washington to put more pressure on Israel.[6]

Until this point Washington had insisted there be no linkage between the invasion of Kuwait and the Palestinian question. The U.S. had favored direct negotiations between Israel and her neighbors as the most promising way to resolve the Arab-Israeli conflict. Now, the reason for the change in long-established American policy was clear: In order to hold the Gulf coalition together, the U.S. had little choice but to appease her newfound allies—and now this would come at the expense of Israel.

Accustomed to shielding Israel in the U.N. Security Council, the U.S. now found herself actually sponsoring a resolution castigating her long-time ally for using excessive force on the Temple Mount. After five days of intensive negotiations, the Security Council voted unanimously to condemn Israel.

Additionally, the resolution directed the U.N. Secretary-General to send a fact-finding mission to the Occupied Territories.[7]

At issue was the precedent of yielding to the U.N. sovereignty over the West Bank. Israel has stated repeatedly that this is out of the question. Despite a personal letter from President Bush urging him to get out of the headlines and let the spotlight return to Iraq,

---

[5] Masland, p. 36.

[6] Masland, p. 35.

[7] The draft resolution "expresses alarm" at the violence in general, thus criticizing only indirectly the rock-throwing Palestinians. At the same time, the draft "condemns especially" the behavior of the Israeli security forces.

Prime Minister Shamir refused to budge. An offended U.S. then supported a follow-up U.N. resolution "deploring" Israel's intransigence. It was the second time in just twelve days that Israel had been condemned in the U.N. Security Council.

The international community was further exasperated when the cabinet of Prime Minister Shamir announced that Israel would not cooperate with any U.N. mission sent to find "ways and means for ensuring the safety and protection of the Palestinian civilians under Israeli occupation." Israel's stubbornness led only to increased hostility in the U.N. as various governments began to stress the need for an international conference to address the Arab-Israeli conflict.

In a parody of justice, only a few days after twenty Arabs died on the Temple Mount, Syrian troops were routing General Michel Aoun and his forces from their Beirut Christian enclave. A devastating air and artillery bombardment finally crushed Aoun's beleaguered army. The Syrians reportedly executed scores of Aoun's officers in cold blood after they had laid down their weapons and surrendered. Scarcely a word of the massacre reached the world's press, obsessed as it was with events in Israel.

One country with an interest in the tragedy of Lebanon was Israel, which resented the double standard being applied to her own situation. There was a growing realization that the sympathy of Israel's powerful benefactor was on the wane.

The downturn in relations between the U.S. and Israel actually began at the onset of the Bush administration. In a speech to the American-Israel Public Affairs Committee on May 22, 1989, Secretary of State James Baker called upon Israel to lay aside once and for all what he termed the "unrealistic vision" of a "greater Israel." *Greater Israel* is a political code-word for the belief that the West Bank, Gaza Strip and Golan Heights should be an integral part of Israel.

Many Israelis are convinced that these territories must remain under Israel's control. For them, Baker's speech was a rude awakening to the new reality. The previous Reagan administration had a greater appreciation for Israel's vulnerability to attack if the

West Bank and Gaza became a Palestinian state. The coastal plain of Israel is the most densely populated region in the country—and it would be directly under the guns of a hostile Palestinian state in the hills to the west. The Israelis know that regardless of any treaty, or even U.N. "supervision" *à la* Lebanon, sooner or later those guns would be there.

Even as the Gulf crisis erupted, the slump in U.S.-Israeli relations was becoming apparent. President Bush's phone log during the invasion of Kuwait tells the story: He consulted directly by telephone with every ally or pro-Western leader in the Middle East, with the notable exception of Prime Minister Shamir. It was only after the first Scud missile attack that, desperate to keep Israel out of the war, the President telephoned the Prime Minister.

The Scud missile attacks upon Israel brought a second honeymoon to American-Israeli relations as U.S. soldiers manning Patriot missile batteries shot down the incoming Soviet-made missiles. But after the hostilities subsided, Israel would once again be pressured to agree to a U.S.-brokered peace. Will Pfaff, writing in the *Los Angeles Times,* put it bluntly:

> There is going to be a larger result [of the Gulf crisis] too. The Palestine-Israel problem has to be addressed. There is no way this coalition so painstakingly assembled by Mr. Bush will disband without making a serious attempt to end a conflict that has disrupted the Middle East and poisoned international relations for two generations.[8]

We should not find it surprising that the world's attention rarely sways from the land of Israel; the Bible indicates that attention cannot help but be fixed on the "center of the world." It is here that the final drama of world history will be played out, and the unresolved Palestinian problem may well be the catalyst. Let's see how the current political situation is shaping up toward the final conjunction of forces in the Middle East.

[8] Will Pfaff, "If We Cannot Avoid War, We Must Prepare for What Comes After," *International Herald Tribune* (December 22, 1990), p. 7.

8
The New World Order

"It is time to pull out this cancerous tumour [Israel] from the body of the Moslem world."[1]

—Hashemi Rafsanjani
President of Iran

A WIZENED ISRAELI WHO HAD LIVED THROUGH the various wars and crises of his country described to me some time ago the feeling of the people of Israel toward the United States.

"You know, Tim," he said, "everybody needs a father, and America is the benevolent father of Israel."

Well put, I thought—especially regarding a tiny country surrounded by hostile neighbors. Who has helped Israel through her difficulties since the beginning of her statehood? It is the economic and military power of the U.S. that has stood between Israel and the world.

America gives approximately $3 billion every year to Israel in the form of direct grants and loans. And even though Israel's army has fought superbly against her Arab enemies, it was the supply and resupply of weaponry that enabled her to fight. The U.S. Patriot missile crews symbolized this paternal relationship. They

---

[1] Laurie Mylroie, "Toward a Sane Gulf Policy," *Jerusalem Post* (October 19, 1990), p. 5.

received an exceedingly friendly response during their stay in Israel. It was wonderful to have a big, powerful friend who would come and protect you from the neighborhood bully.

Between a Rock and a Hard Place

Now the post-war situation in the Gulf has confirmed Israel's worst fears. She would gladly have chosen to confront Saddam's armies in battle rather than face what seems to be the prevailing world view. Because of dramatic changes in the political alignment of the Middle East, it is now clear that the international community will try to accomplish what the Arab armies have been unable to do: force Israel, in effect, to commit national suicide by relinquishing land for peace.

As the foreign troops returned home, President Bush declared that the time was ripe for the United States to address the Arab-Israeli conflict with new vigor and determination. Riding high in the polls at that point with an approval rating of more than eighty percent, the President chose to put his considerable prestige on the line and seize the initiative in the Arab-Israeli dispute.

The operative element in his proposal, the phrase *land for peace*, caused grave concern in Jerusalem. Israel's powerful supporter had finally signaled that it would no longer protect her from facing up to the Palestinian question.

The change of policy was due to the coalition that the U.S. developed with Iraq during the war. The Arabs declared that good relations with the U.S. would continue only at the expense of America's historic relationship with Israel.

"The status quo will be impossible to maintain at the end of this war when all Arab regimes will be shaking," said Nabil Shaath, a political adviser to Yasser Arafat. "We are talking about a nightmare, not a passing phase. There is a deep resentment of the United States' support of Israel accumulated over four decades."[2]

---

[2] Youssef M. Ibrahim, "For Many Arabs, End of War Will Begin the Struggle,"

The Arab states were eager to capitalize on their newfound leverage with Washington. They compared the occupation of Kuwait with Israel's occupation of the West Bank, Gaza Strip and Golan Heights. Why, they argued, did the U.S. spend billions to end one military aggression while continuing to support another?

They touted the emerging Gulf Arab alliance as the replacement for America's traditional relationship with Israel. Israel should no longer be considered an indispensable ally, argued former Jordanian Foreign Minister Taher al-Masri: "If I were an American strategist, I would think that America's interests lie in Egypt and the gulf."[3]

One indication of the force of this argument was Washington's decision during the war to cancel Egypt's $7 billion debt to the U.S. but not Israel's $4.6 billion debt.

The Middle East was not the only place in which alliances were being transformed. Throughout the Gulf crisis President Bush spoke enthusiastically about the new global realities that would emerge after Saddam's aggression was reversed. The world will one day have "a new unity" as never before, he stated, to counter future aggressions.

Could this well-meaning hope turn into a nightmare? Is this what will provide the foundation for the worldwide power of the Antichrist?

The New World Order

We have seen that one day the nations will gather against the land of Israel. But this is a mystery: How will all the nations of the world be joined together for the purpose of invading the Holy Land? The world has never witnessed such a degree of mutual cooperation, and yet one day it will happen:

New York Times Service (February 5, 1991), p. 7.

[3] Melinda Beck, "The Arab World Chooses Sides," *Newsweek* (September 17, 1990), p. 29.

Then I saw three evil spirits that looked like frogs; they came out of the mouth of the dragon, out of the mouth of the beast and out of the mouth of the false prophet. They are spirits of demons performing miraculous signs, and they go out to the kings of the whole world, to gather them for the battle on the great day of God Almighty.

Revelation 16:13–14

Many believe we are already seeing the genesis of this gathering of "the kings of the whole world" in President Bush's proposed New World Order. Granted, the current interest in a unified globe does not necessarily indicate the fulfillment of biblical prophecy; doubtless that political term is often used by those who have no idea there is any such connection. Still, the growing interdependence of nations certainly points toward the gathering described in Revelation and elsewhere.

Fresh with success in the Gulf, Mr. Bush spearheaded the concept, and wanted whatever political entity replacing the U.S.S.R. to be an active partner in the U.S.-led New World Order. (It will be easier to deal with regional conflicts with Moscow as part of the team instead of the antagonist.) It envisions worldwide alliances with America at the helm to contain future aggressors.

As Mr. Bush said in his September 1990 summit in Helsinki with then-Soviet President Mikhail Gorbachev, the goal is an unparalleled era of world peace: "If the nations of the world, acting together, continue as they have been, we will set in place the cornerstone of an international order more peaceful than any we have known."[4]

That summit in itself is a prime example of how the world is becoming interlinked. Only a few years ago, a massive U.S. military presence in the Middle East would have brought the two superpowers to the brink of confrontation. In the Gorbachev era, however, the Soviets began to concentrate more on importing technology than exporting revolution. Thus, the two former adversar-

---

[4] George J. Church, "A New World," *Time* (September 17, 1990), p. 20.

ies met for the first time since World War II as partners with a common goal: the removal of Saddam Hussein's troops from Kuwait. Not only did Moscow refrain from challenging the U.S.-led campaign against Saddam Hussein; it cut off arms to Iraq and voted consistently with the United States in the U.N. Security Council.

Now, of course, with the demise of Marxist-Leninist ideology around the world and the collapse of the Soviet Union at home, Moscow no longer exerts the influence it once did. And, as the Gulf crisis demonstrated, the United States no longer has to worry that sending troops abroad will automatically trigger a clash with the Russian bear.

Even China found itself supporting—or at least not opposing— the U.N. resolutions on Iraq. The reason was simple: It needed Western technology and financial assistance and did not want to antagonize its Western trading partners. "If you want to participate in the world economy," says Robert Hormats, international banker and former State Department official, "you can't support outlaws."[5]

This shows how rapidly our world is changing. In the post-cold war era no single nation can claim world dominance. After forty years of containing Soviet expansionism, a fiscally exhausted United States will have to share global leadership with new superpowers like the European Community and Japan. The tightening web of economic relationships worldwide is making nations more dependent upon one another—and more vulnerable to international pressure.

Thus, as if awakening from a deep slumber, the United Nations is beginning to take on its international role as originally envisioned. For the first 45 years of its existence, the United Nations was capable of little more than endless debates and non-binding resolutions. All that has changed. Diplomats from around the

---

[5] Stephen V. Roberts, "George Bush, Diplomat," *U.S. News & World Report* (September 10, 1990), p. 28.

world now look to the U.N. for solutions to problems, as new life is breathed into the moribund international forum.

And Washington would like to put this newfound power to work in constructing the New World Order. It is becoming apparent that the first major application of the concept of "global collective security" may be none other than the nation of Israel. It may not be the first confrontation, but Bible prophecy indicates that a clash of the nations against Israel is inevitable.

The Gathered Nations

As with the quote from Revelation above, the book of Zechariah foretells a great final battle in Jerusalem:

> I will gather *all the nations* to Jerusalem to fight against it; the city will be captured, the houses ransacked, and the women raped. Half of the city will go into exile, but the rest of the people will not be taken from the city. Then the Lord will go out and fight against those nations, as he fights in the day of battle.
>
> Zechariah 14:2–3, italics added

Here, too, we see reference to "all the nations" being drawn to Jerusalem. This will require a measure of *political and military unity* among the nations of the world—such as the U.N. could offer.

The prophet Joel gives us an idea of where and when this will take place:

> "In those days and at that time, when I restore the fortunes of Judah and Jerusalem, *I will gather all nations* and bring them down to the Valley of Jehoshaphat. There I will enter into judgment against them concerning my inheritance, my people Israel, for they scattered my people among the nations and divided up my land."
>
> Joel 3:1–2, italics added

This apocalyptic battle will be fought in the Valley of Jehoshaphat in Jerusalem at a time when the Lord will "restore the fortunes of Judah and Jerusalem."

Ezekiel pinpoints the time further:

> "After many days you will be summoned; *in the latter years* you will come into the land that is restored from the sword, whose inhabitants have been gathered from many nations to the mountains of Israel which had been a continual waste; but its people were brought out from the nations, and they are living securely, all of them."
>
> Ezekiel 38:8, NASB, italics mine

We read here that the restoration will occur "in the latter years" and that the Jewish people will be brought from many nations. Until now there have been only two historical periods that have seemed to fulfill this prophecy of the return of the Jewish people to the land of Israel—the Hasmonean kingdom and the 1948 statehood of Israel.

The Hasmonean Kingdom

The year was 169 B.C. It was a time of great messianic expectation. Hundreds of years had elapsed since the prophecies of Joel and Zechariah. Surely, people thought, we are in the "latter days" and are seeing the restoration of Israel. At that time the Jewish people were being sorely oppressed by the Seleucid ruler Antiochus (Epiphanes) IV. In the Temple he set up an "abomination of desolation," an altar to Zeus upon which the Jews were commanded to sacrifice.[6]

---

[6] Scripture makes two distinct references to the "abomination of desolation." The first is in Daniel 11:31, which is generally agreed upon to mean the desecration of the Jewish Temple by Antiochus Epiphanes IV in 169 B.C. This is not the same abomination of desolation referred to by Jesus in Matthew 24:15, which in the context clearly occurs at the end of time. If this second abomination of

This final indignity proved to be too much for the Jews, who rose up against their foreign oppressors. The Maccabean brothers led the battle charge against the Seleucids, whose formidable weaponry included a troop of 32 elephants. Certain that the messianic age was at hand, the Jews were ready to give their lives for the freedom of Zion. As Menahem Stern writes:

> Associated with this martyrdom was an eschatological expectation. There was a growing belief that a period of unprecedented suffering was approaching, heralding the downfall of the evil kingdom and the fulfillment of the visions of the end of days.[7]

In a series of brilliant victories, the Maccabees triumphed over their Seleucid oppressors, which led to the establishment of the Hasmonean kingdom. This independent Jewish state, which lasted for nearly one hundred years, was larger and more "religious" than the present state of Israel. Daily sacrifices were offered in the restored Temple, and the Sanhedrin (the supreme Jewish religious council) was sitting in Jerusalem. The Jewish people were convinced that this was the fulfillment of prophecy about the restoration of Israel:

> At the onset of its career the Hasmonean dynasty was borne along on a tide of religious-national enthusiasm. For the Jewish masses it was the dynasty to which the deliverance of Israel had been entrusted.[8]

Their messianic expectations soon faded, however. The Hasmonean dynasty was gradually weakened by internal strife until it was overthrown by Roman intervention in 63 B.C. Clearly, no

---

desolation resembles the first, then we can expect some kind of blasphemous object to be set up in the holy place.

[7] Menahem Stern, "Second Temple (The Hellenistic-Roman Period)," *Encyclopaedia Judaica,* s.v.

[8] Stern.

battle of the Hasmonean period resembles the prophecies of Ezekiel, Joel and Zechariah. The time of the fulfillment of the return of the Jewish people to Israel would be yet in the future.

Israel Reborn

The second historical possibility for fulfilling the prophecy of Joel is in our own day. After 1,900 years of Diaspora the Jewish people once again populate the land of Israel, and in 1948 the state of Israel was reborn. In the words of the *Declaration of the Establishment of the State of Israel:*

> After being forcibly exiled from their land, the people kept faith with it throughout their Dispersion and never ceased to pray and hope for their return to it and for the restoration in it of their political freedom. Impelled by this historic and traditional attachment, Jews strove in every successive generation to re-establish themselves in their ancient homeland. In recent decades they returned in their masses. Pioneers, immigrants, and defenders, they made deserts bloom, revived the Hebrew language, built villages and towns, and created a thriving community, controlling its own economy and culture . . . and aspiring towards independent nationhood.[9]

During the Hasmonean kingdom, the Jewish people had returned from one nation, Babylon. The modern state of Israel is composed of Jews who have returned from more than *one hundred* nations. Up until the end of the nineteenth century, the land of Palestine was a neglected backwater of the Ottoman empire. It was to this land of "continual waste" that succeeding waves of Jewish immigration came.

The indications are that we may indeed be living in the "latter days" forecast by the Hebrew prophets—but we must be cautious. It is still possible that this prophecy is speaking of a time yet in the

---

[9] *Official Gazette* (Tel Aviv, Israel), May 14, 1948.

future beyond the current state of events, perhaps even superseding the modern state of Israel. After all, those living in the second century before the time of Jesus were convinced that the Hasmonean Jewish state was the fulfillment of prophecy. There were a number of good reasons for that conviction, as there are for the modern state of Israel. The divine timetable, however, remains shrouded from human perception.[10]

The Foreboding Article 42

An obscure provision in the United Nations Charter allows for military intervention on a global scale as envisioned by biblical prophecy. Article 42, under chapter VII of the Charter, permits the Security Council to authorize collective military action.

According to the stipulations of the article, a little-known functionary known as the Military Staff Committee will command such a military operation. The committee is composed of the military chiefs of staff of Britain, France, Russia, the United States and China. It is vested with wide powers to engage in military action should the U.N. Security Council so direct.

In addition, chapter XVII authorizes the major powers to take joint military action "as may be necessary for the purpose of maintaining international peace and security." Chapter XVII was designed as an interim option pending the formation of a U.N. army. That army has never materialized but the theoretical structure is in place. Now vis-à-vis the New World Order, as never before, the

---

[10] The absolute identification of the modern state of Israel with the fulfillment of these prophecies is nearly a cardinal article of faith in many circles. A series of relative arguments are strung together to form an absolute position on the matter. The blooming of the desert, for example, is usually given as proof. Yet the same, and even more, occurred during the Hasmonean period, when the Negev Desert of southern Israel was far more developed by the Nabateans than it is under the modern Israelis. See Abraham Negev, "Understanding the Nabateans," *Biblical Archaeology Review*, Vol. 14 (November-December 1988), pp. 26–45. The Roman and Byzantine periods also saw extensive settlement in the Negev. In short, the signposts may be evident, but caution is always prudent.

conditions are ripe for the creation of a U.N. army composed of elements from the nations of the world.[11]

Until the Gulf crisis the only time Article 42 was invoked was just prior to the Korean War. At that time the Soviet ambassador to the U.N. was unable to return quickly enough to New York to veto the Security Council resolution that authorized the use of collective force.

It was a different world in 1991. The superpower confrontation had dissipated and for the first time the U.N. was ready to be the policeman of the world.

And who will be public enemy number one? In the wake of the Gulf War, as Secretary of State James Baker visited several states in the region, the primary focus of discussion was the Arab-Israeli conflict. The Secretary referred repeatedly to a solution *based upon U.N. resolutions.*

At the same time, in an unprecedented move, U.N. Secretary Javier Perez de Cuellar sent letters to all 164 member nations of the U.N. to elicit opinions on whether or not Israel was in violation of the Fourth Geneva Convention. In order to understand the gravity of this move on the part of the Secretary-General, we need to take a look at how the Convention is being used to apply pressure upon Israel.

The Fourth Geneva Convention

Israel is one of the 164 signatories of the 1949 Geneva Convention document, which calls for "the protection of civilian persons in time of war." The document also calls upon any powers that are occupying territories to safeguard the rights of civilian popula-

---

[11] Article 51 of the U.N. Charter recognizes the right of self-defense against armed attack. It covers not only the victim nation but others who may come to assist her. Kuwait appealed for help under Article 51 and the U.N. recognized that appeal, in effect, by passing resolutions condemning Iraq's invasion. The U.S. acted within the U.N. Charter and could legitimately attack Iraq.

tions, to respect their persons, honor, family rights, religious convictions and practices, and manners and customs.

This all sounds reasonable enough. The problem in the Palestinian question is the issue of sovereignty: Who has the ultimate authority over the West Bank, Gaza Strip and Golan Heights? If Israel were to concede that the Geneva Convention applies to the lands in question, that would be an admission that they are indeed occupied territories. And the U.N. claims the right of supervision over territories under military occupation.

The Israeli government has, therefore, rejected repeatedly the applicability of the Convention with regard to what it prefers to call "administered territories." After the U.N. condemnations of Israel in the wake of the Temple Mount shootings, the Israeli mission to the U.N. issued a statement claiming that "the status of Judea and Samaria is not clear under international law, and the Geneva Convention regarding occupied territories does not legally apply."[12]

Israel has no intention, in other words, of granting the U.N. any authority over the West Bank and Gaza Strip. Despite the fact that the Middle East is the main region of the world in which the U.N. has chosen to exercise its "right of supervision," it has actually contributed little to peace.

Israelis have had firsthand experience with the U.N. "peacekeeping forces." Since the 1960s there has been a U.N. peacekeeping force in the Sinai Desert and on the Golan Heights, followed in the 1970s by a peacekeeping force in south Lebanon. Lightly armed and permitted to respond only in self-defense, the U.N. forces have proven, like a toothless dog, to be almost powerless.

All Bark and No Bite

Nowhere was the inability—and unwillingness—of the U.N. to come to Israel's defense more evident than prior to the Six Day

---

[12] The statement went on to declare that Israel "has decided since 1967 to act *de facto* in accordance with the humanitarian provisions of that convention." However: "Israel has the sole responsibility for the administration of these areas, including the duty to maintain law and order. This responsibility is not subject to review or intervention by other authorities."

War. Egypt and Syria, supported by Jordan, Iraq and other Arab armies, were massing their armies on Israel's borders. Finally the time had come to "liberate Palestine" from the scourge of the Zionist occupation. Only one thing stood between the Egyptian armies and Israel: a United Nations emergency force that served as a buffer zone between the two countries.

In May 1967, his war preparations completed, Egyptian President Nasser was on the verge of invading Israel through the Sinai. Reportedly he picked up the telephone and informed the U.N. peacekeeping forces stationed there to leave within 48 hours. In a couple of days the forces had disappeared across the sands, leaving Israel to fend for herself. Israeli President Chaim Herzog describes those dark days:

> Israel was soon ringed by an Arab force of some 250,000 troops, over 2,000 tanks and some 700 front-line fighter and bomber aircraft. The world looked on at what was believed to be the impending destruction of Israel. But no international action was taken. Every effort was made by the Soviet and Arab delegates to the United Nations to preempt any effort that might be made by the West to intervene and obstruct the Arab plans; they went out of the way to minimize the situation and to permit developments to take their course.[13]

When their pleas to the United Nations fell on deaf ears, Israel then went hat-in-hand to various countries, hoping someone would take up their case:

> The Israeli Government, headed by Levi Eshkol, made urgent efforts to solve the crisis by diplomatic means, dispatching Foreign Minister Abba Eban to the heads of governments of the Western great powers. But the mission was in vain.[14]

---

[13] Chaim Herzog, *The Arab-Israeli Wars* (New York: Vintage Books, 1984), p. 149.

[14] Herzog, p. 149.

No wonder Israel has learned she cannot trust the U.N.—or, for that matter, the international community. She has a deep awareness that, in her future hour of need, she will likely stand alone.

The Middle East Peace Conference

In the months following the Gulf War, Secretary of State James Baker persuaded the Arab "confrontation" states and Israel to attend a peace conference co-sponsored by the United States and the Soviet Union. How did the U.S. manage to cajole the Arabs and the Israelis to sit across from each other at the conference table?

The answer to that question has little to do with peace. The Arab participants realized that war, terrorism and finally the Palestinian uprising had each in turn failed to achieve the goal of a Palestinian state. Now, with the U.S. as the sole superpower remaining in the world, they knew their hopes lay in Washington's pressuring Israel. With the cold war over, the Jewish state was no longer needed as a bulwark against Soviet expansionism in the Middle East.

At the same time, Western dependence upon oil remained undiminished, as a senior British diplomat remarked bluntly during the peace talks: "Anyone who suggests that the West, including the U.S., doesn't need Middle East oil is living in a fantasy world."[15]

The tables had turned: Washington was beginning to need the Arabs more than they needed the Israelis. With little to gain and much to lose, the Jewish state approached the Middle East peace talks with fear and trepidation. Yet she dared not refuse to attend lest she antagonize Washington. The depth of the Israeli concern about which way the talks might lead was evident when Prime Minister Shamir decided to head the Israeli delegation personally to assure that things did not "get out of control."

Despite appearances of being willing to come to an agreement, in reality Jerusalem approached the peace talks with one overall

---

[15] James Walsh, "Why Should the World Care?," *Time* (November 11, 1991), p. 17.

strategy: to drag out the negotiations and wear down her Arab opponents until all hopes of a settlement based upon land for peace were squashed. Jerusalem also calculated that domestic pressures would force President Bush to back away from the peace process. As the 1992 elections loomed, the President was already under fire for spending too much time and energy on foreign affairs while the U.S. economy languished. And with Washington withdrawing from active involvement, Jerusalem gambled that the Middle East peace conference would soon fizzle out.

But as long as the talks continued, the bottom line negotiating position would remain the same: Israel's adamant refusal to relinquish control over the Occupied Territories. Instead, Jerusalem was willing to discuss Palestinian "autonomy" that would include "limited self-rule." Palestinians would have more control over their own affairs through the setting up of local Arab governments, police, etc. As the same time, Israel insisted on maintaining control of the land, security arrangements and foreign affairs.

What would all of this mean in practice? Jerusalem's plan for peace amounted to little more than a return to the status quo before the intifada began. To the dismay of Palestinians, the I.D.F. would still be very much in control of the Occupied Territories. (One reason for Israel's adamance is that the Jewish settlements throughout the Occupied Territories would be defenseless without a strong I.D.F. presence to protect them.)

One of the eventual Palestinian demands will be that the Jewish settlements themselves be dismantled as the land is returned to the "rightful" owners. But most of the Jews in the settlements believe passionately that these Territories are an integral part of Israel. Israelis know all too well what a political bomb this issue is: Few can forget the televised pictures of the Israeli military having to remove obstinate Jewish settlers forcibly from the Sinai when the land was returned to Egypt in the late 1970s.

That disturbing scene would be repeated a hundred times over in the strategically more important West Bank and Golan—and at a phenomenal cost. When Israel returned the Sinai to Egypt, she was forced to compensate the Jewish settlers there to the tune of $50,000 for every man, woman and child. Where the Jewish state would get the tens of billions of dollars to pay compensation for a much larger evacuation of the settlements in the Occupied Territories, no one knows. And it is almost inconceivable that the Jewish state will simply pull up roots and walk away from her enormous financial investment in these well-constructed settlements, some of which are veritable cities with tens of thousands of inhabitants.

These, then, are some of the underlying reasons for Israel's stubbornness at the Middle East peace talks. But overshadowing all else is the question of the status of the historic Old City of Jerusalem. Both the Israelis and their Palestinian counterparts at the peace conference resolutely claimed control over the ancient walled city. This issue galvanizes Israelis as no other, and even if they were forced to relinquish parts of the Occupied Territories, they would draw the line at surrendering Jerusalem.

Nevertheless, the authority of the U.N. will increasingly be invoked in order to put an end to Israeli sovereignty over the Jewish capital. The groundwork is already in place: Arab countries have long demanded that Jerusalem be declared an "international city" under the control of the United Nations.

This would represent, of course, the first step toward its "total liberation" as the Arab capital of the state of Palestine. Yasser Arafat has declared repeatedly that there will be no peace until the Palestinian flag flies over Jerusalem, "the capital of Palestine." The Arab world is willing to tolerate it as an international city for one reason: to wrest its control from the Zionists. After that primary goal is accomplished, it will be comparatively easy to oust the "toothless dog" from Palestine.

The government of Israel has no intention of allowing the United Nations to "protect" the city that is the center of the aspirations of the Jewish people. In 1980 the decree "Basic Law: Jerusalem," passed by the Israeli Knesset (Parliament), declared that a "united Jerusalem is the eternal capital of Israel." After 1,900 years of

129

foreign domination, during which Jews were often denied free access to their holy city, one thing is certain: Israel will not yield sovereignty over Jerusalem.

But at the same time we cannot forget that the international community is likely to *step in and determine* control over the territories—and the Old City. One day, in the name of "a just settlement of the Palestinian question," a massive multinational military expedition will, in all probability, be launched against a recalcitrant Israel. The parallels of such a future conflict with the biblical description of the battle of Armageddon are uncanny.

We have seen how the stage is being prepared for a concerted international effort to pressure Israel to relinquish the Occupied Territories. A number of dramatic events on the world scene, including the breakup of the Soviet empire and the Gulf War, have led to fissures between the Jewish state and her major patron, the United States. The question remains: How far along are we toward the biblical description of a time when Israel is totally isolated, facing the armies of Armageddon?

Jesus spoke about "the signs of the times" that will precede the end of the age. In addition to the ones we have already looked at, are there other indications that we are near or even beginning to enter the final phase of this age?

There are. Let's look at some unique developments in today's world that indicate we may be moving toward earth's final chapter.

9
Something Very Wrong in Our World

"If 40,000 spotted owls were dying every day, there would be an outrage. But 40,000 children are dying, and it's hardly noticed."[1]

—Peter Teeley
U.S. representative
to U.N. summit on world hunger

D URING THE GULF CRISIS SWIMMERS AND STROLL-ers along Israel's Mediterranean beaches were treated to a peculiar sight. Huge numbers of snails had washed up all along the coastline. But these were no ordinary mollusks. They were *segulit* snails appearing once again on Israeli shores, and news of their arrival caused excitement in the Jewish Orthodox community.[2]

In ancient times the segulit snail was highly prized as a source of blue dye. Each snail has a pinprick amount of the precious color, which was extracted laboriously by hand. In biblical times the blue dye was used by royalty and commanded huge sums of money.

According to the late Chief Rabbi Yitzhak Halevi Herzog, the pigment was also used for dyeing religious items used in the Temple in Jerusalem and would have been used for the royal blue robes worn by the king. Accordingly, the segulit snails had—and continue to have—messianic significance.

The snails live far from shore and are rarely seen on the beaches.

---

[1] *Time* (October 8, 1991), p. 53.
[2] "Techelot Snails Return," *Jerusalem Post* (October 30, 1990), p. 3.

According to the Talmud the shores of *Eretz Israel,* or the state of Israel, will be inundated once every seventy years with the segulit snail.[3] Rabbis in certain Orthodox Jewish circles have long believed that the first arrival of the snails after the founding of the Jewish state would be a sign that the coming of the Messiah is imminent. Needless to say, when enormous numbers of the snails appeared on the beaches at the height of the Gulf crisis, there was much speculation that the end of the age was soon approaching.

This is a sign that might not be considered earthshaking, but it is certainly one of the most unusual. Other examples, as we will see in a moment, are quite disturbing, causing thoughtful people to wonder more and more if planet earth is racing toward some kind of cataclysmic showdown.

World in Turmoil

We live in a world in which breathtakingly swift changes seem to topple over one another. The decade of the 1980s ended with many parts of the globe in a state of political upheaval. Who would have believed that the Berlin Wall, that offensive symbol of Soviet hegemony over Eastern Europe, would be smashed apart by eager crowds as the world watched by satellite television?

Who could have guessed that a former dock worker would become president of a newly democratic Poland, or that a political dissident would take the helm in Czechoslovakia? That the Sandinistas in Nicaragua and Margaret Thatcher in England would both be out of power, along with Pakistan's Benazir Bhutto and India's V.P. Singh—followed by the tragic assassination of Prime Minister Rajiv Gandhi?

Who had an inkling that Communism everywhere would be so soon on the ropes, especially in the land of Lenin? Soviet President Mikhail Gorbachev faced a losing battle to hold the union together amid profound economic collapse. Few mourned the passing of an era when the red flag of the now-extinct Soviet Union was lowered without fanfare one snowy evening in December 1991. Only a

---

[3] Tractate *Menahot,* 44a.

handful of deputies even bothered to show up for the final session of the Supreme Soviet, convened to formally dissolve the union.

Who would have guessed that Russian schools would now be requesting Christian literature, tapes and videos? That for the first time in nearly half a century, free elections would be held in Bulgaria, Czechoslovakia, Hungary and Romania?

Events are moving quickly—some believe too quickly. Where is it all leading? It is as if planet Earth is poised dangerously on the verge of even greater upheaval.

Jesus warned His followers what to expect at the end of the age:

> "You will hear of wars and rumors of wars, but see to it that you are not alarmed. Such things must happen, but the end is still to come. Nation will rise against nation, and kingdom against kingdom. There will be famines and earthquakes in various places."
>
> Matthew 24:6–7

Christians in every age have hoped and believed that they were living in the time of the Lord's return. And there have always been wars, earthquakes, famines, false teachers and the persecution of believers, as spoken of by Jesus, to encourage Christians to think so. We sometimes assume that ours is the only age to experience such things.

Regardless of whether the end of human history is close at hand or yet in the distance, it is apparent that these are unique times. We may indeed be seeing the fulfillment of biblical prophecy in a number of significant developments in today's world. First and foremost is the return of the Jewish people in our generation to the ancient land of Israel and the growing fear that drives them.

Russian Jewish Immigration

We have seen in the last chapter that up until the twentieth century, Jews had not returned to Israel from a large number of nations around the world. Today more than four million Jews live in Israel, compared to the meager numbers who lived in Palestine up until the nineteenth century. The 1990s have brought a deluge of new immigrants fleeing political upheaval in the republics of the former Soviet Union.

This is the direct result of political changes outside of the Middle East. If the superpowers had not mended their fences and ended the cold war, if the former Soviet Union had not made the momentous decision to start down the tremulous path to democracy, Russian Jews would not have been allowed to leave for Israel.

And many of them still would not have left, except for an ominous development—the resurgence of anti-Semitism in Eastern countries. In Eastern Europe as well as throughout the fragmented Soviet empire, neo-fascism is rearing its ugly head. Fascist and anti-Semitic movements, suppressed under Communism, are flourishing once again.

A journalist who spent six weeks inside a Russian anti-Semitic organization recently emerged with an alarming account of intense animosity toward the Jewish people. The movement, called *Pamyat*, meaning "remembrance," has reportedly compiled extensive lists of names and addresses of Jews.

The journalist, a 22-year-old woman named Yeva Regal, also said a former K.G.B. colonel is one of a seven-member council that runs the organization. Regal was convinced that Pamyat had been funded by and under the control of the K.G.B. and the Interior Ministry. She learned that the group receives large-scale financial support in dollars from Russian monarchists based in the U.S. Without K.G.B. sanction, she added, it would have been impossible to receive such funds.

Pamyat, with an estimated 5,000 supporters in the Moscow area alone, is only one of several similar organizations. Its leader, Dmitri Vasiliyev, denies that Pamyat is anti-Semitic. Jewish Zionism is another thing, however, and Vasiliyev vows that one day the Zionists "will be put to the wall."[4]

---

[4] Walter Ruby, "Penetrating a Pamyat Faction," *Jerusalem Post* (October 26, 1990), p. 8.

It is feared that severe economic instability will bring the same social conditions to the territories of the former Soviet Union and Eastern Europe that led to the rise of Adolf Hitler. A disillusioned public may look for a scapegoat to blame for the problems of society. Many people in the 1920s and 1930s refused to believe that a modern, enlightened society could be transformed into a vicious anti-Semitic regime—until it was too late.

Could it happen again? The beginnings can already be seen in Germany. Berlin police believe that former members of the Stasi, the dreaded secret police, are providing some of the radical groups with weapons and strategy. In addition, a thriving black market in Soviet arms is supplying these groups with everything from guns to rocket launchers.

In times past, alarming signals from Russia and her former allies struck fear in the hearts of the Jewish communities in those lands. They had little choice but to bear whatever pogrom or wave of persecution came their way. But in the midst of a disintegrating Soviet Union, Moscow opened the floodgates and allowed Soviet Jews to emigrate freely.

The floodgates opened in 1990, and a tidal wave of Jews swept into Israel. Arriving at the phenomenal rate of 1,000 per day in the last months of that year, a total of 200,000 new immigrants had arrived by December 31. This was the greatest yearly total since 1949, when 240,000 Jews arrived—mostly from Arab countries.[5] These were followed in 1991 by another 176,000 immigrants, with the promise of similar totals for 1992.

This dramatic upswing shows no sign of tapering off. A second immigration terminal at Ben-Gurion International Airport was opened in 1991 to handle as many as 5,000 newcomers daily. The Israeli government is preparing for an estimated one million Russian Jews to come in the next few years. That will translate into a 25 percent increase in the Jewish population of Israel and a one-third increase in the work force. The magnitude of this population

---

[5] "200,000 New Immigrants Made Israel Home in 1990," *Jerusalem Post International Edition* (January 5, 1991), p. 5.

growth is equivalent to more than *sixty million* immigrants flocking into the U.S. in a period of just a few years.

There is concern in Israel about what is to be done with all the new immigrants, most of whom are fleeing the uncertain political future of the former Soviet Union. Immigration officials are urging the government to declare a state of emergency to handle the influx.

This return of Jews to Israel is truly an unprecedented development and constitutes the single-most-compelling argument that we may indeed be in the last days. But other signs, when viewed against the background of this grand fact, take on new importance.

Famine and Arms: Two Deadly Sisters

It is no secret that the vast territory of the former Soviet Union was never self-sufficient in food production. Year after year, many of the crops were lost through mismanagement and lack of harvesting equipment. Even in recent years as much as one-third of the crop was left to rot in the fields. As the world's largest country lies in political and economic ruin, a disaster of catastrophic proportions looms ahead.

Sadly, there is little hope that the situation will improve in the near future. The collapse of the former Soviet central directorate has resulted in chaos as individual republics strive to organize and distribute their own food supply. To a lesser extent the newly democratic countries of Eastern Europe face the same problems.

Those of us who live in the technologically advanced West tend to assume that poverty and disease around the world are yielding steadily to modern medicine and science. Nothing could be further from the truth. The battle is being lost, not won. The decade of the 1980s actually saw a sharp increase in poverty levels as the per capita income of more than forty Third World countries plummeted.

In a recent study of sub-Saharan Africa, UNICEF (United Nations International Children's Emergency Fund) discovered the primary reason why the battle there against starvation is being lost:

rampant, uncontrolled arms spending. According to the study, entitled *"Arms and the Child,"* the countries surveyed preferred slashing funds for health and education to reducing their arms budgets. Billions of dollars in Western loans were squandered on weapons purchases instead of being used to improve the economic welfare of the population.

The most extreme case was Chad, where an astounding 79 percent of revenues was spent on the military and debt repayment. In Nigeria the figure was 30 percent, compared to a paltry 3 percent for health and education *combined*. The situation becomes all the more appalling when we realize how easily children, in particular, can be helped. Many childhood sicknesses can be cured.

Diarrhea, for example, kills more children than any other disease—an estimated four million every year. Yet the cause of death, dehydration, is easily preventable through a simple oral formula costing only pennies per dosage. When you think that each U.S. copperhead artillery shell fired during the Gulf conflict cost $30,000, and that tens of thousands of such high-tech weapons were fired, some costing hundreds of thousands of dollars each, it is easy to get discouraged about the plight of the suffering.

This is not to say that the Iraqi army should not have been ejected from Kuwait, but it does indicate that countless brutal and senseless military conflicts are draining the world's financial resources at the expense of the poor and needy.

Nor is it the fault only of despotic regimes: Those countries that produce and sell the weapons of destruction must share the blame. It is no secret that the arms merchants of the former Soviet Union, United States, Europe, China and a host of lesser countries are competing in their greed for profits from the sale of deadly weaponry.

According to UNICEF, more than 40,000 children die every day from measles, whooping cough and other easily preventable diseases.[6]

At present rates more than 100 million children will die from such diseases during the decade of the '90s. Untold millions more

---

[6] Eugene Linden, "The Last Drops," *Time* (August 20, 1990), p. 39.

wander the streets uncared for, or are pressed into slave labor—child prostitution. Many simply disappear. The total number of children's deaths eclipses the number of war casualties since World War II.

Consider the following shocking statistics:

- Brazil has as many as 500,000 child prostitutes.
- Mexico City's huge garbage dumps are home to thousands of children, who compete for scraps of discarded food with millions of rats.
- India, despite having signed the International Labor Organization's convention banning child labor, has an estimated 100 million child workers toiling in subhuman conditions, performing endlessly monotonous and dangerous labor.
- More than 30 million children around the world live in the streets. Seven million are refugees from war or famine.[7]

Again, these tragedies caused by famine and arms are prophesied in the Bible:

> Then another horse came out, a fiery red one. Its rider was given power to take peace from the earth and to make men slay each other. To him was given a large sword. When the Lamb opened the third seal, I heard the third living creature say, "Come!" I looked, and there before me was a black horse! Its rider was holding a pair of scales in his hand. Then I heard what sounded like a voice among the four living creatures, saying, "A quart of wheat for a day's wages, and three quarts of barley for a day's wages, and do not damage the oil and the wine!"
>
> Revelation 6:4–6

Worldwide famine is one of the great signs of the end of human history. It is no coincidence that the black horse symbolizing famine gallops close on the heels of the red horse of warfare.

---

[7] Compiled from various news sources.

But not all the tragedies we see around us are humanly inspired. Jesus also foretold a natural catastrophe that can be deadlier than warfare: "There will be . . . *earthquakes* in various places" (Matthew 24:7).

The Travail of Childbirth

Anyone who has experienced an earthquake realizes the helplessness of human beings in the face of the awesome forces of nature. Our family happened to be standing in a cafeteria line at Yosemite National Park in California on October 17, 1989. I was sizing up the possibilities for supper when suddenly there was commotion all around us. People were shouting and running from the room.

Not being from earthquake country, I was slow to catch on to what was happening. Was the food really that bad? When the chandeliers started swaying back and forth, it occurred to me that this was truly something unusual. It did not take long for someone to inform us that we were in the middle of an earthquake and had better dive under the tables like everyone else.

Later we watched the television coverage of what was the worst quake in the United States since the great San Francisco earthquake and fire of 1906. Fifteen seconds of violent tremors measuring 7.1 on the Richter scale, out of the epicenter near Santa Cruz, injured four thousand and left an estimated $6 billion of damage in their wake. Miraculously, only 63 people were killed.

National Geographic reports that despite the magnitude of this quake, "scientists warn that it was merely a dress rehearsal. They see a much more catastrophic event as inevitable in a land locked in the high-pressure grip of the San Andreas fault and its associated fractures."[8]

One of the most forbidding natural phenomena in our world is the frightening increase of seismic activity. Planet Earth is literally

---

[8] Thomas Y. Canby, "California Earthquake—Prelude to the Big One?," *National Geographic* 177 (May 1990), pp. 81–82.

breaking apart. No more apt description of this process can be found than in the epistle of Paul to the Romans: "We know that the whole creation has been groaning as in the pains of childbirth right up to the present time" (Romans 8:22).

If the world is "in the pains of childbirth," then delivery can be expected, perhaps soon. The rate of seismic activity has accelerated dramatically in the twentieth century. The stark fact is that there have been more major earthquakes since 1960—and more resultant deaths—than in all of recorded history *combined*.

Seismologists compare earthquake activity to the breakup of ice on a frozen lake during spring thaw. One crack in the ice is only the beginning of more to follow. Here is a list of some of the major "cracks in the ice" that have occurred since 1960 (it is sobering to realize that most of the victims, by the tens of thousands, perished suddenly):

- February 29 – March 1, 1960; Agadir, Morocco. Two earthquakes killed an estimated 10,000 to 12,000 persons.
- September 1, 1962; northwest Iran. The first of many since 1960 in this quake-prone land killed an estimated 10,000 persons.
- March 27, 1964; southern Alaska. This quake, measuring 8.4 on the Richter scale, was one of the most powerful earthquakes ever recorded. It caused tidal waves that engulfed towns and was felt as far away as Japan and Hawaii.
- August 31 – September 1, 1968; northeastern Iran. Two severe quakes killed an estimated 18,000 to 22,000 persons and left more than 100,000 homeless.
- May 31, 1970; Peru. This massive quake (Richter, 7.75) swept away scores of villages and killed an estimated 50,000.
- December 23, 1972; Nicaragua. This quake leveled much of the capital, Managua, killing more than 10,000.
- February 4, 1976; Guatemala. More than 17,000 were

killed and a million made homeless by this quake measuring 7.5 on the Richter scale.

- July 28, 1976; Tangshan, China. In one of the worst natural disasters in history, more than 250,000 people perished in two massive quakes measuring 7.8 on the Richter scale.
- September 16, 1978; Tabas, Iran. At least 25,000 were killed as a quake leveled this eastern Iranian city.
- September 19–20, 1985; Mexico City. The most powerful quake ever to hit Central America (Richter, 8.1) killed more than 8,500.
- December 7, 1988; Armenia. At least 25,000 were killed in the leveled city of Leninakan and surrounding towns.
- June 21, 1990; northern Iran. More than 35,000 were killed and 400,000 injured by a quake measuring 7.7 on the Richter scale. This is the twelfth major earthquake in this region since 1960 measuring 7.0 or higher on the Richter scale.[9]

True to the prophecy of Jesus, earthquakes are happening in "various places," including some regions that have no previous record of seismic activity. Up until 1960, for example, there had not been a single measurable earthquake in the state of Colorado. Since then seismic equipment has detected several thousand earthquakes.

The astounding increase in seismic activity worldwide is a startling phenomenon—and a sign that human history may be writing its final chapter. Just as the increase of labor pains means that birth is near, the breaking up of the earth's crust signals that the end of the age is approaching.

But this is not the only natural catastrophe the world is facing. There is another equally devastating cataclysm already approaching on the horizon.

---

[9] Compiled from various news sources.

10

The Worldwide Water Crisis

"Wars over water may erupt in the Middle East in the 1990s when states try to control each other's water supplies."[1]
—Arnon Sofer
professor of geography
at Haifa University

ALTHOUGH THREE-QUARTERS OF THE EARTH'S surface is covered by water, 98 percent of it is salt water and unfit for human consumption. Most of the planet's fresh water is in the polar ice caps or stored in underground aquifers. In fact, less than one percent is contained in convenient sources like lakes and rivers. And that supply has been distributed unevenly: Burma has 35 times as much fresh water as Botswana; Canada has 26 times as much as Mexico.

Each year a crisis of mammoth proportions draws closer: Mankind is using fresh water supplies at an alarming rate and polluting those same precious stocks. The World Resources Institute reports that 3.4 billion of the world's 5.5 billion people must get by on one-seventh the amount of water used by the average American.

For much of the world, hunger, disease and poverty are the result of a lack of clean water. And in the future, it may be the basis for war as well—all elements of Jesus' warning. It is almost

---

[1] Eugene Linden, "The Last Drops," *Time* (August 20, 1990), p. 59.

inevitable that water shortages worldwide and the accompanying famines will drive nations into conflict with one another.

Surprising numbers of regions around the world are vulnerable to this threat, but nowhere is the danger more present—as we shall see—than in today's Middle East. The acute lack of water in the lands of the Bible will increase tensions to the breaking point, and may be a factor leading to the final confrontation known as Armageddon.

First, let us examine the ominous water situation around the world.

In sub-Saharan Africa the desert marches southward, turning some 27,000 square miles of productive land into sand dunes every year. In Ethiopia alone more than one million people have starved to death over the past decade. It is feared that millions more will perish in the 1990s.

Other lands are turning into desert because of human mismanagement. The Aral Sea, the second-largest landlocked body of water in Asia, was once a giant lake the size of Ireland. Now it has shrunk to one-third of its former size. Grandiose but ill-advised water projects have drained it over the past thirty years, creating a severe water shortage in the Aral region.

Next door, China chose a unique method of solving her water problem. In the early 1980s a government study concluded that available water resources were sufficient to support 700 million people. That was alarming because the population at that time had already reached 900 million. Unable to increase the water supply, the Politburo did what seemed to be the practical alternative: They revised the study to conclude that there was enough water after all for 1.1 billion. Today, however, the population has exceeded even that mark and more than fifty cities face acute water shortages. One-third of the wells in Beijing have gone dry as the water table drops by as much as six and a half feet per year.[2]

Continental Europe is suffering its worst drought since the 1940s. Groundwater reserves in France are less than forty percent

---

[2] Linden, p. 59.

of their normal levels. Five regions in Italy have asked to be declared disaster zones because of drought. Unusually dry winters, combined with enormously increasing water consumption, have dried up reservoirs across the continent.

In Britain alone, as the supply of water decreases, consumption has increased seventy percent over the past thirty years—to an average of 36 gallons per person per day. It is also estimated that up to one-quarter of all municipal water supplies is lost through antiquated underground piping systems.

In the western United States years of drought have led to stringent controls over water usage in many areas. Southern California receives about half its water from a single, vulnerable canal system, the California Aqueduct. Twenty million people depend upon this 500-mile-long canal bringing water from the Sacramento River Delta. As a result of this pumping, however, the delta is sinking as much as three inches annually, thus becoming increasingly susceptible to seawater intrusion.

To make matters worse, what has been called the worst drought in California history has forced the state to curtail irrigation water to farmers in the central valley. Farm leaders said that the cutoff will cost billions of dollars in losses in what is one of the state's major agricultural regions. Considering that California supplies half of America's fruits and vegetables, a prolonged drought will affect the nation's food supply.

South of the border, upwards of half of Mexico's thirty million people do not have safe drinking water. Ivan Restrepo, head of Mexico's Center for Ecodevelopment, warns: "We've been enduring a crisis for several years now, but it is in this decade that it will explode." Mexico City's burgeoning population of twenty million is causing the city's main aquifer to drop as much as 11 feet per year. Antonia Alcantara, a vendor from a slum outside Mexico City, complains that her tapwater comes out "yellow and full of worms."[3]

---

[3] Linden, p. 59.

The Curse of Irrigation

It was once thought that irrigation was the answer to water-starved lands. The past three decades have seen an irrigation boom that has doubled the amount of arid land being watered around the globe. Today more than seventy percent of the fresh water used by mankind goes for agriculture. But the water that has made the desert bloom is beginning to dry up. According to the Worldwatch Institute in Washington, the amount of irrigated land worldwide has declined by seven percent over the past several years.[4]

The widespread practice of irrigation holds a hidden danger: Without proper drainage, irrigation gradually destroys land through salinization. Surface evaporation leaves an increasing concentration of mineral salts behind, poisoning plant roots and making agriculture impossible. Today it is estimated that 150 million acres of irrigated land around the world have been damaged by salt buildup.

In fact, history reveals that the toxicity of artificially watered land is a major factor in the fall of great civilizations. Both Mesopotamia and Babylon, as well as the Mayan civilization of Central America, may have foundered in large part because of the eventual infertility of their irrigated lands.

The global water shortage may soon restrict food production at a time in history when population growth is expanding faster than ever before. The stark reality is that the world is already consuming more food than it produces. Impoverished countries have managed to avert starvation only by drawing on international reserves of grain—stocks that are themselves being depleted. In just two years, from 1987 to 1989, global grain reserves fell from more than a 100-day supply to a 54-day supply.

Poor weather conditions, especially in the North American grain belt, could put the global food supply in critical condition in a few short years. We would then begin to see the massive famines predicted by Jesus as a sign of the end.

---

[4] Linden, p. 39.

As I mentioned, however, there is one region of the world in particular where the shortage of water will have special significance when viewed in light of biblical prophecy.

Water Shortage in the Middle East

For all the attention given to oil reserves in the Middle East, the one resource that may influence its future most is not oil but water. In a region where rainfall is scarce and less than ten percent of the land is cultivated, the availability of water has been a pressing concern since Bible times. Experts predict that a reduction of the water supply could cause severe economic hardship, rip apart fragile political alliances and plunge the Middle East into a series of bloody conflicts by the end of the century. Douglas Davis writes:

> Warnings are growing steadily louder, both inside and outside the region, that the next major Middle East conflagration will draw its inspiration not from the Arab-Israeli conflict . . . or any of the myriad rivalries, jealousies and suspicions that characterize relationships within the region. The next war, say politicians and scientists, will be over water.[5]

In a widely quoted research paper, the Washington-based Center for Strategic and International Studies analyzed hundreds of key indicators regarding water in the Middle East, such as water flow, consumption patterns and population trends. They expressed the problem in near apocalyptic terms: "Before the 21st century the struggle over limited and threatened water resources could sunder already fragile ties among regional states and lead to *unprecedented upheaval* within the area."[6]

The water policies of some Middle Eastern states border on delusion. Saudi Arabia has spent tens of billions of petrodollars on

---

[5] Douglas Davis, "Future Water Shortages Threaten Middle East Peace," *Jerusalem Post* (May 25, 1990), p. 5.

[6] Davis, p. 5; italics mine.

seawater desalination plants that supply only three percent of her water. At the same time she is using ninety percent of her deep-well water supplies—which cannot be replaced—on agricultural produce. The same fruits and vegetables could be imported at one-tenth the cost, were it not for Saudi Arabia's insistence on self-sufficiency.

Similarly, Libya's Muammar Gaddafi has begun a typically bizarre project to pump underground water from beneath Libya's southern desert. The $24 billion project, termed "the Eighth Wonder of the World" by the eccentric colonel, consists of a system of huge concrete pipes that will transport the water across Libya. Experts predict that the underground lakes will dry up soon after the massive project is completed.

Tourists to the Middle East might be tempted to think that the problem is exaggerated. After all, the hotel pool is filled and water gushes out of the taps in their rooms. There is still a lush green belt of farmland along the Nile, and Israel continues to be an agricultural miracle.

Yet these outward signs are deceiving, masking a situation spiraling out of control. Let's take a quick tour of the region to see just how bad the problem is—all the while keeping an ominous question in mind: "What will happen when the water dries up?"

Egypt

Egypt *is* the Nile. More than ninety percent of the country's population live on the arable three percent of the land along the world's longest river. The country's escalating population is a recipe for disaster as one million people are added to her 55 million population every nine months. The country is already forced to import two-thirds of her food every year. In 1987 the U.S. State Department noted grimly that "there will be insufficient water to sustain Egypt's population by the year 2000 unless dramatic conservation and management improvements are put into place in the next few years."[7]

In the fertile Nile Delta, farmers use twice as much water as necessary because of primitive irrigation techniques. The plumbing in Egypt's swollen cities has become a nightmare. Two-thirds of the drinking water seeps into the ground from cracked and leaking pipes after it leaves the filtration plant. Sewage often backs into houses because of the overtaxed waste removal system. Unless desperate measures are taken in the next few years, a full-blown water catastrophe will engulf Egypt.

On the upper reaches of the Nile River another potentially explosive water problem threatens regional peace. Ethiopia is investigating the possibility of constructing three dams on the Blue Nile, a principle tributary. Cairo fears that such a project would substantially reduce the flow of Nile water to the Delta region.

Addis Ababa has already been warned that Egypt will not tolerate any interference with the flow of the Nile. One Western official predicted bluntly that "Egypt will go to war to protect its Nile waters. There is absolutely no doubt about that."[8]

Egypt is not the only country dependent upon the Nile. Eight other African nations, each with alarmingly high population growth rates, rely on the water of the giant river as well. The balance of water-sharing is so fragile that a major diversion project anywhere along the Nile's 4,000-mile route could lead to conflict.

Jordan

The Hashemite Kingdom is also veering toward the ultimate disaster for a desert nation as her supply of water is drying up. Jordan's 3.1 million residents already consume more water than is deposited on the country every year by rainfall. To relieve this annual deficit, Jordan is pumping from underground water depos-

---

[7] Davis, p. 5.
[8] Davis, p. 5.

its in the south of the country, deposits that cannot be replaced. Meanwhile, her population is doubling every twenty years. Already in many towns water is available only twice a week.

A significant part of Jordan's water comes from the Jordan River and its tributary, the Yarmuk River. Back in 1955 the U.S. helped to negotiate an agreement between Jordan and Israel regarding the use of these waters. Each country guards her allotted share of water jealously. Recently a fracas erupted when Israel reportedly removed a large boulder that slightly increased her share of the water flow. In any event, the Jordan River is now so overused that its water is already too saline to irrigate all but the most salt-resistant crops.

Jordan's King Hussein has warned that a dispute over water is one issue that could provoke his country into a military confrontation with Israel. That day may be growing closer. A $350 million dollar dam on the Yarmuk River is planned to increase the supply to both Jordan and Syria. The proposed dam would cut off one of Israel's vital sources. A similar attempt in the 1960s to cut off Israel's supply of water was one of the provocations leading to the Six Day War.

Israel

Israel cannot hope for any assistance from her Arab neighbors. This makes the situation in the Holy Land especially desperate: If and when the taps run dry Israel will be isolated and helpless. And despite appearances as a twentieth-century agricultural miracle, she is facing a water crisis as severe as any of her neighbors. Many Israelis are hoping that a new Moses will appear to strike a rock and quench the thirst of the present-day children of Israel.

This calamity did not burst upon the scene unexpectedly. From the beginnings of the state of Israel, water experts have known that the country did not have sufficient water resources for an industrial society with a greatly increased population. Now those fears are becoming reality. A 1991 report on the water economy issued by the State Comptroller's Office warned that after 25 years of irresponsible neglect Israel is on the verge of a catastrophic water shortage.

A day's outing to the Sea of Galilee, which supplies one-fourth of Israel's water, illustrates the problem. In some places one has to walk out a third of a mile to reach swimming depth. During the winter of 1990–1991 the lake dropped to its lowest recorded level in more than sixty years. Hydrology experts warn that the biological and chemical balance of the lake may soon be damaged irreparably.

The problem is further illustrated by the lessening flow of the Dan River, which feeds into the Sea of Galilee. In the fall of 1990 its water flow was reduced from its normal peak of 325 cubic yards per second to a feeble 5.2 cubic yards per second.

Because of the dangerously low level of the Sea of Galilee, the National Water Carrier, Israel's water lifeline, has been forced to suspend all pumping operations. This enormously expensive system consumes seventeen percent of Israel's scarce energy resources just moving water around the country. The rest of the country's water comes from huge underground aquifers as well as numerous wells.

The situation with these aquifers and wells is equally perilous. The water level in the underground reservoirs is also dangerously near the red line. The giant Yarkon Hataninim reservoir, for example, is only about a yard above its danger line. As the water level drops, the aquifer will become more and more polluted with seawater intrusion.

A lack of sufficient rainfall over the past several years has led to a water "deficit" of between 1.6 and 2.6 billion cubic yards, or the equivalent of a year's supply. But disaster will not be averted simply with a year or two of above-average rainfall.

Israel's annual population increase of five percent means a corresponding increase in total water usage per year. As it is, there is no extra water to meet this growing demand. And, as I have already mentioned, there is another factor: The dramatic influx of

Russian Jewish immigrants that could add an estimated one million people to Israel's population by the mid-1990s.

No one seems to know where Israel will obtain the considerable amount of new water that this population increase will require. Meanwhile, the water levels in the Sea of Galilee, the aquifers and the wells continue to fall.

Further complicating matters is the pollution of groundwater. Sewage and waste seep through Israel's subsoil and contaminate the fresh water aquifers underneath. This is especially dangerous for Jerusalem, which draws 95 percent of its water from ground sources. Only about one-fifth of the city's sewage is properly treated before being allowed to drain into the countryside.

To top off a list of seemingly insurmountable problems is a political dilemma. No less than forty percent of Israel's fresh water comes from underground aquifers beneath the West Bank and Gaza Strip. Should Israel ever be forced to relinquish those territories, she would lose control over that essential water supply. Indeed, one of the Palestinian demands during the Middle East peace talks was to be given control over the water resources of the West Bank.

Despite the lateness of the hour, there are no ready answers to the problem. Those already suggested are either technologically unfeasible or prohibitively expensive. They range from desalination plants to floating giant water rafts from Turkey. Desalinated water would cost from sixty cents to one dollar per cubic meter (1.3 cubic yards). But this would bring economic catastrophe to farmers in Israel's irrigation-intensive agricultural sector, who now pay only fourteen cents per cubic meter.

Israel faces a water shortage of thirty percent in the next decade alone. For Jordan the figure is fifty percent, while for Syria and Iraq the figure is sixty percent. This can only increase tensions as Israel and her neighbors struggle for control of the scarce water resources.

But the most immediate threat of armed conflict over water comes from a land to the north of Israel.

151

The Ataturk Dam

In southeast Turkey the emerging "water superpower" of the Middle East is constructing a $21 billion project that includes the creation of 21 dams, 17 hydroelectric plants and irrigation channels for an area the size of South Carolina. The centerpiece of the network is the mile-long Ataturk Dam—the highest in the world.

All these dams will cut deeply into the flow of the Euphrates River. Downstream, Syria and Iraq stand to lose up to two-thirds of their water supply from the Euphrates, a disastrous prospect. With running water available for only a few hours a day, Damascus is already approaching a state of crisis.

Turkey has said that she will provide Syria and Iraq with the water they need. She has, nevertheless, rejected all demands for a water-sharing agreement, insisting on full ownership of the waters of the two rivers. Negotiations have broken down over this issue.

To test the first completed stage of the Ataturk Dam in early 1990, Turkey unilaterally shut down the flow of the Euphrates River. Both Syria and Iraq suffered crop failures as well as electrical disruptions from their own hydroelectric installations. The response was swift and forceful: Syria and Iraq threatened war unless the spigot was immediately turned on again. Just one month after it had cut off the Euphrates River, Turkey relented and resumed the normal flow of water.

As the Gulf crisis unfolded, however, Turkey quietly continued with her ambitious dam scheme. The harsh fact remains that the water projects in Ankara could well mean economic disaster for both Syria and Iraq. Even more significantly, the dams may fulfill a cryptic prophecy in the book of Revelation: "The sixth angel poured out his bowl on the great river Euphrates, and its water was dried up to prepare the way for the kings from the East" (Revelation 16:12).

Never in recorded history has this great river dried up, but it will soon be reduced to little more than a trickle. The 1990 test was just a trial run. The completion of the Ataturk and twenty other dams is slated for the mid-1990s. Once the work is finished, the dams will be filled with water. This will take an estimated two years.

It would be necessary for the invading "kings of the East" in Revelation to cross the Euphrates River on their way west. We will look into this turn of events later. Suffice it to say now, it is not necessary for the entire river to become bone-dry. The Greek word in the biblical text can refer to the waters *receding* sufficiently to allow free passage across.

We saw in the Gulf War that the Euphrates River serves as a formidable barrier. In February 1991 the Republican Guard of the Iraqi army was trapped in southern Iraq because the Allied air forces had destroyed the bridges across the Euphrates. The trapped Iraqi armored columns suffered heavy losses because they had no way of escape.

According to the book of Revelation, one day the natural barrier of the mighty Euphrates River will fall. Vast armies will cross it at will on their way to the land of Israel. Let us now look at the setting of this battle and its participants.

Part 4
Back to the Future

11

The Mysterious Gog and Magog

"And now for a roundup of the Lenin monuments attacked today . . . "[1]

—Start of a segment on "Vremya,"
Moscow television's official
evening news program

ONE OF THE MOST ENIGMATIC AND DIFFICULT PAS-sages to interpret in all of the holy writ is in Ezekiel. It is the text found in chapters 38 and 39 describing a great conflict at the end of the age: the battle of Gog from the land of Magog.

This battle has been the subject of endless discussion among Bible scholars—and resultant confusion on the part of lay people.[2] One view, so commonly held as to be almost taken for granted, is that this text refers to a Russian-led invasion of the Middle East—a view that persists in the face of recent convulsive events in the former Soviet Union. So ingrained is this theory that books on biblical prophecy have assumed routinely over the years that it was beyond doubt. Without discussing the evidence, for example, John F. Walvoord simply concluded that the de-

---

[1] *Newsweek* (December 3, 1990), p. 11.

[2] See Ralph H. Alexander, "A Fresh Look at Ezekiel 38 and 39," *Journal of the Evangelical Theological Society* 17 (Summer 1974), pp. 162–165. Alexander discusses five contemporary views as to the nature and time of this battle.

scription in Ezekiel 38 and 39 "could only refer to what we know today as Russia."[3]

What is the evidence for this commonly held belief? In truth, the Russian invasion theory rests upon scanty foundations indeed. Even if Russia retains her military might after the fall of Communism, the evidence has pointed away from that nation as the identity of the biblical Rosh all along.

Let's examine this battle for ourselves and see where the Bible takes us.

The Setting of the Battle

The general context of Ezekiel 36 and 37 presents five stages that precede the battle with Gog and its allies. In the *first* stage, the Israelites suffer grievous judgment because of their wickedness, followed by their dispersion among the nations: "I dispersed them among the nations, and they were scattered through the countries; I judged them according to their conduct and their actions" (Ezekiel 36:19).

This Diaspora began with the destruction of Jerusalem in 586 B.C., when the Israelites were exiled to Babylon. In the following centuries they found their way to distant lands and today there is scarcely a land that does not have some Jewish representation among its peoples. But as we have noted, this worldwide scattering will one day be reversed as, in the *second* stage, they return to Israel: "But you, O mountains of Israel, will produce branches and fruit for my people Israel, for they will soon come home" (Ezekiel 36:8).

In chapter 8 we discussed two historical possibilities for the fulfillment of this return. The Hasmonean kingdom of the second century B.C. does not fulfill the prophecy of the regathering. That

---

[3] John F. Walvoord, *Armageddon, Oil, and the Middle East Crisis*, rev. ed. (Grand Rapids: Zondervan, 1990), p. 141. See also Herman A. Hoyt, *The End Times* (Chicago: Moody Press, 1969), p. 152, and many others.

leaves the modern state of Israel as the only remaining candidate to date.

In the midst of this return to the land there will be a *third* stage: a miraculous spiritual transformation of the people of Israel: "I will . . . put a new spirit in you; I will remove from you your heart of stone and give you a heart of flesh. And I will put my Spirit in you and move you to follow my decrees and be careful to keep my laws" (Ezekiel 36:26–27).

It would be tempting to think of the zealous observance of the Hebrew law by Orthodox Jews in Israel today as the fulfillment of this stage. They take extreme measures, for instance, to avoid working on the Shabbat (Friday evening to Saturday evening). And that is no easy task since almost any physical activity can be considered "work" by the Rabbis.

Thus, many elevators in Israel are programmed to run continuously throughout the entire 24-hour period of Shabbat, stopping on every floor as they ascend and descend. This is so no one will be guilty of breaking the Shabbat by pressing the elevator button.

Apartments throughout Israel have timers that turn lights and other appliances on and off automatically during Shabbat so that, once again, electrical switches do not have to be engaged. Ovens are built with a special Shabbat setting so they do not have to be turned on or off. Likewise, refrigerators built in Israel are designed so that the interior lightbulb does not go on when the door is opened during Shabbat; yes, turning on the refrigerator light by opening the door is considered work.

There is only one exception to these stringent rules: One may work on the Shabbat in a life-threatening situation.

There is an old rabbinic tradition that Messiah will come the moment every Jew in the world observes the Shabbat. This is why Orthodox Jews are so zealous in following self-imposed rules: They believe God is pleased by their efforts. But is this what the passage in Ezekiel is speaking about? The answer lies in the words of Jesus:

"It is written in the Prophets: 'They will all be taught by God.'
Everyone who listens to the Father and learns from him *comes
to me*. No one has seen the Father except the one who is from
God; only he has seen the Father. I tell you the truth, he who
believes has everlasting life. I am the bread of life."

John 6:45–48, italics mine

Jesus told His disciples that the one who truly desires to be
obedient to God will be drawn to Him, "the bread of life." The
spiritual revival foretold by Ezekiel was not one of outward observance, but of inward conversion. Thus, the legalistic observance
of the Shabbat is not a fulfillment of this third stage, but perhaps
another response in the people is. The firstfruits of the spiritual
rebirth foretold by Ezekiel can be seen in the area of faith. Here is
one example.

In the Holy Land one gets accustomed to hearing all sorts of
exaggerated tales. I would not have believed the following story if
I had not heard it directly from the person involved.

A member of the staff at the Garden Tomb related this incident,
which occurred one day as he was waiting to greet visitors at the
entrance. Many Christian visitors to the Holy Land are familiar
with the Garden Tomb, tucked away up a narrow alley near the
Old City. The site is revered by many as the possible site of the
burial and resurrection of Jesus. I have enjoyed many refreshing
visits to the lovely gardens, which are an oasis of serenity in the
midst of the noise and confusion on the other side of the high
walls.

The guide was startled one day to see a Hasidic Jew suddenly
burst through the entrance. These ultra-Orthodox Jews are attired
in the long black coats and knee stockings of eighteenth-century
Prussia, where the sect was founded. They live in reclusive quarters
of the city, keeping to themselves lest they be tainted by contact
with non-religious Jews and Gentiles.

Since the Hasidim are fervently opposed to the belief in Jesus as
the Messiah, the guide was concerned that the man was up to

something. He followed the large, middle-aged Hasid as he made his way quickly through the Garden, looking very much out of place with his untrimmed sideburns flowing from underneath his "stovepipe" black hat. The guide was growing ever more concerned that the man was a fanatic bent upon mischief.

His fears intensified as the Hasid crept up quietly behind a Christian tour group that was having a worship service. *Oh, no!* thought the guide as he quickened his pace to confront the Hasid before he disrupted the service. But just as he was closing in, the guide saw something that made him stop in his tracks: Unnoticed, unobtrusively, the ultra-Orthodox Jew was singing with the group of worshiping Christians.

The guide stood still, dumbfounded. Of all the manifold variety of Jews in Israel, none is more dedicated to Judaism than the Hasidim.

After a while, just as quickly as he had come, the Hasid turned around and began to walk out of the Garden. The guide could restrain himself no longer and caught up with the Hasid just before he exited the Garden.

"Just a minute!" the guide called out, and the man turned to acknowledge him. "I couldn't help observing you back there. . . ."

The two men, from two very different worlds, looked at each other. Then the Hasid, seemingly anticipating his question, said just four words before turning and leaving: "I know Him, too."

Here is a man, existing in the smothering confines of Judaism's most extreme sect, who somehow came to know Jesus as his Messiah.

And he is not alone. While twenty years ago the term *messianic Jew* was almost unheard of in Israel, today there are many Israeli Jews who have accepted Jesus as their Messiah. Estimates in 1991 placed the number between 2,500 and 4,000, including a number who have emigrated from the former Soviet Union. While this constitutes a tiny minority of the population, messianic congregations can be found in cities around the land and the numbers continue to grow.

The *fourth* stage predicted in Ezekiel that will occur before the battle with Gog is the permanent reunification of the land.

Israel was formerly divided into the Northern Kingdom of Israel and the Southern Kingdom of Judah. Through the symbolic joining of two sticks, one representing "Judah" and the other "Ephraim," the prophet predicted that they would again form one undivided land: "I will make them one nation in the land, on the mountains of Israel. There will be one king over all of them and they will never again be two nations or be divided into two kingdoms" (Ezekiel 37:22). In 1967, for the first time in nineteen centuries, the land of Israel was once again united under Jewish control.

The most pressing problem facing the modern Jewish state relates to this fourth stage: the demand for a separate Palestinian state in the midst of the land of Israel. Still, the ancient tribal territory of Ephraim was located squarely in the West Bank, and Ezekiel's prophecy states that "Ephraim" will be forever joined to "Judah." Thus, the West Bank will be joined to the rest of Israel. Even if the demands for a Palestinian state are fulfilled, this passage indicates they are not destined to meet with permanent success.

The *fifth* and last stage is a final attempt to possess the land—not by the returning Jews but by the armies of Gog and its allies:

> "After many days you will be called to arms. In future years you will invade a land that has recovered from war, whose people were gathered from many nations to the mountains of Israel, which had long been desolate. They had been brought out from the nations, and now all of them live in safety."
>
> Ezekiel 38:8

This invasion will occur "after many days," at a time when the regathered Jews "live in safety." Some assume that this means the inhabitants have been lulled by a false sense of peace. But it can also refer to a *high state of security* in the presence of threats.[4] This certainly describes the level of preparedness on the part of the I.D.F., which is ranked among the world's best armed forces.

Visitors to the country soon learn that Israel is extremely security-conscious. Every passenger passes through an elaborate security check at the airport, and armed soldiers are everywhere.

---

[4] See the NASB, which states, "They are living securely, all of them."

Also note that the mention of Gog and Magog again in Revelation 20:7–10 has led to a convoluted explanation that requires one more "final" battle. The premillennialist position holds that there will be yet another satanic rebellion at the end of a thousand-year earthly reign of Jesus Christ. After accepting this view for many years, I finally woke up to its glaring shortcomings. Namely, if the Parousia (Second Coming) of Jesus Christ refers to His return to put a final end to all wickedness and rebellion, why then will Satan and his conspirators be permitted to raise up yet another great rebellion *after* this climactic event? Even D. Pentecost, when attempting to defend this view, acknowledges: "This whole program is admittedly difficult" (Pentecost, p. 551).

Anthony A. Hoekema goes to the heart of the matter: "Why, further, should the glorified Christ return to an earth where sin and death still reign? Why should he after his return in glory still have to rule his enemies with a rod of iron, and still have to crush a final rebellion against him at the close of the millennium? . . . Does not the Bible teach that Christ is coming back in the fullness of his glory to usher in, not an interim period of qualified peace and blessing, but the final state of unqualified perfection?" (Anthony A. Hoekema, *The Bible and the Future* [Exeter: The Paternoster Press, 1979], p. 185).

Is this not what Paul is referring to when he writes in Acts 3:21 that Jesus "must remain in heaven until the time comes for God to restore everything, as he promised long ago through his holy prophets"? Surely Jesus' return "to restore everything" refers to the final state rather than to a world in which sin and death still have not been dealt the final blow, and out of which yet another satanic rebellion arises.

The amillennialist position does not interpret the one thousand years mentioned in Revelation 20 literally. Indeed, it can hardly be denied that the genre of apocalyptic writings is full of symbolism. It is also significant that nowhere else in Scripture is a literal thousand-year millennium taught plainly. One would expect such an important event on the eschatological calendar to find confirmation in other prophetic passages. Accordingly, Hoekema concludes: "Instead of insisting that Revelation 20 affirms a teaching which is not found elsewhere in the Bible, is it not

The public has been trained to watch for suspicious objects as they go about their daily lives. On occasions I have been on Israeli buses when someone raised the alarm about a package or bag that drew his or her attention. If the suspicious item is not claimed by someone immediately, the bus screeches to a halt, the passengers empty out and the bomb disposal squad is called.

These five stages show us the background for the battle with Gog. Our next question is: From where will these invaders with the strange-sounding names come?

The Direction of the Invasion

The identity of Gog and its allies has been the source of considerable speculation. Ezekiel 38 indicates from what direction this mysterious invasion comes: "You will come from your place *in the far north,* you and many nations with you, all of them riding on horses, a great horde, a mighty army" (Ezekiel 38:15).

As I mentioned at the beginning of this chapter, it has been

---

wiser to interpret these difficult verses in an apocalyptic book in the light of and in harmony with the clear teachings of the rest of Scripture?" (Hoekema, p. 185).

If correct, this would indicate that the rebellion of Gog and Magog in Revelation 20 is the same great, final rebellion of Gog and Magog in Ezekiel. As for incongruities in the chronological sequence (notably the occurrence of Christ's return in chapter 19), most commentators recognize that the book of Revelation does not proceed in a strictly chronological fashion. Rather, the sacred writer evidently employs a good deal of recapitulation, that is, the restating of the same events in different ways.

The reader is encouraged to read Revelation 12 for an example of the above principles. Here we find extensive use of symbolism that is not intended to be interpreted literally ("a woman clothed with the sun, with the moon under her feet and a crown of twelve stars on her head," etc.). In addition, the chapter does not follow a strict chronological sequence. Instead, the events of verses 1–6 (the "dragon" being thrown out of heaven and pursuing the "woman") are repeated with more detail in the rest of the chapter. It is this kind of recapitulation that is believed to occur when the final battle is once again described in chapter 20.

While not without its difficulties, the identification of Gog and Magog in Revelation 20 with Ezekiel 38 and 39 would better accord with a simplified approach to biblical prophecy.

widely assumed that this northern confederacy refers to Russia. In one of the most widely published books ever written on the subject of biblical prophecy, *The Late Great Planet Earth,* Hal Lindsey wrote: "For centuries, long before the current events could have influenced the interpreter's ideas, men have recognized that Ezekiel's prophecy about the northern commander referred to Russia."[5]

Indeed, if one takes a map of the world and draws a line north from Israel, it will go directly through Russia. Is this what the Bible means when it refers to the north? Not necessarily.

It may be surprising to learn that, in many cases, the geographical references to north in the Bible actually refer to the east. The book of Jeremiah warns repeatedly of a coming invasion: "Raise the signal to go to Zion! Flee for safety without delay! For I am bringing disaster from the north, even terrible destruction" (Jeremiah 4:6).[6]

This passage refers to the Babylonian invasion that led to the downfall of the kingdom of Judah in 586 B.C. But here is the problem: A quick check of a Middle East map reveals that Babylon is not to the north of Israel. Rather, it is directly east.

We find a similar example in Jeremiah 46 in which the defeat of Pharoah Necho II at Carchemish in 605 B.C. is foretold: "The Daughter of Egypt will be put to shame, handed over to the people of the north" (verse 24).

The Egyptian army was defeated by the neo-Babylonian army led by Nebuchadnezzar. Here again they were said to come from the north, even though Babylon was actually southeast of Carchemish. Other examples include Ezekiel 26:7, which refers to Nebuchadnezzar attacking the city of Tyre in Lebanon "from the north," and Zephaniah 2:13, in which Assyria and her capital, Nineveh, are said to be located in "the north." Assyria, like Babylon, lay almost directly east of the Promised Land.

---

[5] Hal Lindsey and C.C. Carlson, *The Late Great Planet Earth* (Grand Rapids: Zondervan, 1970), p. 63.

[6] See also: Jeremiah 1:14–15; 3:18; 6:1, 22; 10:22; etc.

Why do the biblical prophets speak repeatedly of peoples and invasions as coming from "the north," when they clearly originate from the east? The answer lies in the geography of the region.

The biblical world is sometimes referred to as "the fertile crescent"—a curved swath of arable land that follows the Tigris and Euphrates Rivers to northern Syria and then down through the Promised Land.

Pushing into the middle of this boomerang-shaped region is the inhospitable Syrian/Arabian desert. With little water or human settlement, few but the hardy Bedouin would attempt a *direct* route west from Mesopotamia. Virtually all travelers circumvent the desert, traveling to the north along the fertile crescent. There they find supplies of food and water, as well as the major trading cities of the region. This is the route Abraham took, sojourning at Haran in northern Syria along the way. By the time of the New Testament this situation had changed, and we will see the significance of that development later.

The conquering armies of Assyria and Babylon also marched along this route, which meant that they entered Israel from the north. This is the meaning of the Hebrew prophets. From the perspective of the Holy Land, the invaders came down from the north, even if their place of origin was actually to the east. Ezekiel is giving the *direction* of the invasion, not the place of the invader's origin.

One further point needs addressing: The text in Ezekiel speaks of "the far north." Some take this as proof that Russia is in view. The meaning of the Hebrew words for *far* (*yarkah*—"extreme parts") and *north* (*zaphan*) when used together is difficult to ascertain. The phrase is found only in the above-quoted passages in Ezekiel and, curiously, in Isaiah 14:13 with reference to Lucifer aspiring to the highest heavens.[7]

A similar phrase also using *yarkah,* "the ends of the earth," occurs in Jeremiah 6:22 with reference to the Babylonian inva-

---

[7] Francis Brown, S.R. Driver, Charles A. Briggs, *A Hebrew and English Lexicon of the Old Testament* (Oxford University Press, 1907), p. 861.

sion.[8] And Babylon, as we have seen, was to the east in Mesopotamia. This indicates that such phrases do not necessarily mean extreme geographical distance beyond Mesopotamia. There is actually little support for the belief that the "far north" refers to a distant region beyond the known world of those days.

Perhaps the most telling argument against equating the far north with Russia comes from the immediate context of Ezekiel: "Persia, Cush and Put will be with them, all with shields and helmets, also Gomer with all its troops, and *Beth Togarmah from the far north* with all its troops—the many nations with you" (Ezekiel 38:6, italics mine).

Notice here the same phrase *from the far north* used in conjunction with Beth Togarmah. Thus, if we can locate where Beth Togarmah is, we will have a very good idea what "far north" refers to. Fortunately there is wide agreement as to Beth Togarmah's identification and place of origin. Colin J. Hemer writes:

> Traditionally the place was thought to be in Armenia, but it is now generally equated with the Hittite Tegarama (Assyr. Til-Garimmu), the region of classical Gauraena (Gurun) in Cappadocia . . . on the upper Euphrates.[9]

Thus Beth Togarmah is located in central Asia Minor. To the biblical writer "far north" referred to what is now modern Turkey. Oddly, the location of Beth Togarmah is undisputed even among those who claim that the "far north" refers to Russia, perhaps failing to recognize the inconsistency of insisting elsewhere that the "far north" refers to a different region.

In short, there is no compelling proof that the invasion of Gog and Magog refers to Russia and her allies. This widely held idea seemed to fit the geopolitics of the old cold war era. The dramatic events in Eastern Europe and the former Soviet Union itself, how-

---

[8] Brown, p. 438.

[9] *The International Standard Bible Encyclopedia*, vol. 4, s.v. "Togarmah," by Colin J. Hemer.

ever, have reduced the likelihood of such theories. We will shortly suggest an alternative that fits both the biblical evidence and historical realities in the Middle East. But now we must address a third question: What can we know about the identity of Gog and Magog?

Gog and Magog

The first occurrence of these names is found in the "table of nations" in Genesis 10. There we read that Magog was the son of Japheth, along with Gomer, Tubal and Meshech (Genesis 10:1–2). The historical identity of Gog in Ezekiel 38 and 39 is extremely uncertain.[10] Some Assyrian texts mention a certain king Gugu who is identified as Gyges, king of Lydia (c. 660 B.C.). Lydia was a kingdom in eastern Asia Minor. While most scholars lean toward this identification, it is by no means beyond doubt. Alexander's reasoned judgment is to be preferred to the unsupported claims sometimes found in popularly written books on biblical prophecy:

> None of these proposals addresses Gog's identity clearly. The most that can be said, perhaps, is that Gog is perhaps a personage, whether described by a title or by name. Further speculations are not justified on the basis of available evidence.[11]

The name Magog is unknown in Assyrian literature, which is our primary source of information for the eighth and seventh centuries B.C. By the time of the first century A.D., however, various ideas begin to appear. Josephus wrote: "Magog founded the Magogians, thus named after him, but who by the Greeks are

---

[10] The classic treatment of the subject remains W.F. Albright, "Gog and Magog," *Journal of Biblical Literature* 53 (1924), pp. 378–385; see also J.L. Meyers, "Gog and the Danger from the North in Ezekiel," *Palestine Exploration Fund Quarterly* 64 (1932), pp. 213–219.

[11] Alexander, p. 161.

called Scythians."[12] The Scythians were a tribe of horse-riding nomads, originally from the steppes of southern Russia, who inhabited the region between the Black Sea and Caspian Sea. This would include the southernmost republics of the former U.S.S.R., eastern Turkey and northwest Iran. Other contemporary sources put Magog in southeast Anatolia (Turkey). Later, in Jerome's day (c. A.D. 400), some assumed that Magog referred to the Goths. Still others suggested various Germanic tribes.

The Russian invasion theory relies principally upon the above-quoted remark by Josephus connecting Magog with the Scythians, although the historical reliability of Josephus has often been called into question.[13] In any event, his assertions regarding Magog have found no historical or archaeological confirmation. While this opinion of Josephus is sometimes quoted in popular books about biblical prophecy, it has not found wide support among scholars.

Interestingly, one wonders why proponents of the Russian theory quote Josephus as authoritative, instead of Jewish biblical commentaries from the same age. The answer is that the Jewish scholars of that period do not support the theory. The Targum (Aramaic translations and commentaries), in fact, identified Magog with Rome and Gog with the Roman emperor.[14] In the absence of conclusive evidence, the identity of Magog remains shrouded in mystery.

Rosh, Meshech and Tubal

The terms *Rosh, Meshech* and *Tubal* are often popularly identified as Russia, Moscow and Tobolsk. The origin of this theory can be traced to one common source: a mid-nineteenth-century edition of Gesenius' *Hebrew and English Lexicon*. J. Dwight Pen-

---

[12] Flavius Josephus, *Antiquities of the Jews* I, vi. 1.

[13] Josephus was more accurate in his *Jewish Wars* when he had access to the Roman imperial archives. See Magen Broshi, "The Credibility of Josephus," *Journal of Jewish Studies* 33 (1982), pp. 379–384.

[14] Joseph Blenkinsopp, *Ezekiel* (Louisville: John Knox Press, 1990), p. 181.

tecost, for instance, in his standard textbook on eschatology (the doctrine of future things), merely quotes other writers for authority on this point, including Louis Bauman—who in turn relies upon Gesenius:

> . . . Gesenius, whose Hebrew Lexicon has never been superceded, says that "Gog" is "undoubtedly the Russians." He declared that "Rosh" was a designation for the tribes then north of the Taurus mountains, . . . and in this name and tribe we have the first trace in history of the "Russ" or Russian nation. Gesenius also identified "Meshech" as Moscow, the capital of modern Russia in Europe. "Tubal" he identified as Tobolsk, the earliest province of Asiatic Russia to be colonized.[15]

All this may sound impressive but, in fact, the whole edifice rests upon an Achilles' heel. It is certainly not correct to state that the work of Gesenius, who died in 1842, "has never been superceded."[16] His own lexicon has had extensive revisions, the most important of which was completed by Francis Brown, S.R. Driver and Charles A. Briggs in 1907. This work, which remains a valuable scholarly tool, has itself been corrected several times. In addition, other valuable Hebrew dictionaries have appeared since Gesenius' time.[17]

Why is an outdated nineteenth-century lexicon quoted while the widely available revisions of that same lexicon are ignored? Be-

---

[15] Louis Bauman, *Russian Events in the Light of Biblical Prophecy* (Philadelphia: The Balkiston Co., 1942), pp. 23–25, cited by J. Dwight Pentecost, *Things to Come: A Study in Biblical Eschatology* (Grand Rapids: Zondervan Corporation, 1958), p. 328.

[16] Lindsey adapts the same phraseology as Pentecost, professor at the seminary where he studied, referring to Gesenius and his "unsurpassed Hebrew Lexicon" (p. 64).

[17] One standard work, in which the views of Gesenius are nowhere to be found, is G. Johannes Botterweck and Helmer Ringgren, eds., *Theological Dictionary of the Old Testament*, trans. John T. Willis (Grand Rapids: Eerdmans).

cause the later works have corrected some of Gesenius' unwarranted conclusions—including his oft-quoted but misinformed remarks about Rosh, Meshech and Tubal.

D.J. Wiseman, the eminent assyriologist of the University of London, rejected this notion regarding Rosh: "Gesenius suggested Russia, but this name is not attested in the area, and a very distant people named this early is unlikely in the context."[18] John W. Wevers reflects the scholarly consensus when he speaks of "the bizarre identification by the misinformed with Russia."[19]

Popularly written books about prophecy continue to propagate this view, however, sometimes appealing to the phonetic similarity of the names. This method of determining origin is, of course, not linguistically sound.

We do have historical documentation, on the other hand, that identifies Rosh with the Assyrian "Rashu" on the northwest border of Elam, that is, in Media. Media was located in the area of what is now northern Iran and Iraq and the republic of Azerbaijan.

This ancient Rosh did include part of some of the southern republics of the former Soviet Union, but the southern republics were not part of the Russian empire until the rule of Alexander I in the first part of the nineteenth century.[20] And with the uncertain future of the current Commonwealth of Independent States, they may one day separate themselves completely from the northern Slavic republics. This is yet another reason why there is no basis for the claim that Rosh refers to Russia, and we conclude with Joseph Blenkinsopp:

> So it is still necessary to repeat that *ro'sh meshech* has nothing
> to do, etymologically or otherwise, with Russia and Moscow

---

[18] *New Bible Dictionary*, 1962 ed., s.v. "Rosh," by D.J. Wiseman.

[19] John W. Wevers, *Ezekiel* (London: Thomas Nelson & Sons, Ltd., 1969), p. 287.

[20] "Russia had reached the Terek River and Kabarda, just north of the Caucasus, in the sixteenth century, but the subjugation of the areas between the Black and Caspian seas was not completed until 1878." Allen F. Chew, *An Atlas of Russian History* (New Haven: Yale University Press, 1967), p. 72.

and that therefore some other means will have to be found to identify the evil empire described in these chapters.[21]

We also have solid historical data as to the identity of Meshech and Tubal. It must first be noted that any connection of Tubal with the Russian city of Tobolsk is completely specious. A latecomer on the stage of history, Tobolsk was only founded in 1587 when Siberia was being colonized by the expanding Russian empire.

On much firmer footing is the view expressed by T.C. Mitchell that Meshech and Tubal are to be associated "with the people referred to as Tabal and Musku in the Assyrian inscriptions and Tibarenoi and Moschoi in Herodotus, in both of which sources these names are closely associated."[22]

Where did they come from? The Assyrian cuneiform texts clearly locate Musku and Tabal in central and eastern Anatolia.[23] This corresponds to the region southeast of the Black Sea. On the modern map, it includes the region where Turkey, Iran and the southernmost republics of the former Soviet Union converge.

There is a modern counterpart to the ancient lands of Rosh and company, which, as we will see in a moment, accounts for the historical data and also fits the description of the "evil empire" described by Ezekiel. First, let's see what can be said about the other four participants mentioned with Beth Togarmah in Ezekiel 38:5–6 (NASB).

The Allies of Gog

There is little doubt as to the identity of the first three confederates. *Persia* is clear enough, being the ancient name of modern Iran, although some scholars disagree.[24] *Ethiopia,* the kingdom of

---

[21] Blenkinsopp, p. 181.

[22] *New Bible Dictionary,* "Meshech," by T.C. Mitchell.

[23] See Yamauchi, "Meshech, Tubal, and Company," pp. 243–245, for a full discussion.

[24] See Carley, *Ezekiel,* p. 255. Carley holds that *Pharas* was, along with *Put,* a North African tribe.

the Nubians, retains her biblical name. *Put,* when translated into Egyptian, means Libya, and is so translated in the Septuagint.[25] It is also possible that the original Ethiopians and Libyans have spread beyond the modern borders of the countries by the same names.

There has been considerable speculation about the identity of *Gomer.* Lindsey, among others, has popularized the view that it refers to East Germany: "The conclusion is that Gomer and its hordes are part of the vast area of modern Eastern Europe which is totally behind the Iron Curtain. This includes East Germany and the Slovak countries."[26]

Back in the 1970s, during the cold war era, it was common for prophecy books to identify Gog and its allies with countries that were either Communist or about to fall under Communist control. East Germany was then part of the now-defunct Warsaw Pact, and seemed to fit into the picture of a massive Russian-led invasion. Now, of course, East Germany no longer exists as a separate country.

Once again Lindsey relied upon Gesenius, who stood alone among linguists with his novel identifications. One may search in vain among critical and exegetical commentaries to find Gomer identified as Germany. Walther Eichrodt expresses the scholarly consensus:

> [The people of Gomer are] referred to by the Assyrians as Gimirrai, and by the Greeks as Cimmerians. They emerge in the eighth century as conquerors of Urartu (Armenia) in Asia Minor and then as invaders of the territory of the Phrygians and Lydians.[27]

The Cimmerians occupied what is now eastern Turkey on the southern shores of the Black Sea. Beth Togarmah, we have already

---

[25] See *The International Standard Bible Encyclopedia,* vol. 3, s.v. "Put," by William Sanford LaSor.

[26] Lindsey, p. 70.

[27] Walther Eichrodt, *Ezekiel, A Commentary* (Philadelphia: The Westminster Press, 1970), p. 518.

seen, occupied central Asia Minor, located in the same general region as Meshech, Tubal and Gomer.

These are the participants of the great future invasion of Israel and they come from two geographical areas. The first is the conjunction of eastern Turkey, northwest Iran and the southern central Asian republics, and the second is the general region of Libya and Ethiopia in Africa.

How Many "Final" Destructions?

The true identity of Gog, Magog and company is not the only problem with the Russian invasion theory. The most widely held timeline in this theory places the battle just before the midpoint of the Tribulation.

On the basis of Ezekiel 38 and 39, Walvoord concludes: "Russia will attempt a final bid for power for the Middle East, and her armies will be supernaturally destroyed."[28]

Louis Goldberg concurs: "This northern bloc of nations will be defeated *finally and completely* on the soil of the land of Israel."[29]

We might conclude from this that the military power of Russia comes to an end. Surprisingly, according to this theory, that is not the case. This is because Russia is represented at another conflict just three years later at the end of the Tribulation.

Thus, after speaking of "Russia's mysterious annihilation" in the middle of the Tribulation, she "apparently will have been able to recoup her losses enough to put another army in the field."[30]

It seems unlikely, to say the least, that after a devastating, supernatural destruction at the hand of God that Russia could turn around in three years and mount another massive attack against Israel.

---

[28] Walvoord, p. 28.

[29] Louis Goldberg, *Turbulence Over the Middle East* (Neptune, New Jersey: Loizeaux Brothers, 1982), p. 174, italics mine.

[30] Walvoord, pp. 159, 179.

Alexander describes it this way:

> The burning of weapons for seven years while being perse-
> cuted by the beast, and the burying of the bones of Gog's
> hordes in order to cleanse the land, while the abomination of
> desolation is transpiring and judgment is at its apex, is incon-
> ceivable.[31]

Will Gog (supposedly Russia) live to fight another day soon
after this? The Bible text, speaking of Gog, gives no hint of this
possibility: "On the mountains of Israel you will fall, you and all
your troops and the nations with you. I will give you as food to all
kinds of carrion birds and to the wild animals" (Ezekiel 39:4).

Two Hundred Million Invaders from China?

There is another biblical prophecy about the end-time battle that
complicates the prophecy charts. As mentioned already in chapter
10, the drying up of the Euphrates River opens the way for "the
kings of the East" (Revelation 16:12). Is this yet another battle?
Lindsey typifies a common identification of this military force:

> We believe that China is the beginning of the formation of this
> great power called "the kings of the east" by the apostle
> John. . . . In fact, a recent television documentary on Red
> China . . . quoted the boast of the Chinese themselves that
> they could field a "people's army" of 200 million militiamen.
> In their own boast they named the same number as the Bib-
> lical prediction. Coincidence?[32]

This identification of the kings of the East with China comes
from the connection of two separate passages in the book of Rev-

---

[31] Alexander, p. 163.
[32] Lindsey, p. 86. Walvoord, p. 179, concurs with this identification.

elation. In chapter 16 verse 12 there is no mention of two hundred million men in the armies of the kings of the East. Writers on biblical prophecy who believe in the connection take a verse from chapter 9 to prove their point:

> And the four angels who had been kept ready for this very hour and day and month and year were released to kill a third of mankind. The number of the mounted troops was two hundred million. I heard their number.
>
> Revelation 9:15–16

China with her huge population, they argue, is the only country that can fit this bill.

The biblical text, however, does not support this popularly taught idea. To begin with, there is no direct relation between the two passages: Revelation 9:15–16 does not mention any kings. It does not indicate that the two hundred million horses and riders are soldiers. Rather, they appear to be fearsome demonic beings spewing "fire, smoke and sulfur" out of their mouths (see verses 17–18).

On the practical side, has anyone ever stopped to calculate what such an invasion would entail? The necessary logistics make a literal Chinese invasion quite unbelievable. Just for fun let's take a moment to make a few calculations.

By comparison, in the greatest and most expedient airlift of military history the United States moved approximately one-half million troops and their equipment to the Middle East in a six-month period during 1990–1991.

At that rate it would take *two hundred years* to move a two-hundred-million-man army from China to the Middle East. Furthermore, this theory has the kings of the East crossing the Euphrates riverbed, meaning, they are traveling not by air or sea, but overland. Since overland transport is considerably slower, we would need to allow even more time for this army to arrive in Israel.

The most direct overland route from China follows the ancient trade route known as the "Silk Road," which skirts India and the almost impassable Himalayas. But that would mean the armies of China would be traveling through the central Asian republics of the former U.S.S.R.—hostile territory if China is supposedly at war with the rest of the world at this point.[33] It is not likely that they will be allowed safe passage through all the countries along their route.

Another consideration in moving such a huge army is the size of the convoy. To describe it as gigantic is an understatement. One might conservatively estimate that about ten million vehicles, including tank carriers and other military vehicles, trucks carrying troops, fuel, food supplies, weapons and ammunition, etc., would be required to move an army this size.[34]

If each vehicle occupies an average of forty yards of road space, including the space between vehicles, the convoy would stretch for 227,272 miles, or *almost ten times around the circumference of the earth!*

Some might object, saying that not *everybody* would have to be moved together at one time. But in truth they would or else run up against the problem of time. In fact, the transport would need to start *decades before* the beginning of the Tribulation just to get everyone there on time! And there would be the added problem of fitting them all into the tiny country of Israel once they got there.

The whole idea is patently unrealistic, even though the vast majority of popularly written books about biblical prophecy assume without question its plausibility. How did we get off on the wrong track? By failing to observe a basic principle of biblical

---

[33] In *There's a New World Coming* Lindsey states: "The sixth stage is the mobilization of all the rest of the world's armies to fight under the command of the Antichrist against the 'kings of the East' (Rev. 16:12)" (New York: Bantam Books, 1975), p. 213. Walvoord puts it the other way around, with the armies of the world attacking the Antichrist (pp. 170–181).

[34] A common military truck carries about forty soldiers with their personal effects. Thus, it would take five million trucks just to move the troops.

interpretation. Simply put: Don't build a teaching around one verse.

Two Hundred Million?

As we have seen, the Chinese invasion theory comes from the two hundred million horses and riders mentioned in Revelation 9:16. What is this verse actually talking about? One possibility, already mentioned, is that it refers to a demonic force that rains plagues upon the earth.

Others might insist that it refers to a human army. This is also a possibility, but even if it does refer to humans it is not describing two hundred million troops. While the Greek word used in the passage means literally "twice 10,000 times 10,000" or "two myriads of myriads," it is meant to signify a number too large to calculate. A similar expression is found in Genesis, where the descendants of Jacob would be "like the sand of the sea, which cannot be counted" (Genesis 32:12).

The ancient world had no use for the mathematical number of two hundred million. The expression simply conveys the picture of an awesome gathering "more than the eye can see." Robert H. Mounce observes:

> Attempts to reduce this expression to arithmetic miss the point. A "double myriad of myriads" is an indefinite number of incalculable immensity. Reference to a *Time* article which reports the People's Republic of China as having a militia of 200,000,000 is interesting but of no special help.[35]

Another look at the map of the Middle East will yield a more plausible explanation for the identity of the kings of the East. The Euphrates River neatly divides the land of Israel from the kings of

---

[35] Robert H. Mounce, *The Book of Revelation* (Grand Rapids: Eerdmans Publishing Company, 1977), p. 201. See also William F. Arndt and F. Wilbur Gingrich, *A Greek-English Lexicon of the New Testament and Other Early Christian Literature*, rev. 2nd ed. (Chicago: The University of Chicago Press, 1979), p.199.

the North already discussed—the areas of Turkey, Iran and the southern republics of the former Soviet Union.

So why are they referred to as coming from the north in Ezekiel and then from the east in Revelation 16:12? For the answer we must look again at the historical geography of the region. In the time of Ezekiel all major travel routes followed the fertile crescent in a big hook around the Syrian desert. By the time of the New Testament, however, other routes had been opened up from the East.

After the death of Alexander the Great, the Seleucid kingdom stretched eastward to India. In the third century B.C. a major trading route was forged directly through the desert to gain access to the eastern part of the kingdom. Two major cities developed along this route by the Seleucids, and the Romans after them, were Palmyra in central Syria and Dura Europos on the northern reaches of the Euphrates. They were major links of the new trading route connecting the Mediterranean with Parthia and points east.

At the end of the first century, when the book of Revelation was written, this eastern route was a major international highway of the day. It had become commonplace to think of passage directly from the east, and therefore John speaks of the "kings of the East." Likewise, the "Magi from the east who came to worship Jesus (Matthew 2:1) are believed to have journeyed from Babylon. But another look at the map of the Middle East will show that these "eastern" lands across the Euphrates are actually the *very same* geographical region as the Old Testament lands of the "north" we have already discussed.

Since the precise direction of the lands of Gog and Magog is neither directly north nor east but rather almost exactly *northeast*, the directions given in Ezekiel and Revelation can be easily correlated. It is also reasonable to assume that all available routes from that general direction would be used by the invading armies.

There we have it. The kings of the East in Revelation are in all likelihood from the same general region as Gog, Magog and company in Ezekiel 38 and 39. There is no reason to consider two separate invasions here, and our confusing prophecy outlines can be simplified accordingly.

179

So Who Are They?

Now that the Russians and the Chinese are probably out of the picture, how then do we explain the invasion of Gog and its allies? There is one possible scenario that fits the evidence, both past and present. One common thread runs through each one of the places we have examined—from North Africa to Turkey, Iran and the southern republics of the former Soviet Union. Each one—even today—has a compelling reason for participating in an invasion of Israel. Perhaps you have guessed it already: Every one of these lands is part of the *dar al-Islam*—the realm of Islam.

We can already see the genesis of this Muslim power bloc in today's world. Let us examine the rationale found in the Koran for the destruction of Israel, and how frighteningly close we may be to that final attempt.

12
Unbottling the Islamic Genie

"Anyone who fights America's aggression has engaged in a holy war in the cause of Allah, and anyone who is killed on that path is a martyr."[1]

Iranian religious leader
Ayatullah Ali Khamenei

THE SCENE WAS THE BLEAK FRONTIER BETWEEN IRAN and Iraq in the spring of 1982. This war-ravaged battlefield had already changed hands several times during the war between these two countries. Now a major Iranian offensive was about to be launched across the seven-hundred-mile border.

Newsmen brought to witness the spectacle waited nervously, aware that they were within range of the Iraqi guns. But the Iraqis were waiting also for the attack to begin. The cause for the delay was soon apparent: From behind the low hills to the rear, a long line of old buses filled with Iranian soldiers was lumbering toward the staging area. No—hardly soldiers: These were children between the ages of twelve and seventeen. Eyes glazed with religious fervor, they chanted in unison as they disembarked, alternately praising Khomeini and damning their Iraqi enemies.

They wore ordinary clothes, but each jacket was stenciled with the Ayatollah's permission to enter heaven, confirmed by a chain with a metal "key to paradise" around each neck. Tied around their heads were black cloth headbands inked with religious slogans. They carried no weapons or equipment of any kind.

---

[1] Bruce Nelan, "Call to Arms," *Time* (September 24, 1990), p. 33.

The only preparation they had received was an incessant barrage of propaganda extolling the glories of martyrdom for Allah's sake. Bidding farewell to their families, they had embarked upon what was considered the most noble of all missions. This, for them, would be a short walk to eternity.

As a precaution against faint hearts, they were roped together in groups by uniformed officers from the Iranian army and Revolutionary Guards. No one complained. For Allah's sake they were more than willing to submit to earthly chains that would soon dissolve as they approached the abode of bliss. Visions of the brown-eyed consorts of paradise, of whom it is said no man tires, were already dancing before their eyes.

Soon the order was given and the long lines of rag-tag youths moved rapidly forward to a marked-off area. The air was filled with shrill voices chanting verses from the Koran as they ran toward the Iraqi lines. When one wave of boys moved about fifty yards, the officers sent another after them. Behind them other men in uniform watched with indifference, cradling their rifles and smoking cigarettes. To an Austrian journalist, the only foreigner present, the grotesque scene resembled "children racing down a beach to enter the water for a swim."[2] But the real purpose of the rush would soon become apparent.

Suddenly a boom reverberated across the battlefield, followed by others, as the human chains were shorn by powerful land mines. The martyrs were being used to detonate the land mines with their feet, thus helping to preserve the Iranian tank force. Many were blown to pieces as the shocked Austrian watched incredulously. The scene became confused as boys found themselves tied to mangled bodies. Still, incredibly, those who were unmaimed continued to run forward to almost certain death.

The mine-clearing operation lasted perhaps ten minutes. The ground was littered with the silent dead and stirring wounded. The confident shouting had been replaced by pitiful cries of agony. Those few who managed, miraculously, to make it through the

---

[2] John Laffin, *Holy War: Islam Fights* (London: Grafton Books, 1988), p. 63.

killing zone cowered together in a state of shock. No one had made provision for those who, to their shame, had failed to gain martyrdom.

The Iranian soldiers began to stir. In the distance the low, guttural roar of the tanks, followed by armored personnel carriers filled with troops, could be heard moving up to the front lines. Soon they were riding over the just-cleared minefields, mowing down dead and wounded alike, the engines drowning out any final screams on their way to engage the waiting Iraqis.

Back home, the families of the young boys would be congratulated at the successful entrance into paradise of their loved ones. They would receive official "martyrs' certificates" from the Iranian government. With rare exception, parents did not complain. Especially in the beginning, many parents willingly surrendered their sons for the holy war.

Iranian newspapers were filled with photographs and long lists of the names of the dead children. They reported the gruesome details of the slaughters—not with revulsion but with pride. Here were the martyrs of the revolution! The accounts turned the cruel deaths of the youths into a sacred event ordered by Allah. In one account, the victims were likened to "blossoms" who turned the minefield into "a rose garden." One newspaper commended the boys for ingeniously preserving their soon-to-be mutilated bodies:

> Some of the children had found a way of keeping their bodies more or less intact at the time of their heroic end. They covered themselves with blankets before walking over the mines. Thus the bits and pieces that were left could be gathered together more easily for dispatch to their proud parents back home. They did this partly to facilitate the task of our orientation officials, who needed bodies to show to other young ones, to incite them to take the same path to Paradise. . . . [3]

---

[3] *Ettelaat* daily (Tehran), January 30, 1982, cited by Amir Taheri, *Holy Terror* (London: Sphere Books, 1987), pp. 239–240.

Untold thousands of young men and boys met a similar fate during the eight-year Iran-Iraq war. What is the cause of such madness? How does a nation become engulfed with unimaginable savagery so as to use their children as cannon fodder—and to exult in it? Iran is not alone: Many in the West are perplexed at the seemingly irrational violence that seems to have gripped the Middle East. To understand this veritable explosion of fanaticism we must leave the comforts of our Judeo-Christian Western heritage and enter a wholly different realm: the dark, macabre world of Islam.

Kingdom of Darkness

Christianity is founded upon love, mercy and tolerance. One need only descend into the depths of darkness to appreciate the light—even if that light becomes obscured by clouds. The religion founded by Jesus, despite the many failures of His followers, is worlds apart from that of Muhammad.

Westerners often assume mistakenly that all religions teach the same basic values. That is to say, Muslims are taught to obey the same moral precepts that we take for granted. Unfortunately, this is not always the case. Not all Muslims lack a proper moral foundation: Our experience living in a predominantly Muslim region has taught us to appreciate the fact that individuals of whatever descent or religion often have a high personal standard of morality.

Little incidents stick in one's mind as a reminder of the admirable qualities often displayed by the Arab people. Being absent-minded, I have on occasion walked out of a shop before receiving the change due me. Once in the Nablus *suk*, the charming old covered market street, I left a shop oblivious to the fact that I had overpaid the proprietor. Here was a perfect chance for the man to make a little extra profit. We were obviously foreigners who in all probability would never return. And even if we did, what was the chance that we would remember this man's shop among so many others in the maze of the suk? Yet a few minutes later a boy caught up to me with my change.

On another occasion, our Volkswagen bug broke down at what I thought was just about the worst possible time and place. I was on my way home at dusk next to a refugee camp when the engine suddenly went dead. Our yellow (Israeli) license plates made the car an automatic target. I was anxious, not wanting to abandon the car for fear it would be burned, but unable to find the problem.

Often we are placed—all of us—in situations beyond our control to teach us something. And I had a lesson to learn. I feared the Muslim people in the refugee camps, those hotbeds of discontent and radicalism, but that did not make it right to prejudge every individual.

So what happened? A group of young men gathered around my car—not to attack it, but to help. And when all their efforts failed, they pushed my car all the way home, inch by inch up an incline. Then they ran off cheerfully before I could thank them properly. I sometimes wonder what the chances are in America that people would offer to push a stranger's car up a hill.

This leaves us with a tremendous paradox between barbaric and virtuous behavior. The Muslim people can indeed exhibit moral traits that are lacking in the West. But our experience has convinced us that they do so to a large extent *despite* the oppressive influence of Islam upon Arab culture. The fact that individuals succeed in this is a testimony to the God-given sense of morality triumphing in the face of difficult odds.

Popularly written texts on Islam often gloss over unsavory aspects of the religion and attempt to paint a more enlightened portrait. Well-meaning apologists excuse the penchant for violence and war in the Koran, claiming that Islam has "risen above" such a primitive reading of the text. Indeed, Islam in Western countries appears to be much more reasonable and tolerant than in its Eastern counterparts.

The temperate Islam of the West, however, can be attributed to the moderating influence of democratic values, which are derived from the Christian heritage. The Middle East, having been steeped in Islam for centuries, knows little of such values and would consider them corrupting influences. The oppressive nature of the religion of Islam is perhaps best illustrated by how it treats its women.

The Veil of Islam

In mid-November 1990 an incident of feminine rebellion took place in Saudi Arabia, shocking even reformist segments of the Muslim society. What was this revolutionary act—a real-life Middle East version of the film "Nine-to-Five"? Not quite.

In an unheard of act of defiance, a group of Saudi women who had obtained drivers' licenses while living abroad did the unthinkable. They dismissed their chauffeurs and *drove themselves* through downtown Riyadh. They were soon cornered by police, who raced to the scene to arrest the women.

The policemen, however, soon had to protect the women from infuriated *mutawain*—the zealous Islamic guardians who patrol the streets. The particularly virulent form of Islam found in Saudi Arabia, called the *Wahhabiyah,* is a rigidly puritanical form of Sunni Islam. Its followers include many Afghans and the Saudi ruling family. Wahhabi women may travel only in the company of a husband or male blood relative.

The resulting furor led to the suspension of several of the women from their teaching positions (instructing women) at King Saud University. Their names, phone numbers and addresses were distributed publicly, followed by telephone threats against them. The intimidation of the women was led by Sheik Abdul Aziz ibn Baz, who achieved a certain notoriety in the 1960s by insisting that the sun revolved around the earth.

Such is the inbred conservatism of Saudi society that the women found no solace even on the university campus, where they were met with angry protests against them: "Not one of my students understood what I was trying to accomplish," said a stunned victim.[4] What would have been a harmless protest to the Western way of thinking became a nightmare for the women, who face perpetual isolation in their society.

The place of women in Saudi society is controlled rigidly in all respects: They are not permitted to work alongside men, and are confined largely to jobs in fields such as teaching and nursing. They dare not trespass the bounds set by their religion. Islamic laws are adhered to rigorously, and in city squares around Saudi Arabia the hands of thieves are chopped off, adulterers are stoned to death, murderers and rapists are beheaded, and lesser offenders are flogged.

The 1970s brought some modest reforms: Women appeared on TV for the first time and had more educational opportunities. That all changed, however, when 250 armed Shi'ite extremists stormed the Grand Mosque and occupied it for two weeks at a cost of hundreds of lives. Almost overnight the Saudi regime became more devout. The religious police began patrolling the streets. Offenders, such as "immodest" women not wearing the head-to-foot Muslim *hejab*, were beaten with sticks.

Elsewhere in the Muslim world, women challenge Islamic society at their peril. In the refugee centers of Peshawar, Pakistan, more than a dozen Afghan women have disappeared. Their crime was offending extremist Islamic groups by working in women's centers and with foreign humanitarian aid organizations.

In Islamic society women are under the control of male family members. Grown unmarried women answer to their brothers. In the Algerian town of Mascara a Muslim nurse was doused with alcohol and set on fire by her brother. He was infuriated because his sister was treating male patients. While such acts of violence are not yet the norm everywhere, women are coming under pressure wherever radical Islam is growing in strength.

In 1984 Algeria adapted a "Family Code," which gives a husband the right to divorce his wife and eject her from his home for

---

[4] William Dowell, "Life in the Slow Lane," *Time* (November 26, 1990), p. 46.

almost any reason. The legislators even debated the length of the stick that could be used by husbands to beat their wives, as commanded by the Koran:

> Men have authority over women because Allah has made the one superior to the other, and because they spend their wealth to support them. . . . As for those from whom you fear disobedience, admonish them and send them to beds apart and beat them (*Women*, 4.34).

The Koran decrees that a man can have up to four wives at a time. The Muslim wife lives in a state of perpetual insecurity, as Anis A. Shorrosh explains:

> A Muslim husband may cast his wife adrift without giving a single reason or even notice. The husband possesses absolute, immediate, and unquestioned power of divorce. No privilege of a corresponding nature is reserved for the wife.[5]

The Koran also states that the value of a woman's testimony in court is worth only half that of a man's. The basis for the superiority of men is because, according to the Koran, they have "more strength." This reinforces the claim that Islam is a religion based on the exercise of power. Those who are able to rule from a position of strength do so on all levels of society. Throughout the Middle East, rule by brute force is condoned by the religion of Islam.

The widow of Major Abboud al-Zammor, one of the assassins of Egyptian President Anwar Sadat, describes the transformation of her husband, who was "originally a man like any other, one who smoked and even allowed me to attend university unveiled." Then he became involved in Islamic radicalism:

---

[5] Anis A. Shorrish, *Islam Revealed: A Christian Arab's View of Islam* (Nashville: Thomas Nelson, 1988), p. 167.

> First he told me and his mother that we ought not to eat cucumbers, as this could awaken in us instincts that are hard to control. Then he forbade us to watch television. He also ordered us not to serve stuffed vine leaves any more as this would—according to his organization—heat our blood and lead to deviations.[6]

Other women who refused to conform had acid thrown in their faces, an all-too-common technique used by fanatics in Muslim countries for punishing "unruly" women. Horror stories like these are becoming more commonplace.

In times when Arab countries have fallen under Western influence the status of women has risen considerably. This is not due to a genuine development in Islamic theology, since the Koran is considered to be unchangeable. Rather, the *ulema* (Muslem religious scholars) merely follow the prevailing winds of the times. In a symposium organized by Colonel Muammar Gaddafi, Egyptian writer Ahmed Bahaeddine mocked the capricious guidance of these religious authorities:

> Throughout history we meet Moslem theologians and religious scholars twice, and consistently. We meet them once prior to change, when they rule that it is forbidden, and once after the change has taken place, when they protest that Allah had already envisioned such change long ago and permitted it. . . .[7]

The issue of the education of women is an example of this vacillation. Since the time of Muhammad there was little reason for women to go to school. Their place in the Muslim world was clear: They were the "fertile gardens" for their husbands and re-

---

[6] *Al-Akhbar* (Cairo), January 16, 1985, cited by Taheri, p. 215.

[7] Ahmed Bahaeddine, "Islam Can Justify Anything," *Jerusalem Post* (November 2, 1990), p. 4.

sponsible for rearing the children and taking care of the household. One did not need an academic education for this very restricted role in society. But then came the British and French colonialists, who established schools and insisted that women also be given the opportunity for an education. Bahaeddine describes the reaction of the Muslim scholars:

> For 100 years or so the ulema kept issuing edicts to the effect that education for women was strictly forbidden. However, now that all the ladies have attended school . . . [the religious leaders] all proclaim that Mrs. Aisha Abdul Rahman (Egyptian Moslem scholar) is one of the authorities on the Hadith, Islam's oral law. Well, why had such verdicts not been pronounced long ago?[8]

The answer to Bahaeddine's rhetorical question is, once again, that Islam is a religion based upon power, not justice. The religious authorities will always bend to whoever wields the most power. Thus, when the British ruled Egypt after World War I, the ulema were forced to abandon their long-standing opposition to female education.

To understand the true essence of Islam, one need only listen to the statements of its spokesmen. Ayatollah Ruhollah Khomeini, arguably the most important Shi'ite leader of the twentieth century, poured contempt upon those who explained away the violent aspects of Islam:

> Those who know nothing about Islam pretend that Islam counsels against war. Those [who say this] are witless. Islam says: Kill all the unbelievers just as they would kill you all! . . . Islam says: Kill them [the non-Muslims], put them to the sword and scatter [their armies]. . . . Whatever good there is exists thanks to the sword [of Islam] and in the shadow of the sword! People cannot be made obedient except with the

---

[8] Bahaeddine, p. 4.

sword! The sword is the key to Paradise, which can be opened only for Holy Warriors! There are hundreds of other [Koranic] psalms and Hadiths [sayings of the prophet] urging Muslims to value war and to fight. Does all that mean that Islam is a religion that prevents men from waging war? I spit upon those foolish souls who make such a claim.[9]

When I read such vituperative statements I sit back for a moment and try to imagine the founder of Christianity talking in a manner like this. It is, of course, unthinkable. This brings the contrast between Islam and Christianity into sharp focus once again. The Ayatollah's words seethe with arrogant contempt for everything non-Muslim. Compare this blackness with the pure light of Jesus:

> "Here is my servant whom I have chosen,
>   the one I love, in whom I delight;
> I will put my Spirit on him,
>   and he will proclaim justice to the nations.
> He will not quarrel or cry out;
>   no one will hear his voice in the streets.
> A bruised reed he will not break,
>   and a smoldering wick he will not snuff out,
> till he leads justice to victory."
>   Matthew 12:18–20

It is no coincidence that Western countries, even those that may be considered "post-Christian," generally embody the values that arise out of Christianity. There is a foundation, however obscured, for positive values such as love, justice and toleration. The phrase "a bruised reed he will not break" speaks of the gentleness of Jesus in not forcing Himself upon anyone. Biblical religion grants to every person the freedom of choice. And God will respect that gift

---

[9] Ayatollah Ruhollah Khomeini, *Kashf al-Asrar* (Key to the Secrets) (Qom, 1986); cited in Taheri, *Holy Terror,* pp. 226–227.

of choice—even if it is utterly wrong and leading to damnation. Yet "a smoldering wick he will not snuff out"—as long as there is life, there is hope.

The Muslim world does not have the benefit of these life-affirming values. While it is true that one may find statements in the Koran that present a positive view of God, they are twisted around to justify acts of violence and hatred. John Laffin gives as an example the Koranic invocation that accompanies almost everything that is written or said in Islam:

> It means "In the name of Allah, the merciful, the compassionate." Ayatollah Khomeini uses this language when calling for death to his enemies. Islamic Jihad terror squads and spokesmen use it to preface each announcement they might make about some act of holy war.[10]

Thus, people are killed ruthlessly in the name of "Allah, the merciful and compassionate." To the radical Muslim there is no contradiction in this. Those who defy the religion of Muhammad have no right to expect mercy. They are obstructing the divine order and must be resisted with every ounce of the believer's energy. This perennial struggle is the duty of every Muslim.

Jihad!

The concept of Jihad, the constant state of war until the world falls under the rule of Islam, is not a perversion of the Koran by extremist political sects within Islam. Rather, it occupies a central place in the religion. Jihad finds its origin in Muhammad himself, who was no stranger to warfare and bloodshed. Muhammad realized that unless the strong family and tribal allegiances of Arabian culture were broken, his new religion would not spread beyond any single tribe. His first task was to teach his early fol-

---

[10] Laffin, p. 97.

lowers to disregard their qualms about killing even family members who rejected the new "messenger of God":

> To overcome the age-old tradition of never spilling common blood was a considerable psychological victory. The new religion had no tribal boundaries. The son of Abd Allah Ubayy asked Muhammad's permission to kill his father for his "treachery" against Muhammad. It was necessary for him to be his father's executioner; had anybody else killed him the son would have to seek blood vengeance.[11]

Muhammad insisted that his followers break all family ties. The only "brothers" a believer was allowed were his fellow Muslims. Many were destitute because they had left everything to follow the new prophet. Muhammad and his men, therefore, relied upon a time-honored tradition in Arabia to support themselves: plundering caravans in the desert. The fighting skills that his followers honed in those early days were later put to use against those who resisted his message. According to Islamic history, Muhammad participated in no fewer than 81 military campaigns in Arabia between A.D. 622–632. It is no wonder, then, that the Koran is riddled with references commanding the faithful to fight for Allah:

> When the sacred months are over slay the idolaters wherever you find them. Arrest them, besiege them, and lie in ambush everywhere for them. . . . Prophet, make war on the unbelievers and the hypocrites and deal rigorously with them. Hell shall be their home: an evil fate (*Repentance* 9.5, 73).

According to the Koran, Christians are included among the idolaters because they worship Jesus as God. They are also called unbelievers because they reject Muhammad as the final revelation

---

[11] Laffin, p. 97.

of God. From the time of Muhammad the "brothers" have considered it a sacred duty to impose the religion of their prophet upon the entire world.

After Muhammad's death in A.D. 632, Abu Bakr, the first *caliph* (successor to Muhammad), galvanized the followers of Muhammad into an formidable fighting force. Brandishing the sword, nearly twenty thousand faithful set out across the desert in search of conquest. In just a few years they were already in Transjordan gazing on the bastion of Christianity in the Middle East, the land of Palestine.

Weakened by internal divisions and exhausted by a costly struggle with Persia, the Byzantine empire in the Holy Land could offer little resistance to the new threat from the eastern desert. Their mercenary army proved to be no match for the ferociously single-minded Muslim warriors. In 638 Jerusalem surrendered to the Caliph without a struggle.

Forty thousand more soldiers of Islam then marched to North Africa, which was soon subdued by the sword. Europe was next. Crossing Gibraltar, they swept across all of Spain. It seemed nothing could stop the Muslim hordes. But in one of the decisive battles of history, the armies of Islam finally met their match. In 732 the Christian army of Charles Martel stopped and turned back the armies of Islam in the Battle of Tours.

It took another eight centuries before Spain was finally released from the grip of Islam by the capture of Granada in 1492. Other Muslim armies advanced across Eastern Europe, and on several occasions nearly succeeded in capturing Vienna. In the succeeding centuries, as we shall see, the Muslims still have not conceded their former European territory.

The Ayatollah's Map

Muslims believe that Islam is the final and superior revelation of God, and has been destined to rule over mankind. This means that, if at all possible, Muslems should never accept the position of being ruled over by non-Muslems. Thus, any land that once was Muslim *can never be relinquished,* even if it falls under the power of non-Muslims.

In 1985 Iran's Ayatollah Khomeini commissioned a map dividing the world into spheres of Muslim and Christian influence. Spain and parts of Eastern Europe were included in the Muslim sphere of influence even though they have not been controlled by Islam for hundreds of years. Why? To the Muslim they were once under the control of Islam and must forever be considered Muslim. The whole Levant, including the land of Israel, was also included within the Muslim sphere of influence. Israel is viewed by Muslims as a reversal of history, producing the intolerable situation of Jews ruling over Muslims. It is, therefore, the duty of Muslims everywhere to return the Holy Land to Islamic control.

In the meantime the Islamic presence must be made as conspicuous as possible. When a mosque is constructed in an Arab community, Muslims go to great lengths to ensure that the minaret is higher than any church tower in the vicinity. Such symbolism is important for Muslims, confirming their belief in the superiority of the religion of Muhammad. The call to prayer is broadcast from the minaret into the community—disturbing the peace of non-Muslims within hearing range. I discovered this for myself when living across the street from a mosque in Bethlehem. The loudspeakers blasted me out of bed many a morning in the pre-dawn darkness, when the first call to prayer is given.

In January 1992 the issue finally came to a head in Jerusalem when the *muezzin* (who calls Muslims to prayer) of the Sheik Jarrah mosque was fined for disturbing the peace of Jews in the neighborhood.[12] The muezzin's call to prayer was measured at nearly sixty decibels, considerably over the forty-decibel limit permitted by the Jerusalem municipality. Jewish residents complained that the volume was cranked up even higher on the Sab-

---

[12] Clyde Haberman, "Jerusalem Judge Orders Mosque to Lower Voice," *The New York Times* (January 25, 1992), p. 5.

bath and other special occasions. The message is clear: Until Palestine is once again Muslim territory, the power of Islam must be brazenly asserted at every opportunity. Should that day come, as in all Arab lands today, no Jew would dare to protest the muezzin's call.

Muslim teaching implies that the kingdom of God will be established only after the last Jews are killed. In one of the most authoritative collections of Islamic traditions, the *Hadith* (Traditions of the Prophet), we read:

> Allah's Messenger [may peace be upon him] said: "You will fight against the Jews and you will kill them until even a stone would say: Come here, Moslem, there is a Jew hiding himself behind me, kill him."[13]

So deep is their aversion that many Muslims still cannot bring themselves to speak of "Israel." To utter the word would be to grant the Jewish state a reality that they wish to deny. Rather, they refer to "the Zionist entity," which for them is but a temporary imposition on the Muslim land of Palestine.

The last few years have seen a flood of anti-Semitic literature in the Arab world, depicting the Jew as evil incarnate. Much of this hate-filled literature was produced—ironically—in Kuwait. Schoolchildren throughout the Arab world are indoctrinated with vivid descriptions of how Jews secretly obtain the blood of Muslims (preferably children) for their Passover matza bread and Purim cakes. Anti-Semitic literature from the West is published and widely read in the Arab world. The infamous and rabidly anti-Semitic forgery composed by the pre-Bolshevik Russian secret police, *Protocols of the Elders of Zion*, is still a brisk seller throughout the Middle East.

The fact is that the Middle East is on the verge of being overwhelmed by a floodtide of Muslim fanaticism. And there is one

---

[13] *Sahih Moslem*, English trans., vol. 4 (Beirut, Dar al Arabia), p. 1510.

common denominator throughout the region: enmity toward the Jewish state. One day that collective abhorrence will in all probability strike at the tiny land of Israel. Let us now see how the various countries of the Middle East are being prepared for that apocalyptic confrontation.

13
Treacherous Alliances

"The beginning of every war is like opening a door into a dark room. One never knows what is hidden in the darkness."[1]
—Adolf Hitler
on the eve of his
invasion of Russia

O N OCTOBER 12, 1990, TWO YOUNG ARAB MEN waited restlessly outside a luxury hotel in downtown Cairo. They seemed out of place in this small island of affluence contrasted with the sea of poverty that characterizes the city. No one took notice of them or the bulky tote bags at their feet. They themselves took little notice of other pedestrians, anxiously scanning the traffic flowing past on the busy boulevard.

They glanced at their watches. It was just before 11 A.M.—and there it was. A shiny black Mercedes appeared with its armed escort car. Inside was Dr. Rifaat Mahgoub, the Speaker of the Egyptian Parliament and second-highest-ranking politician in Egypt after President Hosni Mubarak.

The two young men instantly went into action. Out of the tote bags came automatic weapons. As the Mercedes passed they blasted away, spraying a row of neat holes in the polished exterior of the car. The windows shattered and inside lay Mahgoub, mortally wounded. As the Mercedes slammed to a halt the gunmen

---

[1] William Pfaff, "If We Cannot Avoid War, We Must Prepare for What Comes After," *International Herald Tribune* (December 22, 1990), p. 7.

finished off the Speaker of the Parliament at close range. Before the bodyguards in the escort car could react, the young men jumped on the backs of two Suzuki motorbikes and disappeared into the Cairo traffic.

The assassination was the most spectacular attack on an Egyptian politician since the killing of President Anwar Sadat in 1981. The attack was so well-planned and executed that at first Egyptian police believed it was an act of retaliation by Iraq-backed terrorists. Just a few days before, President Hosni Mubarak had confidently declared that the security situation in Egypt was under control.

Later it became clear that Iraqi sympathizers were not responsible for the assassination. In all likelihood it was the work of Islamic extremists. The killing may have been a case of mistaken identity, the real target being the Interior Minister Abdul Halim Moussa, who has been accused by the Muslem Brotherhood of waging a campaign of repression against them. It was reported that his own automobile passed the site of the ambush just minutes before Mahgoub's car.

The stunning growth of Muslim fundamentalism in Egypt is symptomatic of the trend throughout the entire Middle East. President Mubarak's regime remains pro-Western because of the massive American financial aid that was the Egyptian "price" for signing the 1979 Camp David Accords, which established a fragile peace between Israel and Egypt.

Financial backing was also one reason why Egypt was a solid member of the Western coalition against Iraq. Mubarak's anger with Saddam Hussein translated into the commitment of two divisions—some 30,000 soldiers—to Saudi Arabia. In return, the city of Riyadh has contributed an initial $800 million to help prop up the Egyptian economy while Washington generously forgave Egypt's multi-billion-dollar debt.

Political instability in Egypt, however, means that Mubarak has embarked upon a risky gamble in joining with the West against a fellow Muslim country. The indications are that the same Muslim fundamentalist undercurrents in Egyptian society that assassinated his predecessor will soon be targeting him.

The land of the Nile is a key player in the Arab-Israeli dispute. The Arab countries have never been able to go to war with Israel without the armies of Egypt. Since Camp David, however, the southern front of Israel has been quiet. Without the manpower of Egypt, Jordan and Syria would not dare challenge the Jewish state.

But should a fundamentalist Muslim revolution succeed one day in Egypt—and it appears all but inevitable—that would change. Egypt would be a powerful ally for the Arab lands bent on Israel's destruction. Let's see how conditions in two other neighboring nations, Jordan and Syria, are growing dangerous for Israel, and then we will take a look at four other members of this growing alliance of nations, those from the lands of Gog and Magog.

King Hussein and Jordan

Until the twentieth century the modern country of Jordan was mostly desert, her population consisting of Bedouin tribes and a few impoverished villages. King Hussein deserves credit for almost singlehandedly forging a modern nation on the windswept plateaus of the trans-Jordanian highlands.

With no oil and few natural resources, the Hashemite Kingdom remains heavily dependent upon the largess of the Gulf states and other foreign aid. This is the essence of the Hashemite Kingdom's vulnerability, and King Hussein has proved to be an astute player in the turbulent politics of the Middle East. Known locally as the man who has "changed his skin a million times," the king has managed to survive longer than most Middle Eastern leaders. This time, however, he is finding himself increasingly cornered as the Hashemite Kingdom of Jordan teeters on the brink of takeover by radical Muslims.

The king's attempts to contain this wave of fanaticism have backfired. His natural inclinations were to sit on the sidelines, hoping to preserve his weak and vulnerable kingdom. He soon realized, however, that his only hope for survival was to drift with the radical wave lest he be drowned in it. This led to the absurd pretense of joining with two of the fiercest enemies of the Hashemite Kingdom: George Habash and Nayef Hawatmeh of the Popular Front, and the Democratic Front for the Liberation of Palestine. They were welcomed by the king to a pro-Saddam conference in Amman.

In his attempt to prevent these radical elements from being turned against his regime, the king allowed them free expression, thus opening a Pandora's box of new threats to his regime. Dan Schueftan describes the turbid mood in the Hashemite Kingdom:

> The political climate in Jordan is extremely hostile to Israel, perhaps more so than in any Arab country. Radical Moslems and Palestinians dominate the public scene and fill the air in an unprecedented manner with hysterical battle-cries against Israel and demonic antisemitic images of Jews.[2]

Israelis watch these developments with increasing concern. Jordan shares the longest border with Israel, and until the war against Iraq that frontier was relatively quiet. In 1991, however, after the Gulf War, the number of cross-border terrorist incursions began to increase. Demonstrations calling for the destruction of Israel erupted in the streets of Amman.

If the king resists the fanatical Muslims they will simply overthrow him, so great is their power and popular appeal at this juncture. And if he goes along with them, playing for time, they will eventually overwhelm him anyway. All it will take is a flash point to ignite the Islamic fundamentalists' aversion to his monarchy. And when King Hussein is gone, there will be little to prevent a radical Islamic regime from joining an offensive against the Jewish state.[3]

---

[2] Dan Schueftan, "Is the Hashemite Imbroglio Getting Out of Control?," *Jerusalem Post* (January 4, 1991), p. 4.

[3] Even if the monarchy should survive, the Hashemite Kingdom will be markedly more radical. Next in line for the scepter is Crown Prince ibn Talal, who has closer ties with the Muslim extremists than does King Hussein.

This means that Jordan, across the river from Israel, like Egypt to the south, will almost inevitably be a front opening up against her. The third front, Syria, is an ancient adversary to the north.

The Syrian Lion

The name of Syria's president, Hafez al-Assad, literally means "lion." Known as a shrewd player in Middle East politics, Hafez al-Assad played his cards early in the Gulf crisis. He pledged quickly to send his entire 9th Armored Division, totaling 15,000 men and 270 tanks, to join the alliance against his arch foe, Saddam Hussein. He was promptly rewarded: Saudi Arabia reportedly provided at least $1 billion in immediate aid to Syria's debilitated economy.

One paradox of the Gulf crisis was the positioning of soldiers from Syria's perennial anti-American regime alongside U.S forces in Saudi Arabia. Their uneasy coexistence is understandable: Syria has been implicated in the deaths of American and French soldiers in Lebanon, including 241 American casualties in the 1983 bombing of the Marine barracks at the Beirut airport.

The regime of President Assad is the most blatant example of state-sponsored terrorism in the Middle East. It has supported terrorist groups and operations in the Middle East and around the world. The primary target is Israel, which Assad considers to be an integral part of Syria. The U.S., viewed as the protector of the Zionist enemy, has also been targeted. In addition to the Beirut bombing, Syria has been directly involved in terrorist attacks that have killed hundreds of Americans in the last decade.

Responding to Syria's involvement in worldwide terrorism, in 1986 the U.S. and the European Community imposed diplomatic and economic sanctions on Damascus. Despite this, an unrepentant Assad still maintains an elaborate terrorism apparatus. Damascus funds and directs terrorist groups, supplying them with explosives and weapons through Syrian Arab Airline offices and

Syrian embassies abroad. Thus, terrorists have access to false passports and official Syrian documents, diplomatic pouches, safe
houses and logistical support. Syrian military attachés have been
directly implicated in a number of terrorist incidents in Western
Europe.

Syria has provided the P.L.O. with training facilities, equipment
and personnel, and also has its own organizations within the
P.L.O. One example is As-Saiqa and Ahmed Jibril's Popular Front
for the Liberation of Palestine, General Command. This is believed
responsible, among other things, for the explosion aboard Pan Am
flight 103 in December 1988, which killed 270 people—most of
whom were Americans. A.M. Rosenthal describes Jibril's organization:

> It is based in Syria, trained by Syria, armed and sheltered by
> Syria. Its chief, Ahmed Jibril, lives in Damascus, was a Syrian
> army officer and is part of the Syrian terrorist apparatus.
> Intelligence agents around the world say that Iran probably
> paid the gang for the bombing, in revenge for the downing of
> an Iranian airliner by the U.S. cruiser Vincennes.... The
> United States is so convinced that the Jibril gang was respon-
> sible that last year it asked Mr. Assad at least to close the
> camps. He refused.[4]

Despite Syria's dismal record involving terrorism, Washington
was surprisingly forgetful when trying to woo President Assad into
joining the Gulf coalition. "We share a common purpose with
respect to problems in the Gulf," declared Secretary of State James
Baker while in Damascus.[5] President Bush went so far as to make
a special stop in Geneva in order to meet the Syrian president,
prompting Rosenthal to comment:

---

[4] A.M. Rosenthal, "What Bush Told the Victim's Family," *International Herald Tribune* (December 22–23, 1990), p. 4.

[5] Christopher Dickey, "A 'Common Purpose' or a Common Enemy?," *Newsweek* (September 24, 1990), p. 24.

Syria is using the Gulf crisis to scoop up billions for arms. Someday Mr. Assad will use his new strength to expand his empire. And those pictures of Presidents Bush and Assad grinning away will look even sadder than they do now.[6]

Given Syria's abominable record on yet another front, Washington's eagerness to improve its relationship with Damascus becomes all the more incomprehensible. According to Yonah Alexander, research professor at Georgetown University:

Syria is deeply involved in the cultivation, production and distribution of illegal narcotics, including heroin and hashish. According to American and European government sources, the Syrian government funds some of its terrorist activities against the West, Israel, and other target countries primarily with money generated by drug trafficking.[7]

The Beka'a, a valley in Lebanon, is a major source of the illegal drugs. The U.S. Drug Enforcement Agency estimates that Damascus reaps a yearly profit of about $1 billion from the Beka'a alone. Syrian army trucks, helicopters and naval vessels routinely bring the drugs to Syrian ports and smuggling points along the Turkish border.

Vice-President Rifaat Assad, the notorious brother of the Syrian president, controls the illegal narcotic operations. International law enforcement officials have traced connections between Rifaat Assad, the Sicilian mafia and the Colombian Medellin drug cartel. Closer to home, it is believed that twenty percent of the heroin sold in the U.S. comes from the Syrian-controlled Beka'a.

Syria and her four-hundred-thousand-man army remains a formidable opponent that would almost certainly one day join another concerted attack on Israel. The billions in financial assistance that President Assad received during the Gulf crisis have already

---

[6] Rosenthal, p. 4.

[7] Yonah Alexander, "Still the Terror-Master," *Jerusalem Post* (December 28, 1990), p. 5.

been spent—not to improve the lot of his needy people or to pay off his country's immense debt, but to buy yet more weapons of destruction.

Syrian arms agents are reportedly buying up everything in sight, including a huge arms purchase from the Kremlin worth at least $2 billion, including Mig-29 fighter aircraft and T-72 tanks. Hundreds more T-72s have already been purchased from Czechoslovakia. Since the end of the Gulf War, Israeli intelligence has observed the docking in Syria of several North Korean ships carrying shipments of Scud-B missiles. These ominous developments indicate a real prospect of another Saddam Hussein arising in the region.

The likely target of those weapons will once again be Israel. And this time the Arab armies will be markedly better equipped—and fanatically motivated. If this were the extent of the threat that Israel faced, perhaps it would still prevail against these formidable opponents. If other Muslim lands join the battle, however, then Israel would face truly *overwhelming* odds.

We have seen how the conditions in Egypt, Jordan and Syria are moving toward such a confrontation with Israel. Let us now look beyond the Arab world to the modern lands of Gog, Magog and company.

The Restless Land of Ataturk

The land of Turkey straddles two continents: Europe and Asia. This division symbolizes the tremendous contradictions of a people who are attracted to the West but increasingly bound by their Muslim heritage. A member of NATO (North Atlantic Treaty Organization), Turkey is clamoring for membership in the European Economic Community. At the same time, Muslim fundamentalism is pulling the country back to her Islamic roots.

The last Muslim caliphate (centralized Islamic authority) was the Ottoman empire, which ruled from Istanbul. It lasted exactly four hundred years, from 1517 to the end of World War I. Istanbul ruled over a vast area including the Middle East, North Africa,

Southeast Europe and Western Asia. All of that was lost after the first World War. In the aftermath of that disaster, a new strongman by the name of Mustafa Kemal Ataturk began to transform Turkey's Islamic culture.

Ataturk, who ruled from 1922 until 1938, blamed the Muslim religion for Turkey's decline and defeat in the war. Accordingly, he recast Turkish society into a modern secular state. The *shari'a* was replaced by a Western-style legal code. Education was secularized and the Arabic alphabet was replaced by Latin characters.

This anti-Islamic revolution has not gone unchallenged. There has been a growing reaction to Western values in the midst of great political instability in the country. Between 1961 and 1980 there were nineteen different governments, an average of one shaky coalition per year. During the 1970s Turkey was terrorized by rightwing, left-wing and Islamic terrorists battling in a campaign of murderous violence.

Finally in 1980 the army intervened to restore order. Three years later Turgut Ozal of the Motherland Party was elected president. President Ozal has attempted to steer his country down a middle course between East and West, but that is proving increasingly difficult. There has been an upsurge of Muslim fundamentalism in Turkey, supported by neighboring Islamic countries—notably Iran.

One significant incident was the decision, amid heated debate, to build a mosque on the premises of the Turkish parliament. The decree was accompanied by a law calling for heavy penalties for anyone making "insulting remarks against Allah and the Prophet Muhammad." Such laws are directed squarely at the Christian population of Turkey, which has never recovered from the Armenian genocide at the beginning of the century. There are estimated to be fewer than a thousand evangelical believers in a country of more than 55 million people.[8]

---

[8] See Patrick Johnstone, *Operation World,* 4th ed. (London: STL Publishers & WEC Publications, 1986), pp. 414–416. This statistic actually represents an

The Gulf crisis exposed the deep East-West tensions in Turkish society. A poll in August 1990 showed that 72 percent of Turks opposed any kind of military involvement in the Gulf crisis.[9] All the main opposition parties and even President Ozal's own military have opposed Turkey's involvement in the Gulf coalition. The chief of staff of the army, as well as President Ozal's foreign and defense ministers, resigned in protest.

Disenchantment with the West may increase when it becomes clear that Turkey's support will not make the dream of joining the European Community come any closer. The twelve current members of the EEC are stalling, unenthusiastic about admitting Turkey and her mixed first- and third-world economy. Meanwhile, the Muslim world is making a concerted effort to lure Turkey back, as Laffin writes:

> The difficulty for the liberals and moderates is that the leaders of Islamic Jihad as well as the fundamentalist Saudi Arabian government and the imperialist Gaddafi have all made it clear to the Turkish leaders that by re-embracing Islam in the fight against the West they can gain a great deal of money for Turkey—money from oil.[10]

At the moment, Turkey is a major recipient of U.S. aid and also derives benefits from her NATO membership. But should the inflow of Western money dry up, Muslim countries would be more than willing to support a repentant Turkey that returned to the Islamic fold. That day may not be too far in the future: In October 1991 Ozal's governing Motherland Party was defeated in general elections by the nationalist True Path party. This signaled a shift away from the strongly pro-Western policies of the Turkish leader. With a runaway seventy percent annual rate of inflation and grow-

---

encouraging improvement. When I visited Turkey in the late 1970s there were only an estimated fifty believers in the country.

[9] Lisa Beyer, "Hanging Together—or Separately?," *Time* (August 27, 1990), p. 32.

[10] John Laffin, *Holy War: Islam Fights* (London: Grafton Books, 1988), p. 161.

ing economic problems, the land of Ataturk may soon be looking east to its Islamic roots.

We have seen that Turkey is likely where Gog of the land of Magog, along with several allies, is historically located. Despite being a non-Arab country, a newly "Islamicized" Turkey would surely join an invasion to "reclaim the land of Palestine."

After Egypt, Turkey has the largest population in the Middle East—one that is expected to top one hundred million by 2030. The military potential of Turkey can only increase: With more than half a million men, it is one of the largest standing armies in the world.

From the land of Ataturk will, in all probability, one day come forth hordes of warriors heading south through allied Muslim territory toward the land of Israel. But there are still more participants from the historic lands of Gog and Magog.

The Central Asian Republics

Most people tended to regard the Soviet Union as one huge monolithic entity. In fact, as the world's largest country it was an extraordinary mosaic of nationalities and ethnic groups that comprised the fifteen republics. Until the end of the 1980s there was little organized resistance to centralized Soviet authority. All that has now changed, of course. The Russian bear has broken up altogether, with the various republics struggling to redefine themselves as a Commonwealth of Independent States.

As we have seen, there is a natural cleavage within the now-collapsed Soviet Union that is a prime candidate for total separation: the central Asian republics adjoining Iran, Afghanistan and China. These lands were conquered by Islamic armies in the seventh and eighth centuries A.D. when the Muslim empire had become the largest yet known in history.

Central Asia has remained part of the Muslim world ever since. In the nineteenth century the Russian empire expanded south across the Caucasus and west to present-day Kazakhstan. For the first time Russia with her Orthodox Church became the master of a Muslim people. The central Asian republics constituted an alien civilization, with a separate religion and culture, in the midst of the Slavic-dominated Soviet Union. Today these republics constitute a considerable Muslim demographic block:

> Six Soviet republics with substantial numbers of Muslims have a combined population of about 55 million. Two of the republics, Azerbaijan and Turkmenistan, share a border with Iran, and 80 percent of their combined population is Muslim. The four others are Uzbekistan, Tadzhikistan, Kirghizia and Kazakhstan.[11]

The Islamic world has begun a major effort to hasten the secession of the Muslim southern republics from the new Commonwealth of Independent States. Saudi Arabia, Iran and Pakistan are beaming radio programs into these areas. Cassettes and literature preaching the virtues of Islamic fundamentalism are being shipped by the ton across the border to a ready audience. Thus, after decades of suppression, Islam is once again flourishing with thousands of new mosques being constructed.

It may be only a matter of time before these central Asian republics separate from the Commonwealth of Independent States. If this happens, the odds are that they will become Islamic republics on the Iranian model and join in the liberation of Palestine.

There will be another participant from the biblical lands of Gog and Magog.

The Persian Wild Card

Iran is the ideological leader of Islamic fundamentalism worldwide. It is the stronghold of militant Shi'ite Islam—the fiery branch

---

[11] Patrick E. Tyler, "Tehran Quietly Backs Soviet Muslims," *International Herald Tribune* (September 20, 1991), p. 2.

of the Muslim faith that also predominates in the republics of Central Asia.

At the moment, the bottom line for Iran, like so many other countries in the region, is foreign aid: Tens of billions of dollars are needed for reconstruction and modernization after the costly war with Iraq. Still, the Iranians are clearly revolted by the prospect of appearing to cooperate with the U.S.

In September 1990 Iran's National Security Council voted reluctantly to continue respecting the embargo against Iraq. The very next day, however, the Iranian parliament voted by a two-thirds majority to support a call by Ayatullah Ali Khamenei for a jihad against America.

It appears that Iraq's nuclear facilities have been put out of commission, partly by American bombs and missiles and partly by the U.N. disposal team. Saddam Hussein is so crafty, however, he may still become a threat in this area unless he is deposed. Meanwhile, Washington is becoming increasingly concerned that another nuclear-armed nation may come to dominate the Persian Gulf. Intelligence officials believe that Iran is trying to purchase the technology necessary to build atomic weapons. Accordingly, the U.S. and her allies are quietly launching an international effort to prevent that from happening.

Undaunted, Iran has already embarked upon an ambitious program to purchase the latest in conventional arms. The Chinese, British, Swedish and remnants of the Soviet empire head a long list of arms suppliers eager to sell to the Islamic republic. In June 1989 Iran concluded a $6 billion defense and industrial contract with Moscow. In September they unveiled Mig-29 advanced fighter jets acquired under the deal. American-made weapons are not absent, either: The infamous arms-for-hostages deal in 1985–1986, during President Ronald Reagan's term, saw the U.S. shipping Hawk anti-aircraft missile batteries to Iran.

Now that the debilitating Iran-Iraq war is over, Iran should have sufficient revenues to pay for her military buildup. Despite an oil production exceeding two million barrels per day, the long war drained an estimated seventy percent of Iran's resources every year. Now Iran is poised to take the wreath of Islamic leadership and become the new regional superpower. Along with Iran, the remaining southern allies of Gog will also likely join the Islamic crusade to reclaim Palestine.

African Confederates

Two additional nations from Africa will undoubtedly join with Gog—Ethiopia and Libya. The first of these, Ethiopia, refers to the area of the horn of Africa. Two countries now occupy that region: modern Ethiopia and Somalia. Ethiopia has a mixed Christian and Muslim population, while Somalia is virtually entirely Muslim. Ezekiel's reference to Ethiopia may also include next-door Sudan, proclaimed an Islamic republic in 1983. Muslim fundamentalists strongly supported Saddam's call for jihad in that country as well.

In recent years the Mengistu regime in Ethiopia attempted to impose Marxist-Islamic rule over the Christian areas of the country, which fiercely opposed him, leading to the overthrow of his regime in 1991.

With regard to Libya, little need be added about the regime of Colonel Gaddafi, which has proved itself to be fanatically opposed to the Jewish state. Gaddafi's involvement in international terrorism is also well-established. In the late 1980s the American Navy was involved in naval engagements in which several vessels of the Libyan navy were sunk, followed by the bombardment of Tripoli by the U.S. Air Force.

Gaddafi has turned Libya into one of the world's most militarized nations. Every child begins military training at age fourteen. Every Libyan, male and female, is a specialist in some military field by the time of graduation from high school or university. In 1986 Gaddafi attempted to launch what he termed an "International People's Front," which was intended to become a huge mercenary army. Advertisements were placed in newspapers around the Arab and Muslim world in which the elimination of Zionism was explicitly mentioned as a major goal of the army.

The World's View

Not only are more and more Middle Eastern nations bowing to the rule of Islam, but Muslims themselves are undergoing a population explosion that is increasing the numbers of believers in those countries—and around the world:

> The birthrate of Muslims exceeds that of all other religions. . . . In 1990, the world population exceeded 5.4 billion, of which 1.1 billion were Muslims. Every fifth person on our planet follows Islam. The world population doubles every 40 years. Muslims alone double every 24–30 years; excluding them, the rest of the world doubles in 50 years.[12]

The driving force behind Muslim expansionist aims is petrodollars. Since the 1973 OPEC oil embargo the Persian Gulf states have reaped fantastic oil wealth. Muslims believe that this is proof of Allah's blessing upon the "true faith," and is to be used for the propagation of Islam around the world.

We have seen that virtually every land mentioned in Ezekiel 38 is now under Muslim control. We have also observed the tide of Islamic fundamentalism now engulfing the Middle East, and that the return of Palestine to Islamic rule remains a paramount objective. And we know that the numbers of Muslims are increasing at a dramatic rate.

All of which reinforces the ominous reality that there will not be peace in this region but rather continually expanding levels of conflict until the end of the age.

Who will lead these hosts and when will this greatest conflagration in history occur? That is the subject of the next chapter.

---

[12] Abd al-Masih, *World Muslim Population Growth—1970–2000* (Villach, Austria: Light of Life, 1990), p. 3.

14
Field Marshal of Armageddon

ANYONE WHO ENJOYS LEARNING ABOUT BIBLICAL prophecy is bound to have asked the following questions: Why are there so many conflicting ideas about the timetable of future events? Why are there so many guesses as to who the Antichrist is?

A survey of the popular literature will reveal various opinions about the prophetic timetable—each one with detailed charts and reams of biblical references. The layman is often bewildered by these detailed diagrams, no two of which seem to agree exactly. Nevertheless, the writers must know what they are talking about. After all, they are the experts, aren't they?

Not necessarily. Citing numerous biblical references and presenting detailed prophecy charts does not guarantee accuracy. In fact, the closer one looks at some of these complicated presentations the more baffling they become.

For many years I assumed that the prophetic ideas I was brought up on were the only possible way of understanding the Scriptures. Moreover, I even doubted the faith of those who took different views. Such was the degree of pride and exclusivism that my denominational tradition tended to instill regarding biblical prophecy. Looking back, I realize that I had never examined the Scriptures with an open mind to see whether or not my ideas about prophecy were sound and consistent. Years later, when I finally took the effort to make a careful study of the Scriptures, I was disappointed to discover that the Bible did not agree with some of my ideas!

We have looked at other commonly accepted ideas that find little support in Scripture. Let's check now some current theories on the final battle and the evil "field marshal" who will lead the armies of the world against Israel.

The Atomization of Biblical Prophecy

All neatly laid out blueprints for the prophetic future have their shortcomings. A major drawback of the whole enterprise is the "atomization" of biblical prophecy. The dictionary defines *atomize* as: 1) to reduce to minute separate units, or 2) to subject to atomic bombing. While it may be true that either of these definitions at times rightly describes what expositors do to the biblical text, we will focus on the first. That is, instead of focusing on the *general prophetic themes* that have been held by Christians throughout history, Bible teachers compete with each other in "breaking apart" prophetic passages into smaller and smaller *distinct units*.

Let's begin at the beginning. What have the majority of Christians of all ages believed about the prophetic future? We may summarize these themes, each of which can be readily seen in Scripture, as follows:

First, despite our best efforts to evangelize the world, one day there will be an organized spiritual rebellion against the heavenlies. This grim picture of the future was painted by Jesus in the Mount of Olives discourse:

> Jesus answered: "Watch out that no one deceives you. For many will come in my name, claiming, 'I am the Christ,' and will deceive many. You will hear of wars and rumors of wars,

but see to it that you are not alarmed. Such things must happen, but the end is still to come. . . . All these are the beginning of birth pains. Then you will be handed over to be persecuted and put to death, and you will be hated by all nations because of me. At that time many will turn away from the faith and will betray and hate each other, and many false prophets will appear and deceive many people. Because of the increase of wickedness, the love of most will grow cold, but he who stands firm to the end will be saved."

Matthew 24:4–6, 8–13

Second, at the end of the age the situation will deteriorate into a dark period of human history that has been called the "Great Tribulation":

"For then there will be great distress, unequaled from the beginning of the world until now—and never to be equaled again. . . . At that time if anyone says to you, 'Look, here is the Christ!' or, 'There he is!' do not believe it. For false Christs and false prophets will appear and perform great signs and miracles to deceive even the elect—if that were possible."

Matthew 24:21, 23–24

Third, this "reign of wickedness" will lead to a final confrontation between God and the forces of evil. That battle will culminate in the Second Coming of Jesus Christ:

"Immediately after the distress of those days 'the sun will be darkened, and the moon will not give its light. . . .' At that time the sign of the Son of Man will appear in the sky, and all the nations of the earth will mourn. They will see the Son of Man coming on the clouds of the sky, with power and great glory. And he will send his angels with a loud trumpet call, and they will gather his elect from the four winds, from one end of the heavens to the other."

Matthew 24:29–31

Fourth, this final confrontation will be followed by the Day of Judgment for the whole world:

215

In the past God overlooked such ignorance, but now he commands all people everywhere to repent. For he has set a day when he will judge the world with justice by the man he has appointed. He has given proof of this to all men by raising him from the dead.

Acts 17:30–31

Then I saw a great white throne and him who was seated on it. Earth and sky fled from his presence, and there was no place for them. And I saw the dead, great and small, standing before the throne, and books were opened. Another book was opened, which is the book of life. The dead were judged according to what they had done as recorded in the books.

Revelation 20:11–12

Finally, for those who have trusted Christ as their Savior, and whose names are written in "the book of life," the reward of eternal life awaits:

Then I saw a new heaven and a new earth, for the first heaven and the first earth had passed away, and there was no longer any sea. . . . And I heard a loud voice from the throne saying, "Now the dwelling of God is with men, and he will live with them. They will be his people, and God himself will be with them and be their God. He will wipe every tear from their eyes. There will be no more death or mourning or crying or pain, for the old order of things has passed away."

Revelation 21:1, 3–4

This then is the essence of what the Bible says about the prophetic future; to go further is to tread on less-certain and controversial territory. To be sure, some will want to expand this brief presentation to include other detailed events. Those who do so might consider a wise motto I heard long ago: "Let us speak loudly where the Bible speaks loudly, and softly where the Bible speaks softly."

In no other area of biblical study is this basic principle ignored more than in the area of eschatology. Instead of focusing on what the Bible clearly says about the future, we want to hear about novel ideas that may have very little support in Scripture.

The problem began when Bible teachers began to atomize or break apart the different accounts of the end of time in the Bible. I believe that a prime motivation for this was the desire to bring a new teaching about the subject that audiences would find interesting. Thus, instead of viewing minor divergences in the prophetic passages as complementary, they began to teach that the differences indicated completely separate events. Soon we had a complicated succession of end-time events.

The details of the battle of Gog and Magog in Ezekiel 38 and 39, for example, differ in some respects from those of the battle of Armageddon described in Revelation. And both of these passages are difficult to reconcile in every respect with the prophet Daniel's description of future battles.[1]

The atomizing solution is to separate the Ezekiel and Revelation accounts and make two completely different battles out of them. Those holding to the Russian invasion theory separate the battle of Gog and Magog from the battle of Armageddon. But then, as we have seen, you have the incongruous situation of Russia being annihilated *a short time after already being completely destroyed.*

The Western mind places great emphasis upon the rational faculties. We are uncomfortable with anything that cannot be re-

---

[1] A discussion of the notoriously thorny problems involved with the interpretation of the prophecies of Daniel is beyond the scope of the present book. Commentators are divided, for example, as to the meaning of one key passage, Daniel 11:40–45, which is thought to refer either to the career of Antiochus IV or to the future Antichrist. The "Antiochus" side claims that there is no break in the progress of chapter 11, which describes the battles of the second-century B.C. Seleucid ruler. The "Antichrist" side connects those verses to the beginning of chapter 12, which appears to speak about the events at the end of the age. In my view, popular commentators often play "fast and loose" with these verses, quoting them to support their particular prophecy timelines.

duced to clear definition. Since God's purposes are infinitely beyond human understanding, however, there will always be an element of "mystery" to our faith:

> "For my thoughts are not your thoughts, neither are your ways my ways," declares the Lord. "As the heavens are higher than the earth, so are my ways higher than your ways and my thoughts than your thoughts."
>
> Isaiah 55:8–9

Apocalyptic literature, which employs imagery and symbolism to convey truths about the future, especially reflects the element of mystery. The very nature of this literary genre defies mathematical precision. That is why various well-meaning attempts to chart the prophetic future invariably contradict each other, as Paul Thigpen observes:

> The resulting discussions throughout conservative, evangelical and charismatic/Pentecostal circles are uncovering a bewildering array of conflicting teachings. Supporters of each position claim a biblical basis for their thought, and point to respected Christians of the past whose thinking apparently agrees with them.[2]

Do divergences in these accounts mean that we are necessarily talking about *different* battles? Not at all. Let's compare another similar situation in Scripture.

The four Gospels all approach the life and ministry of Jesus from different perspectives. Each Gospel account includes unique information and incidents that the others do not. We also find diverging accounts of the same incidents from Jesus' life that are at times hard to reconcile.

---

[2] Paul Thigpen, "The Second Coming: How Many Views?" *Charisma & Christian Life* 14 (February 1989), p. 42.

Do we then postulate from this that there must be four different people called Jesus? Of course not. Each Gospel was written for a particular audience. And each of the evangelists, under the inspiration of the Holy Spirit, emphasized what was appropriate for his distinctive message. We may compare this to an automobile accident seen by several observers from different vantage points. Each account of the accident will include unique details, but they will all be, nonetheless, true accounts of the same event.

In the same way, the various accounts of the last battle express the same basic truths in unique ways. We should not expect exact correlation in every detail. Rather, in many instances the accounts should be considered *complementary* descriptions of the same prophetic future.

It is true that different names and terms are used to describe the participants in Ezekiel and in Revelation, but this, again, does not mean that two separate battles are being described. After all, various terms are used to describe the personage called the Antichrist: In 2 Thessalonians 2:8–9 he is called "the lawless one," in Revelation he is called the "beast," and in Ezekiel he is called by the name we have discussed numerous times, "Gog, of the land of Magog." The apostle John refers to "the spirit of the antichrist" that was already in the world in his day (1 John 4:3).

As John B. Taylor states, "The origin of the name is less significant that what it symbolizes, namely the personified head of the forces of evil which are intent on destroying the people of God."[3]

Which Final Battle?

The truth about the final battle in which God destroys the forces of evil is simpler than some would have us believe. Scripture indicates that there is only one final, cataclysmic war. It is known in Ezekiel as the battle with Gog of the land of Magog and in Revelation as Armageddon.

---

[3] John B. Taylor, *Ezekiel, An Introduction and Commentary* (Leicester: Inter-Varsity Press, 1978), p. 244.

A considerable portion of the text in Ezekiel 38 and 39 is given to a vivid description of the *final, utter destruction* of Gog and company at the hand of the Lord. We have seen that this is more than just a temporary setback for Gog and Magog. But perhaps most telling is the proclamation of the Lord after their defeat: "I will make known my holy name among my people Israel. *I will no longer let my holy name be profaned,* and the nations will know that I the Lord am the Holy One in Israel" (Ezekiel 39:7, italics mine).

Here the Lord declares that one result of this final confrontation is that His holy name will *no longer be defiled.*

This creates more problems for those who hold to the theory of two battles: The book of Revelation says that the beast will open his mouth "to blaspheme God, and to slander his name and his dwelling place and those who live in heaven" (Revelation 13:6). Likewise, Paul describes the profanity of the "man of lawlessness" who "opposes and exalts himself over everything that is called God or is worshiped, and even sets himself up in God's temple, proclaiming himself to be God" (2 Thessalonians 2:4). This is a level of insult against the one true God that is difficult to imagine.

The question is: When does this blasphemy take place? The commonly accepted view puts it *after* the battle of Gog and Magog in the time leading up to Armageddon. But this cannot be: After the battle of Gog and Magog the world will *no longer* be filled with blasphemy against the true God.

It goes beyond reason to imagine that the profane utterances of the Beast will begin *after* the battle of Gog and Magog. The text of Ezekiel 38 and 39 does not lend itself to any other interpretation except that of one final, decisive confrontation between God and Satan.

The Last Battle

Scripture has a name for this final confrontation in which the Lord defeats the forces of evil. It is generally referred to as "the Day of the Lord," spoken of by the prophet Joel:

"The sun will be turned to darkness and the moon to blood before the coming of the great and dreadful day of the Lord. And everyone who calls on the name of the Lord will be saved; for on Mount Zion and in Jerusalem there will be deliverance, as the Lord has said, among the survivors whom the Lord calls. In those days and at that time, when I restore the fortunes of Judah and Jerusalem, I will gather all nations and bring them down to the Valley of Jehoshaphat. There I will enter into judgment against them concerning my inheritance, my people Israel."

Joel 2:31–3:2

This apocalyptic Day of the Lord is the final day of human history when the Lord intervenes to put an end to all evil rebellion. It is Gog and Magog, the Antichrist and Armageddon all rolled into one climactic struggle. In the announcement of the battle of Gog and Magog, Ezekiel confirms: "It is coming! It will surely take place, declares the Sovereign Lord. This is the day I have spoken of" (Ezekiel 39:8).

A Nefarious World Leader

We have seen that Islam is in a state of perpetual war with all "unbelievers." It is a fight to the death, and Muslims are confident that the religion of Muhammad will prevail. It is eminently reasonable to expect that Islam will be a major force confronting Israel at the end of time. But there will also be another power, who will—incredibly—even be able to exercise a degree of control over the Islamic world.

The book of Revelation tells us that at the end of the age, when the world will be unified as never before, a mysterious figure of consummate evil will arise:

The beast was given a mouth to utter proud words and blasphemies and to exercise his authority for forty-two months. He opened his mouth to blaspheme God, and to slander his name and his dwelling place and those who live in heaven. He was given power to make war against the saints and to conquer them. And he was given authority *over every tribe, people, language and nation.*

Revelation 13:5–7, italics mine

World history is the story of the succession of great empires. None of them, however, has been capable of dominating the world's political system to the degree portrayed here. Until the present day no world leader ever possessed such far-reaching powers "over every tribe, people, language and nation." The Beast of Revelation will also exercise unheard-of authority over the economic affairs of the world:

He also forced everyone, small and great, rich and poor, free and slave, to receive a mark on his right hand or on his forehead, so that no one could buy or sell unless he had the mark, which is the name of the beast or the number of his name.

Revelation 13:16–17

This Antichrist, or Beast, will, along with the false prophet of Revelation 16, make war with the saints and lead the world in a final rebellion against God. Led by Satan, the "great red dragon," they form a satanic trinity. The Antichrist will command the worship of the nations: "All inhabitants of the earth will worship the beast—all whose names have not been written in the book of life belonging to the Lamb that was slain from the creation of the world" (Revelation 13:8).

From this we must conclude that a political leader will one day arise who will have authority to rule over the nations of the world. He will be demonically inspired, and will have the power to perform unimaginable feats: "He was given power to give breath to the image of the . . . beast, so that it could speak and cause all who refused to worship the image to be killed" (Revelation 13:15).

222

The world will be in a state of terrible confusion as such satanic miracles are performed—especially those in the Western world who have come to deny the existence of the supernatural. Witnessing for the first time undeniable and terrifying spiritual phenomena will cause shock and paranoia among the masses, who will come to accept the Antichrist as the only solution to the overwhelming problems facing planet Earth. The purpose of the satanic trinity is to draw the nations of the world into the final battle we have discussed (see Revelation 16:13–14).

One perplexing problem remains: How can we understand the relationship between the various political and military forces that will descend upon the land of Israel on that day?

The Lands of Japheth

We are now moving into the realm of speculation. Scripture does not elaborate regarding such particulars, and we can only make an educated guess about how things *might* transpire. But there is nevertheless one fascinating clue worth passing on.

The ancient Jewish rabbinic literature is a valuable source of information for biblical interpretation. The rabbis were once engaged in endless discussion about the prophetic books, and their insights often shed light on hard-to-understand passages.

Commenting on the battle of Gog, Magog and company, the rabbinic sages agreed that Gog and Magog originate from the Caucasian region between the Black and Caspian Seas. According to the table of nations in Genesis 10, Magog was the son of Japheth. The descendants of Japheth settled in the regions to the north and west of the Near East, especially Anatolia (Turkey) and the Aegean.

Some have connected the Greek mythological figure *Iapetos* with Japheth, thereby extending the lands of Japheth to include the European heritage. The rabbis concluded that Japhethic peoples will be in the forefront of the battle. If true, the implications are significant, for this would also include Greece and, by implication, the civilization of Europe.

This posed a problem for the rabbis, however. In the Scriptures it is Edom, not Japheth, that is the one irreconcilable enemy of Israel. The Edomites are the descendants of Esau who inhabited what is now the southern Jordanian desert. The Edomites have long been associated with the Arabs, who first overran their territory in the fifth century B.C.

The rabbinic tradition had an intriguing solution to the relation of Edom in all of this: There is wide agreement in the literature that Gog himself is a descendant of Esau.[4] In this he will follow in the footsteps of his ancestors, the Edomites, who have never ceased their bitter enmity toward the house of Jacob. Indeed, Edom is the perennial archenemy of the children of Israel. For this the prophets foretold judgment upon Mount Seir:

> "Because you rejoiced when the inheritance of the house of Israel became desolate, that is how I will treat you. You will be desolate, O Mount Seir, you and all of Edom. Then they will know that I am the Lord."
>
> Ezekiel 35:15

and:

> "Your warriors, O Teman, will be terrified, and everyone in Esau's mountains will be cut down in the slaughter. Because of the violence against your brother Jacob, you will be covered with shame; you will be destroyed forever."
>
> Obadiah 9–10

It is fitting—in a macabre way—that the leader of the final great battle should come from Edom. The rabbis also believed that this

---

[4] See Rabbis Nosson Scherman and Meir Zlotowitz, eds., *Ezekiel: A New Translation with a Commentary Anthologized from Talmudic, Midrashic and Rabbinic Sources,* vol. 2 (Brooklyn: Mesorah, 1980), pp. 581–582.

Edomic Gog would lead the Japhethic nations—which would include Europe and the Western nations—to fight against God in that conflict. But how would this world leader be related to the Western world?

One possibility is that he will be a Middle Eastern leader who will succeed in exercising control over the Western world. One way of achieving this could be through economic blackmail. We have already seen the growing dependence of the West upon Persian Gulf oil. It is entirely conceivable that a powerful Middle Eastern leader could force the West to do his bidding or face the cut-off of this vital commodity.

The Name of the Antichrist?

There is another possibility, however. He might be Occidental (that is, born in the West) but of Middle Eastern descent. This would harmonize with another aspect of the coming ruler: He will lead a revived Roman Empire. The prophet Daniel experienced a series of mysterious visions and prophecies regarding this future potentate:

> "In the latter period of their reign, when rebels have become completely wicked, a stern-faced king, a master of intrigue, will arise. He will become very strong, but not by his own power. He will cause astounding devastation and will succeed in whatever he does. He will destroy the mighty men and the holy people. He will cause deceit to prosper, and he will consider himself superior. When they feel secure, he will destroy many and take his stand against the Prince of princes. Yet he will be destroyed, but not by human power."
>
> Daniel 8:23–25

Here we have a summary of the characteristics of the end-time ruler. He will be demonically empowered to fight against the "holy people," and will even oppose the Prince of princes—the Messiah. But at the apex of his power, he will suddenly meet his end through divine intervention. In the next chapter Daniel mentions this future ruler again—and here we have a clue to the seat of his power:

> "After the sixty-two 'sevens,' the Anointed One will be cut off and will have nothing. *The people of the ruler who will come* will destroy the city and the sanctuary. The end will come like a flood: War will continue until the end, and desolations have been decreed."
>
> Daniel 9:26, italics mine

The "Anointed One" is a reference to the Messiah. He will be "cut off," and then "the people of the ruler who will come" will destroy Jerusalem. There is no doubt as to the identity of the people mentioned here: It is the Roman army that destroyed Jerusalem and its Temple in A.D. 70. And so we know that the ruler spoken of in these passages will be connected to the people who destroyed Jerusalem—the Romans.

It is believed that the Roman Empire will once again rise from the ashes of history. And since Rome controlled much of what is today called Europe, one should expect the emergence of a new, unified Europe. Many believe we are already seeing this in the European Economic Community that is once again transforming the continent into a politically and economically united empire.

The ancient Jewish commentaries on the Scriptures yield one more tantalizing piece of information about this future world leader: They give his name. It is a name that is pregnant with meaning for Roman history. It symbolizes the mystical, personified force behind one of the greatest empires that the world has ever known—and which will be again. What is this name? In the Midrashic Jewish literature Gog is often called *Armilus*—a variant of Romulus, none other than the founder of Rome.[5]

We have now come to the end of our deliberations regarding the final confrontation between God and the forces of evil. Now it is time to sit back and transport ourselves into the future to take an imaginative look at how it might all transpire.

[5] Scherman and Zlotowitz, p. 581.

15
Final Battle, Final Hope[1]

"You Christians believe that the Messiah has already come. We Jews believe that he is yet to come. Whether it is this or that, let us all pray that it may be soon!"[2]

—Jerusalem Mayor
Teddy Kollek

The Beginning of the End

I looked, and there before me was a black horse! Its rider was holding a pair of scales in his hand. Then I heard what sounded like a voice among the four living creatures, saying, "A quart of wheat for a day's wages, and three quarts of barley for a day's wages, and do not damage the oil and the wine!"

Revelation 6:5–6

It was a sunless, gloomy day as the limousines lined up to disgorge their diplomatic passengers at the United Nations buildings in lower Manhattan. The mood was somber, like that of the city itself.

---

[1] Note: The following is a possible scenario of the last days of human history. It is not intended to be a comprehensive description of every aspect of biblical prophecy, but rather to present a glimpse of the setting of the final battle described in the book of Revelation.

[2] Address to the International Christian Embassy Feast of Tabernacles Celebration in Jerusalem, October 16, 1991.

This was a different New York. A closer look would send the senses reeling. Gone were the glitter and opulence of one of the world's premier cities. Abandoned cars littered the broad avenue in front of the U.N. tower. Even the chauffeured limousines looked worn. Traffic was sparse. Indeed, no automobiles had been produced in the United States, and virtually none around the world, for several years.

A visual sweep of the skyline would reveal that New York was a city in its death throes. The bottom floor windows of the U.N. —as with most buildings in view—were boarded up. At least one skyscraper in the distance appeared to be a burned-out hulk. The U.N. buildings were heavily barricaded and guarded by soldiers and armored vehicles.

The city was in a state of siege. Most municipal services were curtailed. Water and electricity were available only intermittently. Crime was rampant: Violent battles between the rival gangs that ruled the streets were an everyday occurrence. The Army and National Guard were present in force to preserve the order. The military also supervised the distribution of basic necessities.

The delivery of foodstuffs was beginning to slow down. Even the most pessimistic of climatologists could not have predicted the recent changes in the world's climate. It seemed as though planet Earth was turning on a different axis. Whole regions of the world had been transformed into either frigid regions or desert wastelands. In just a few years food production had plummeted. No one counted anymore, but hundreds of millions were starving.

The diminished harvests had little chance of making it to the cities, teeming with millions of refugees from rural poverty. Transportation systems had broken down. The U.S. interstate system was in shambles. The sparse traffic crawled along, snaking around endless wrecked obstructions in the broken roadway, avoiding the unsafe bridges. Civilian air travel was a thing of the past. Equipment and spare parts were no longer available to keep more than a few non-military planes flying. Most airports had been abandoned; a few were converted to military use.

Almost all heavy industry had ceased—except that related to weapons production. At the end of the previous century, the level of worldwide petroleum consumption had steadily increased. Continued instability—especially in the Middle East—had prevented a corresponding increase in oil production. This growing shortfall led to astronomical price increases as countries around the world competed for dwindling supplies of oil.

The cumulative effect was a chronic worldwide depression as the industrial machine of the West slowly ground to a halt. Violent labor and social unrest erupted as factories shut down one by one. People sought desperately for a means of survival. Bartering for basic necessities had become a way of life.

The U.S. had been rocked by major earthquakes that had killed and injured hundreds of thousands. On the West Coast the big one had finally come, and California had not recovered from the fractures that left the coastal cities in ruins. The state was also in the throes of a persistent drought: The California aqueduct was now reduced to a trickle. Running water was becoming a rarity and large areas gradually reverted to desert land. In a mass exodus Californians sought more habitable regions of the U.S.

The rest of the globe had experienced the same cataclysmic undoing. Particularly hard hit were the cities of the world, which had become concrete jungles. Millions found themselves trapped in decaying urban areas without adequate food or water. Epidemics broke out as basic health care became a thing of the past. The desperate conditions laid bare the brutal side of human nature, and violent revolution plunged country after country into political chaos.

War Breaks Out

"He will confirm a covenant with many for one 'seven,' but in the middle of that 'seven' he will put an end to sacrifice and offering."

Daniel 9:27

The focal point of conflict remained the Middle East, where beleaguered Israel was surrounded by implacable enemies. International pressure was growing to force Israel to yield her sovereignty over the Occupied Territories and to abide by a U.N. decree placing the city of Jerusalem under U.N. supervision as an international zone. Washington threatened a ten percent reduction in her foreign aid package *every year* until she complied with U.N. resolutions by vacating the West Bank and Gaza.

At first the Jewish state was obstinate. Vigorous budget reductions were initiated as the country tightened her economic belt, hoping to outlast the embargo of U.S. dollars. Then an extraordinary natural disaster occurred that many in Israel took as a sign of divine favor upon the Jewish people.

It came as a result of the longest and deepest fault line in the surface of the earth. Running for 6,000 miles, this Syrio-African rift extended from Mozambique in southern Africa to Armenia in the north. It passed through the Dead Sea, the Jordan valley and the Sea of Galilee on its way northward. A secondary fault line split off west toward Jerusalem, running directly through the ridge of the Mount of Olives bordering the Holy City. On average, the land of Israel experienced a major earthquake every fifty years. The last major quake had struck back in 1927, and seismologists were bracing for the next one, which was long overdue.

It happened one evening. An earthquake struck along the Mount of Olives rift, causing major damage in Jerusalem. The Old City, which lay directly opposite the Mount of Olives, was particularly hard hit. But the focus of the world's astonished attention was the Temple Mount. The Muslim shrine of the Dome of the Rock, which had stood in the middle of the Haram esh-Sharif since the eighth century, was reduced to rubble by the tremors.

The structure was damaged beyond repair. The Muslim world demanded that another Islamic edifice be erected on the spot without delay. Some in Israel argued that this was the reasonable—indeed the only—option open to the nation. Anything less would be exceedingly perilous, especially at this moment in history when the Jewish state was already under tremendous international pressure.

Recent dramatic events in and around Israel, however, had awakened a tremendous religious consciousness in many who were convinced that the dawn of the messianic age was near. The religious parties in the Knesset had experienced a surge of support in the last elections. Their voice now represented the majority sentiment and could not be ignored.

It was decided that to allow the Muslims to build another structure on the most holy place in all the earth for the Jewish people was out of the question. The earthquake was an act of divine providence. To return to the former state of affairs would be to ignore the will of God. It was widely believed that this event signaled the end of the country's hopeless position: Now that the pagan offense on the holy Temple Mount had been destroyed, surely God would once again bless His people.

The Jews had waited almost 2,000 years to rebuild their Temple Mount. The glories of the Temple of Solomon could never be duplicated, but plans were set in motion to build a modest structure to commemorate the holy ground.

The Memorial Temple, as it would be called, would not disturb any of the Muslim structures still standing on the Temple Mount—save one: a small, domed cupola that stood about 75 feet north of the now-ruined Dome of the Rock. Known as the "Dome of the Spirits," this cupola went unnoticed by most visitors to the Temple Mount. Since it covered a piece of original bedrock that was thought to be the exact location of the Holy of Holies of Solomon's Temple, it was carefully removed and construction began over the revered ancient bedrock. The Orthodox religious community prepared to reinstate the sacrifices and offerings that had been the central purpose of the ancient Temple.

It was hoped that the continued respect shown to the remaining Muslim structures would deflect international disapprobation at the Jewish construction on the Temple Mount. The al-Aksa mosque on the southern end of the Temple Mount was relatively undamaged and would continue to serve for Muslim prayers. It proved to be a vain hope: While the West registered its disapproval, the Muslim world acted.

This was the *casus belli* that the Arab world had been waiting for. By this time the Arab states in the Middle East had become Islamic republics. The moderate regimes had long been overthrown by Muslim fundamentalists who made little pretense about their hostility toward the Jewish state. The call to jihad went forth, and brought a swift response.

The Arab League declared war immediately against Israel. Egypt, Jordan and Syria led the attack, supported by other Arab countries. The Egyptian armies broke through into the Israeli Negev, while the Syrian armored forces along with Jordan penetrated deep into the Golan. As in the last major Arab-Israeli conflict, the 1973 Yom Kippur War, the heavily outnumbered Israelis fought valiantly to halt the advance of the Arab armies.

This time, however, they were unable to push back the invading armies with their seemingly limitless reserves of manpower. After a week of intense fighting, the battle lines had redrawn the map of Israel. While the I.D.F. continued to hold the Hebron range in the south, the Egyptians overran Beersheba. In the north the Syrians held the Golan down to the eastern side of the Sea of Galilee.

On the other hand, I.D.F. forces had swept around from the Mount Hermon area eastward into Syrian territory, cutting off the invading forces. Similarly, I.D.F. Southern Command, in an armored thrust from the Eilat sector, was slicing through the Egyptian lines. In a repeat of the Yom Kippur War, the overextended Egyptian forces were once again in danger of being completely cut off.

The United Nations, under the direction of its dynamic new Secretary-General, was called in to mediate a cease-fire. The proposed conditions were at first rejected outright by Israel: The Arab belligerents were demanding, as the price of a permanent cease-fire, that Israel comply with the U.N. resolutions regarding Jerusalem, which would become international land under the supervision of the U.N., and the Occupied Territories, which would be turned over to the Palestinians. Having been severely weakened by the war, Israel could ill afford the tremendous expense of weaponry and equipment. And this time there was no rapid military resupply from the United States.

Vulnerable to another attack, Israel had her back against the wall. There was little choice but to accede to the demands of the international community before the Arabs regrouped and mounted another offensive. After firm assurances from the Secretary-General, who was personally involved in brokering the peace treaty, the agonizing decision was made to evacuate all Israeli presence from the Occupied Territories. In return, the Arab armies would withdraw from Israeli territory.

Fierce opposition erupted at this sudden reversal in long-standing Israeli policy. The embittered inhabitants of the Israeli settlements in the West Bank and Gaza Strip resisted and were forcibly removed by the army. There was open revolt as armed radical Jewish groups tried to sabotage the withdrawal. For the first time in the history of the modern state of Israel, Jews fought Jews in armed confrontation.

Finally the dream of Arabs around the world was realized. The borders were closed and the state of Palestine was jubilantly proclaimed. And when the walled city of Old Jerusalem was declared an international zone, the Arab world was awash with hysterical excitement. For their part, the Palestinian leadership awaited the day when the Old City would be the full-fledged capital of the new state of Palestine.

The euphoria over the new state of Palestine soon evaporated in the face of hard reality. A bloodbath of revenge erupted and thousands died. There was a brutal purge of all who had cooperated with the Jewish state. Businessmen who had traded with Jews, along with common workmen who had held jobs inside Israel, were marked and executed by roving "justice squads." Students who had studied in Israeli universities were also suspect. The Christian Arab minority was an easy target and suffered heavily.

Many were driven from their homes and property by Muslim mobs. Lacking a unified central government, the various cities of the West Bank and Gaza Strip operated more or less independently, controlled by powerful henchmen.

The expected incoming flood of financial aid never materialized. Western countries, exhausted by the protracted oil embargo, were in no frame of mind to assist the fledgling Palestinian state even if they could. The Gulf states, still possessing substantial financial reserves, as usual found excuses to avoid any real commitment to their Arab "brothers."

As a result, Palestine foundered in chaos. The state was unable to provide even basic services for its people. In the flush of excitement few stopped to realize that the Territories had little electrical generating capacity—and not so much as a single factory to produce candles. The water supply, which had been integrated into the Israeli system, was no longer operative.

For lack of funds, the shallow-water port of Gaza could not be developed to handle the needed traffic for the new state. There was little economic development and the few meager existing industries suffered from lack of capital. The stores were even emptier than during the self-imposed perennial intifada. Many secretly regretted the end of Israeli rule, which by comparison was beginning to resemble a golden age of prosperity.

Yet no one dared say a word. The abiding hatred of Israel was more intense than ever. The Palestinian state was viewed as the first step to the eventual liberation of the rest of the land from Israeli rule. This ultimate goal had been skillfully concealed lest the naïve Westerners realize the true nature of Palestinian aspirations.

But now it was time to call openly for the dissolution of the Jewish state altogether. As the incipient Palestinian army acquired arms, it was not long before cross-border incursions increased. The close proximity of the state of Palestine put the heartland of Israel within easy range of rockets and artillery fire.

Israel's strenuous objections to the U.N. about these incursions accomplished little. The Arab nations considered them isolated incidents by extremist factions. There were, in any event, other more pressing problems occupying the attention of the world community. Israel responded to the cross-border attacks in kind, which in turn escalated the conflict.

The proverbial straw that broke the camel's back came when a barrage of rocket and artillery fire, timed to interrupt the Jewish New Year holiday festivities, slammed into West Jerusalem. Scores were killed when several rounds fell among a large crowd gathered in a park.

The Israeli Defense Forces reacted swiftly. An armored column punched into the West Bank and was soon in control of the region south of Jerusalem. Other forces surrounded Nablus in the north, another center of hostile activity against Israel. Large stores of weapons and ammunition were rounded up and destroyed. Within a week, to everybody's astonishment, the West Bank was in effect under Israeli "occupation" once again.

A Terror of Spirits

> And out of the smoke locusts came down upon the earth and were given power like that of scorpions of the earth. They were told not to harm the grass of the earth or any plant or tree, but only those people who did not have the seal of God on their foreheads. They were not given power to kill them, but only to torture them for five months. And the agony they suffered was like that of the sting of a scorpion when it strikes a man. During those days men will seek death, but will not find it; they will long to die, but death will elude them.
>
> Revelation 9:3–6

Not only the Middle East but planet Earth itself was at the end of its tether. Hopelessness and despair were everywhere—and frightening confusion at the supernatural phenomena that were being manifested. Gone were the days of cultured skepticism regarding spiritual realities. Few could deny the existence of the unearthly forces that were now being unleashed. But Christians stood alone in renouncing them as tools of the devil.

As dark-winged creatures, actually flying scorpions, began sweeping across continents, panic gripped people that went beyond words. They would appear and disappear unpredictably, leaving the population on the raw edge of tension. Whole communities locked themselves inside boarded-up buildings and houses in a vain attempt to escape them. Yet they appeared to possess a kind of malignant intelligence that enabled them to find entrance through vents and minute openings.

The insidious creatures were impervious to the strenuous attempts at eradication, and there was no escape from their horrible sting—with one curious exception. Inexplicably, one segment of the population was maddeningly impervious to their vicious attacks. It was none other than the very people who were suffering the brunt of the United Nations Emergency Regulations—the hated Christians.

Even more terrifying were the occult powers being exhibited by the mysterious personage known as the Minister, a shortened form of his official U.N. title of Minister for International Relations. He functioned as the regent of the President of the U.N. Formerly a clergyman from one of the more apostate Christian denominations, he had abandoned church work years before for politics. That was where the real power lay, he was fond of boasting.

Such talk was only in jest. Long ago he had given himself over to the spiritual realities that propelled him, forces that were now coming to the forefront. At first they were little more than unconfirmed reports: Rumors of his magical incantations that could alternately cure or cause sickness or even death; or that he could levitate objects at will and transport them great distances. On one occasion, as a demonstration of occultic power at a religious gathering, the Minister was reported to have caused an electrical blackout throughout the city.

He preferred not to call these powers "demonic" or "satanic"; such terms had unfortunately been given a negative connotation by Christian culture. In time all prejudice against the spiritual world would be overcome. Only when the world was united in openness to the occult forces would they be able to exercise their powers fully on behalf of humankind. These powers alone possessed the ancient, infinite wisdom necessary to lift the planet out of the morass.

Indeed, this was the driving mission of the Minister: to bring about a revolution in the acceptance of these forces. Nonetheless, significant numbers of Christians still opposed his efforts, which only spurred the Minister on in his wrath against them. The whole world would not continue to suffer because of the few who refused to accept his wisdom.

In his hidden chambers, the Minister was in regular communication with these spiritual forces. They appeared as angels of light before him in the night as he awaited their presence, mesmerizing him with profound discourses filled with benevolence toward the human race. He did not realize how they had drained him of all genuine personality, indeed, of his very humanness. Without them he was a limp, empty shell, a helpless puppet no longer able to resist their control over him.

But (and this was part of the delusion) he did not think so. As far as the Minister was concerned, it was he who was shrewdly manipulating these powers for his own self-advancement. It did not occur to him to wonder why he still shuddered at every encounter with the spirits, despite their assuring words of love and peace, or why after every session he was drenched in sweat. If his eyes had been opened for an instant, he would have recoiled in horror at the true nature of the beings that were beguiling him.

As it was, the Minister was for the moment a useful tool in drawing the world behind the President of the United Nations. This enigmatic man was almost unknown until recent years when he was selected for the post of Secretary-General, the same Secretary-General who had mediated the Arab/Israeli "peace" arrangement. The President was undeniably in possession of an irresistible charisma combined with uncanny powers of diplomacy that had helped him achieve a meteoric rise to power.

A Wound Unto Death

> The dragon gave the beast his power and his throne and great authority. One of the heads of the beast seemed to have had a fatal wound, but the fatal wound had been healed. The whole world was astonished and followed the beast. Men worshiped the dragon because he had given authority to the beast, and they also worshiped the beast and asked, "Who is like the beast? Who can make war against him?"
>
> Revelation 13:2–4

The creation of the office of President of the U.N. was a new development. At first there was opposition to modifying the U.N. Charter to allow for this position. It was argued that the concentration of so much authority in the hands of one man was contrary to the democratic spirit of the U.N. Others countered that the Security Council was hopelessly divided and that the magnitude of the problems facing the world necessitated strong leadership.

All resistance to the idea, however, soon melted away in the face of a bizarre demonstration of unearthly power. A crazed diplomat who managed to smuggle a knife into the U.N. stabbed the President on his way to address the General Assembly. The President was reported dead, and an extravagant funeral was nearly underway when the unimaginable happened. Suddenly, to an aghast world, he appeared alive.

It was at this time that the Minister began to display astonishing powers that left many around the world in an unbelieving daze—as though the world itself had suddenly become a giant horror movie. But this was one show that nobody could escape by walking out or flicking a switch. The evening news—what was left of it—brought the latest installments. Viewers gaped, staggered by each new manifestation of occultic power.

Along with extraordinary personal appeal that had brought him to the pinnacle of earthly power, the President could exhibit a dark side as well. He raged incessantly against all who dared oppose him. His public utterances were filled with execrable abuse heaped upon Christianity. Churches and denominations that did not have the stamp of official approval were ordered closed; those that persisted were suppressed ruthlessly.

There was no escape for his political enemies either. In a series of military campaigns that consolidated his power, the President defeated by supernatural means any remaining forces that rebelled against his authority. At the command of the Minister fearsome pillars of fire struck from heaven, consuming assembled armies in the field. Modern weapons of warfare proved utterly futile against these otherworldly forces.

Worshiping the Image of the Beast

And he performed great and miraculous signs, even causing fire to come down from heaven to earth in full view of men. Because of the signs he was given power to do on behalf of the first beast, he deceived the inhabitants of the earth.

Revelation 13:13–14

And then there was the ultimate test of loyalty. The President announced that the gravity of the world situation demanded a united front against the Herculean problems facing the planet. As a visible demonstration of unity, people of all nations were now required to show reverence to a tangible symbol of the oneness of humankind. They would do this by bowing physically to a large human-like marble structure, whose image was televised at strategic times and locations. It was, in fact, referred to as "the Image" and stood behind hallowed halls in the U.N.

There would be no exceptions. The President warned that all who refused at this critical juncture were subverting progress toward the solution of Earth's problems. There would be no tolerating those who resisted.

Accordingly, they would not be included in the U.N. Uniform Identification System—a painless electronic tattoo visible in ultraviolet light—until they made common cause with the rest of humankind. This in effect made them outcasts and pariahs. Without an identity number such people would have great difficulty purchasing the few goods that were available or selling their own products. Still, many refused to participate in the "Unity Ceremony." These were hounded and arrested, forcing many into hiding. Friend turned against friend, and brother against brother.

The Unity Ceremony ignited intense controversy in the Christian Church worldwide. Part of the ceremony involved the recitation of the Unity Creed, which included the specific rejection of the central doctrines of Christianity. Eminent theologians gave assurances that this should not in itself cause alarm. They argued that one had to understand the necessary purpose behind denying that Jesus Christ was the Savior of the world. Such dogmatic affirmations, they claimed, have always blocked unity with those of other faiths.

In fact, as the President stated persuasively, such teachings had been a major cause of conflict around the world. To put it bluntly, they were nothing less than dangerous. It was time for a new, vital faith that could be embraced by all of humankind. This would be a faith—a religion, if you like—that would free the world from hoping vainly in an "otherworldly" salvation. The primitive conception of a "God" descending to give His own life for the sins of the people, then being resurrected and ascending into heaven, was no longer meaningful in the modern age. Rather than negative teachings about the sinfulness of man, the new creed would emphasize human potential.

Numerous church leaders accepted the new Unity Creed. Some embraced it with enthusiasm and received special recognition for their cooperative attitude. They argued that, after all, Jesus Himself prayed for unity among the brethren. The Great Teacher would be more in agreement with this spirit of toleration and brotherhood than with rigid dogma. And surely Jesus would lend His support to the survival of the human race! If the recitation of mere words helped to unite the world against destruction, they were ready and willing to humble themselves for that noble task.

For the first time in many years, religious broadcasts were permitted in order to help the population adjust to the Unity Ceremony, which was incorporated into the revamped church services. Church leaders recited the Unity Creed unabashedly from the pulpit. Denominational creedal statements were hastily rewritten to reflect the laws against the propagation of historic Christian beliefs. With the clever manipulation of religious language, they so marvelously resembled the original creeds that many hardly noticed the difference.

People became cold and hard like the sky above them, eager to grasp at any savior who would make their unimaginable nightmare go away. Those who formerly took great pride in liberality turned their backs when resisters were publicly executed for treason. Now was not the time for latitude; the stakes were too great. Many of the persecuted were those who refused to deny the historic teachings of Christianity. They steadfastly refused to bow before the Image, which they considered blasphemous idolatry.

These gave testimony to their faith in Jesus Christ, to whom alone they bowed the knee. The world was under divine judgment, they said, because of the rebellion of the human race against the true and living God. And trust in anyone or anything else but Jesus Christ—the only hope of the world—was utterly futile. This confession enraged the many, but there were others who believed their testimony even at great cost.

The Minister's ceaseless efforts had one target: all those who resisted the absolute rule of the President and refused to show reverence to him. In one fear-inspiring incident, a group of Christians in a large city were rounded up and taken to the local sports stadium. There, as the Minister invoked a curse upon the Christian religion and its founder, they were burned to death by a mysterious fire that seemed to descend from above.

To the Minister's consternation, however, it seemed that when a city had been pronounced "clean" of the defiant Christians, others would spring up to take their places. Sensing that the President and his Minister were evil incarnate, they were looking for true hope in the midst of a collapsing world. They were moved by the courage of the Christians in the face of persecution. It seemed that the only light and love to be found in a darkening world were in their radiant testimony. Regardless of the price they would pay, they recognized the truth and worshiped Jesus Christ as their Lord and Savior.

The Invasion of Israel

> I will gather all the nations to Jerusalem to fight against it; the city will be captured, the houses ransacked, and the women raped. Half of the city will go into exile, but the rest of the people will not be taken from the city. Then the Lord will go out and fight against those nations, as he fights in the day of battle.
>
> Zechariah 14:2–3

Back in Israel, the "reoccupation" of the West Bank by the Jews as a result of the Palestinian shelling of Jerusalem roused the wrath of the Arab world. In a matter of weeks war had begun.

In the best of times, the I.D.F. was prepared to blunt such an attack. But times had changed. The first Arab attack had sapped Israel's military strength, and the U.S. was no longer Israel's chief arms supplier. Stores of equipment and ammunition were already at minimal levels. Fighting under these restrictions, the I.D.F. lost ground steadily against seemingly endless waves of assaults.

There was a new, critical factor this time. The Arabs were using a new weapon of terror: long-range ballistic missiles equipped with both conventional and chemical warheads. Repeated volleys were fired at Israeli cities, which were soon abandoned by tens of thousands. The economy ground to a halt as the population huddled in underground shelters. On every front, the I.D.F. fought a losing battle against the relentless advance of the combined Arab armies.

Finally the war cabinet of the Israeli Prime Minister met in closed session in an underground bunker. They listened soberly as weary generals from Northern and Southern Commands gave their battlefield assessments. It was becoming frighteningly clear that the very existence of the state hung in the balance. The I.D.F. had fought well against overwhelming odds, but stocks of weapons and ammunition were depleted. The Army Chief of Staff estimated that his men had only a few days' supply left, and by then the enemy would be at the approaches of Jerusalem and Tel Aviv.

Gone was the characteristic Israeli self-assuredness. A look of shock and alarm registered on every face. Everyone knew the decision that had to be made. Now was the time for the doomsday weapons reserved for the dark days when the state of Israel faced imminent destruction. A Pandora's box of unknown consequences would be opened, but there was no longer any choice. And if the end was to come, Israel and her enemies would descend into the abyss together. After a brief, muted discussion of the situation and the available options, the Prime Minister gave the command.

Deep in the Negev desert at a secret airbase that was even then threatened by an Egyptian armored column, the reinforced concrete roof of several underground silos slid open. The tips of Israeli-made Jericho II ballistic missiles soon appeared, pointing upward into the desert sky. In an instant they shot into the sky and out of sight, each leaving a white trail of smoke.

In less than five minutes the city of Cairo had received direct hits with three separate one-megaton nuclear warheads. Amman, Damascus and Baghdad each received two warheads. In five minutes a quarter of a million people perished under mushroom clouds hundreds of times more powerful than those that struck Hiroshima and Nagasaki.

There was a collective pause as the invading armies digested the enormity of the devastation. Their governments no longer existed;

they had been incinerated in their capital cities. The advancing field armies halted in their tracks, uncertain of what to do next. There was no longer a military command to give instructions. In the next few days they slowly withdrew.

When the news reached a stunned world, all eyes looked to the U.N. Until then the President had remained peculiarly silent about the war, and Israel was still hoping that he would remain so.

But the President now sprang into action: The time had finally arrived. Under the direction of the President, the U.N. High Command was activated under Article 42 of the U.N. Charter. Preparations were soon underway to mobilize a United Nations army. Within a matter of weeks the largest combined military force in the history of the world was preparing to converge on the Middle East.

No Turning Back

> Then I saw three evil spirits that looked like frogs; they came out of the mouth of the dragon, out of the mouth of the beast and out of the mouth of the false prophet. They are spirits of demons performing miraculous signs, and they go out to the kings of the whole world, to gather them for the battle on the great day of God Almighty.
>
> Revelation 16:13–14

Two stormy months passed. There had been more missile exchanges between Israel and her neighbors. Syria had fired three tactical nuclear warheads that she had obtained covertly from China. One fell into the sea but two others caused massive destruction in the Tel Aviv area. It was as if the world were teetering on the edge of a precipice. But there was no drawing back as the President marshaled the armies of the world inexorably toward the Middle East.

Back at the U.N. the national representatives filed into the assembly chamber. It would be an extraordinary session. The President would be addressing the delegates via satellite. A huge screen had been erected at the front of the hall. Around the world people would be gathered in front of flickering television sets to witness the same oration. Everyone was anxiously awaiting his word about the progress of the raging Middle East campaign.

It was a time of war such as the world had never before witnessed. Never before had such an impressive display of men and equipment been assembled under the banner of the United Nations. Every major Western power contributed its heaviest fighting units; their navies and air forces transported the immense war machine to the Middle East. The forces disembarked and assembled at various points along the eastern Mediterranean.

Diplomacy had run its course. The time had come to impose—by force—a lasting peace on the Middle East. The first pressing objective was to secure the land of Israel-Palestine, followed by the enforcement of a U.N.-supervised peace. Once the focal problem of the region was dealt with, the stranglehold on oil, still the lifeblood of the West, would be relieved. Later, the President would muster his considerable powers to deal with the other calamities that had befallen the planet.

A second major group of forces, with its own agenda, moved toward Israel in a giant pincer movement from the North and East. These were the armies of the Islamic nations of the region, intent on avenging the nuclear holocaust that Israel had inflicted on her Muslim neighbors.

Turkey was now firmly back among the Muslim nations. After nearly a century of flirtation with the West, the legacy of Ataturk had finally been overthrown. The end came when Turkey's hopes for membership in the European Economic Community were dashed and there had no longer been any reason to identify with the West. Under increasing pressure from Muslim fundamentalism, Ankara proclaimed itself an Islamic state. Trained and equipped by the now-defunct NATO, the Turkish army would be a major component of the northern thrust into the Holy Land.

Close at its heels were contingents of the central Asian republics of the former Soviet Union. Now also Islamic republics, Azerbaijan, Turkmenistan, Uzbekistan and Kazakhstan all were eager to contribute to the liberation of Palestine. These were joined by the armies of Iran, whose militant fundamentalists had played an instrumental role in the Islamic transformation of the Middle East.

Several of these nations had had serious disputes with each other that had led to armed conflict. But for now their differences could be shelved. No one wanted to be left out of the glorious task of recovering the sacred soil of Palestine for Islam. The great natural barrier of the Euphrates River would normally have obstructed the passage of the enormous numbers of soldiers and equipment. But the Turkish dams and prolonged drought had reduced the river to a muddy stream.

Other Muslim nations within striking distance of the Holy Land joined eagerly in the final battle for the liberation of Palestine. Intensive proselytizing in the twentieth century had transformed the northern half of Africa into a stronghold of Islam. Thus, the armored thrusts from the North and East were linked with another group of forces making their way up from the south, past devastated Egypt. These were from the North African Islamic countries as well as from Ethiopia and her neighbors.

The allegiance of these Islamic nations to the United Nations was purely nominal. It may have proved impossible to draw them into alliance with the Western powers except for one significant fact: The President, although born in Europe, was himself of Middle Eastern descent. Even more remarkable, he drew his lineage from the ancient Hashemite family, and was therefore a legitimate descendant of the Prophet Muhammad. As such he could command a measure of respect and loyalty from Muslims despite his deviant religious beliefs.

Despite their tentative alliance with the President, the Islamic nations would wait no longer. They were in a race against time—to seize the land of Israel before the United Nations Army did in order to ensure that it was firmly in Muslim hands.

The combination of these two forces, attacking on all fronts, proved overwhelming to the I.D.F. With concentrated air strikes against the approaching armored columns, the I.D.F. made a determined effort to prevent the invaders from reaching the borders of Israel. There was no longer any hesitation to use the ultimate weapon. Israel expended her tactical nuclear weapons in a desperate attempt to halt the advancing armies, who replied in kind. Thousands perished in minutes on both sides as the land hung under a radioactive pall.

As the I.D.F. air force was gradually decimated by enemy fire, their situation became futile. Now it was up to the army to hold back the vastly superior forces that were already on the horizon. A feeling of despondency settled over the defenders of the various approaches into Israel. Where was the God of Israel now?

The Beast Speaks

> He ordered them to set up an image in honor of the beast who was wounded by the sword and yet lived. He was given power to give breath to the image of the first beast, so that it could speak and cause all who refused to worship the image to be killed.
>
> Revelation 13:14–15

As the delegates took their seats at the U.N. in New York, the first strategic objective had already been secured. After furious combat the joint U.N. armies had succeeded in breaking through the Israeli border defenses in the north and south. Armies flying the Muslim scepter had met with even greater success. Penetrating from the comparatively lightly defended east, armored columns had managed to reach Jerusalem, where a terrible slaughter was continuing.

As the huge screen came alive with signals from the satellite transmission, the U.N. members shifted nervously in their seats, knowing what was coming next. Many, especially those from Western countries, were uncomfortable with this ritual, necessary as it was. It seemed a throwback to, well, paganism. But they buried these doubts, attributing them to the specter of the Christian religion that still haunted their cultural heritage.

And there it was. The delegates rose as one before the Image that glowered down at them from the screen. The Image itself, which was normally sequestered in the hallowed inner recesses of the U.N., had recently been moved—to Jerusalem. Taking advantage of the status of the Old City as a U.N.-administered zone, the President had taken the liberty of moving the Image to what he termed a fitting setting for a symbol of the new "religious consciousness."

What could be more appropriate than for the Image to be residing in the very center of three of the world's great religious traditions—Judaism, Christianity and Islam? Despite strenuous and violent protests by the Israelis, the President had a special enclosed platform constructed on the Temple Mount to exhibit the Image. It was from there that the Image was visually transmitted around the world—and into the U.N.

The Image was actually about nine feet tall, taller than the largest of men, but displayed on screen it somehow appeared much larger. It was straight out of the Roman Empire. It resembled the busts of past emperors displayed in the great museums of the world, with the same haunting realism.

The figure appeared, as the emperor Hadrian often did, with a gold breastplate signifying military conquest. Strangely, though, while the caesars usually preferred the short sword in hand, the Image bore a spear. Upon closer examination—which none of the delegates was privileged to do—another oddity would be revealed. The head of the spear was not, like the rest of the sculpture, a new creation.

The lance was old, even ancient. It was reputed to be the very spear of Longinus, the lance with which the Roman soldier pierced the side of Jesus. It was known to have existed during Crusader times, when it was supposedly recovered from Palestine. According to legend, the one who claims the spear holds the destiny of the world in his hand—for good or evil.

But it was the face of the Image that all eyes were focused upon. Many shuddered, still unable to cope with the reality of a statue whose marble lips parted and spoke, and whose jeweled eyes came alive with penetrating gaze. This time the Image remained silent as the delegates were frozen in hushed silence, momentarily expecting the stone to begin twitching with life.

The signal was given and the diplomats rose as one. After reciting the Pledge of World Unity and Brotherhood, they bent awkwardly down on one knee—some were still not accustomed to such rituals—and pledged allegiance to the President. After a minute of reverence, they resumed their seats. A scattered few still felt vague, annoying pangs of defilement.

The screen changed and suddenly there he was. The President of the United Nations was standing at the summit of the archaeological site of Megiddo with the backdrop of the Valley of Megiddo behind him. It was the same spot where Napoleon had stood and marveled that the valley was ideally situated for warfare. But Napoleon's armies would have been swallowed up by the vast forces arrayed in the valley below the site.

As far as the eye could see, the verdant twenty-mile-long by ten-mile-wide valley was covered with the assembled weapons of war, as men and machines swarmed over the landscape. The rumor was that the President was fielding terrible new weapons never before unveiled. Indeed, in the distance loomed the silhouettes of huge, strange machines projecting menacingly upward into the sky. These were the products of an unearthly technology and were kept isolated in a separate sector. They were not intended for use against mere mortals.

The U.N. General Assembly sat transfixed before the President. To a man they were all considered leaders, but here was one who embodied the very apex of earthly authority. None from their midst, or any combination of them, would dare to challenge him. He was both feared and loathed, yet they were drawn to this man as the only remaining answer to the world's problems. If he were not there, they would be wholly without hope.

From the screen the President spoke: His deep, resonant voice filled the hall and commanded absolute attention. The intensity, the profundity of his face gripped them. His look was one of sheer omnipotence—as if nothing could stop him from what he set his mind to accomplish. He spoke with supreme confidence on the progress of the campaign. Recalcitrant Israel would soon be completely subdued. If the seditious Jews did not surrender quickly he would not guarantee the life of a single one. Even as he spoke the thunder of forces battering the Israelis echoed in the distance.

Mourning in the Land

> "They will look on me, the one they have pierced, and they will mourn for him as one mourns for an only child, and grieve bitterly for him as one grieves for a firstborn son. On that day the weeping in Jerusalem will be great, like the weeping of Hadad Rimmon in the plain of Megiddo."
>
> Zechariah 12:10–11

In the foothills of the Carmel range the Jewish defenders put up a futile resistance. They were now cut off from I.D.F. Northern Command in Galilee. Using the terrain to their advantage, they sought to block enemy penetration through the critical Yokneam, Megiddo and Iron Passes. They knew that once their lines broke, the enemy would sweep unopposed down upon the Sharon plain where the majority of Israelis lived.

The end was near: They could only delay the inevitable. The disheartening news reached them that Jerusalem had fallen, and now the Jewish population centers faced certain annihilation. The soldiers, crouched in their makeshift trenches, mourned for themselves and for their loved ones, who—if not already dead—would soon face massacre. Fathers wept for their children, stricken by memories of last, awkward partings. No one imagined it would come to this. All the hopes and dreams of the Jewish state would soon be crushed in the iron teeth of this monstrous power that had now descended upon the land.

It was at this time that a spontaneous outpouring of desolate grief spread from man to man, from trench to trench, and throughout the scattered Israeli forces. The same national convulsion of woe seized their families behind the lines as they awaited the end, huddled in underground shelters. At last, like never before—even during the Holocaust—many of the surviving Jewish people cried out to the living God with broken hearts. For the first time they truly sought the Messiah. They were given understanding about their wickedness and disobedience against the living God—and they repented with wretched desolation.

Then they were granted peace. Even as death and destruction rained down all around them, their eyes miraculously perceived a glorious reality unfolding in the heavens above them. They saw their Messiah, the One whom they had rejected up until the very end. Seeing Him, they loved Him and marveled that they had resisted so long.

His appearance was the very essence of all things good and true. To gaze upon Him was to long to serve Him. Here was a Leader of leaders, worthy of being followed to the ends of the earth. The charisma of earthly rulers was repulsive in comparison to His glorious countenance. He had come at last to put an end to wickedness, and none could stand against Him. Yet He exuded gentleness and humility. He knew the name of all who belonged to Him, and they were loved with an inexpressible love. The moment had come when they would never fear again.

An End to Wickedness

Don't let anyone deceive you in any way, for that day will not come until the rebellion occurs and the man of lawlessness is revealed, the man doomed to destruction. He opposes and exalts himself over everything that is called God or is worshiped, and even sets himself up in God's temple, proclaiming himself to be God.

2 Thessalonians 2:3–4

The President was prepared, or so he thought. No one but himself, the Minister and their master knew the real reason he was there. It was not because of the poor Palestinians—he scoffed at the idea. It was to remove the scourge of the Jews from the planet. The Messiah was from the seed of this despised race, and they must be obliterated.

Spiritual forces on behalf of the Jews could be expected to intervene, but the President had prepared for this eventuality. Psychic forces in possession of intelligence light years beyond the human mind had guided the construction of fearsome weapons for the occasion. These weapons, capable of incinerating planets, were now at the ready in the valley of Jezreel. The Minister assured him that nothing, mortal or spirit, could survive their devastating effects.

The world was his, and nothing would stop his will from being performed. The President exalted himself greatly in his heart and mocked the God of his fathers. There was no god in this world but him.

His master, however, knew otherwise. Unbeknown to the President, he himself, like the Minister, was but a pawn. The Dragon from the pit, knowing that his time was short, had sent them on a murderous quest to avenge his own approaching destruction. And he despised his willing dupes none the less for their servitude. They would all join him in eternal damnation.

The very essence of loathsome, hideous enmity toward all that is good, the evil one was rightly called the Destroyer. From the moment of the Great Rebellion in eternity past, he had only one means whereby he could touch the Holy One who thwarted his bid for supremacy in the heavens: by depriving Him of the eternal fellowship of those whom He loved. This was his consuming passion: the destruction of souls.

At the darkest moment, the end of human history came. What the newly believing Jews envisioned was soon beheld by the horrified eyes of the gathered armies. What they experienced was also seen in a heavenly vision by the apostle John:

I saw heaven standing open and there before me was a white horse, whose rider is called Faithful and True. With justice he judges and makes war. His eyes are like blazing fire, and on his head are many crowns. He has a name written on him that no one but he himself knows. He is dressed in a robe dipped in blood, and his name is the Word of God. The armies of heaven were following him, riding on white horses and dressed in fine linen, white and clean. Out of his mouth comes a sharp sword with which to strike down the nations. "He will rule them with an iron scepter." He treads the winepress of the fury of the wrath of God Almighty. On his robe and on his thigh he has this name written:

KING OF KINGS AND LORD OF LORDS.

. . . Then I saw the beast and the kings of the earth and their armies gathered together to make war against the rider on the horse and his army. But the beast was captured, and with him the false prophet who had performed the miraculous signs on his behalf. With these signs he had deluded those who had received the mark of the beast and worshiped his image. The two of them were thrown alive into the fiery lake of burning sulfur. The rest of them were killed with the sword that came out of the mouth of the rider on the horse, and all the birds gorged themselves on their flesh.

And I saw an angel coming down out of heaven, having the key to the Abyss and holding in his hand a great chain. He seized the dragon, that ancient serpent, who is the devil, or Satan, and bound him for a thousand years. He threw him into the Abyss, and locked and sealed it over him. . . .

And I saw the souls of those who had been beheaded because of their testimony for Jesus and because of the word of God. They had not worshiped the beast or his image and had not received his mark on their foreheads or their hands. They came to life and reigned with Christ a thousand years.

Revelation 19:11–16; 19:19–20:4

Epilogue

THE END OF THE WORLD MAY NOT RESEMBLE THIS scenario. But it will surely come, and will probably exceed the portrayal attempted here. There is, however, one truth that must be emphasized in the midst of all the expected horror: Jesus Christ is the King of kings and the Lord of lords. Yet He did not come to earth to destroy it. In His own words, He expressed the eternal purpose of the incarnation: "The thief comes only to steal and kill and destroy; I have come that they may have life, and have it to the full. I am the good shepherd. The good shepherd lays down his life for the sheep" (John 10:10–11).

The offer of eternal salvation is open to all, regardless of how far they have strayed or how inadequate they may feel. Conversely, no one can "earn" entrance to heaven by his or her own efforts: "For it is by grace you have been saved, through faith—and this is not from yourselves, it is the gift of God—not by works, so that no one can boast" (Ephesians 2:8–9).

One thing is certain. As long as there is life there is hope. If you are reading this, then you are not beyond hope. These words of Jesus are meant for you:

"Those whom I love I rebuke and discipline. So be earnest, and repent. Here I am! I stand at the door and knock. If anyone hears my voice and opens the door, I will come in and eat with him, and he with me."

Revelation 3:19–20

Will I see you there?